CREATING

CHARACTERS

WD

WRITER'S DIGEST
BOOKS

WritersDigest.com
Cincinnati, Ohio

For more resources for writers, visit www.writersdigest.com.

To receive a free weekly e-mail newsletter delivering tips and updates about writing and about Writer's Digest products, register directly at www.writersdigest.com/enews.

18 17 16 15 14   5 4 3 2 1

Distributed in Canada by Fraser Direct
100 Armstrong Avenue
Georgetown, Ontario, Canada L7G 5S4
Tel: (905) 877-4411

Distributed in the U.K. and Europe by F&W Media International
Brunel House, Newton Abbot, Devon, TQ12 4PU, England
Tel: (+44) 1626-323200, Fax: (+44) 1626-323319
E-mail: postmaster@davidandcharles.co.uk

Distributed in Australia by Capricorn Link
P.O. Box 704, Windsor, NSW 2756 Australia
Tel: (02) 4577-3555

ISBN-13: 978-1-59963-876-8

Edited by Cris Freese
Interior designed by Laura Spencer
Cover designed by Rebecca Kuhlman
Production coordinated by Debbie Thomas

TABLE OF CONTENTS

PART I: GETTING STARTED

PART II: POINT OF VIEW

PART III: DIALOGUE

PART IV: PROTAGONISTS

PART V: ANTAGONISTS

PART VI: SUPPORTING CHARACTERS

PART VII: CONFLICT

PART VIII: MOTIVATIONS & RELATIONSHIPS

PART IX: CHARACTER ARCS

FOREWORD

BY STEVEN JAMES

I heard a saying once: "The fish is in the ocean, and the ocean is in the fish."

It sounds either very self-evident and hardly worth mentioning or very Zen.

Let's go with Zen.

A nugget of wisdom that's paradoxically both easy and hard to crack.

What is the relationship of character to plot? Well, they're inextricably connected.

How can you pull them apart without unraveling a story?

You can't.

Why not?

Because the character is in the plot, and the plot is in the character.

Stories are more than accounts of events occurring, and they're more than character studies. Rather, in a narrative, we find characters being revealed and transformed as they face struggles that, while defining them, refine them.

The plot and the character are in each other, serving each other, informing each other.

At its core, a story is about an interesting character trying to accomplish something difficult. If the character isn't captivating or the task isn't compelling, the story suffers. So, when a story drags, you simply make your character more fascinating or the task tougher to accomplish.

No big deal, right?

In theory, yes.

In practice, there's a bit more to it than that.

Once I was reading a novel and the main character was so whiny and immature and annoying that I kept wanting the author to just kill her off and get on with the story.

Needless to say, that's not what you want your readers thinking. They have to care about what happens. If they don't care about the character, they won't care about the conflict. And if they don't care about the conflict, they won't care about the story.

Struggle.

Character.

Plot.

Emotion.

All interwoven when a story is told.

And you have to be at the top of your game as a storyteller these days because you're in a war for people's attention, and there's never been a time in history when the battle has been fiercer. Think of all the websites, books, video games, movies, apps, and TV shows out there that are vying for your readers' time. (Not to mention work and family obligations, hobbies to pursue, 5Ks to run, drag races to attend, bathrooms to remodel, gluten-free cookies to eat.)

It's overwhelming to think about how many distractions and delights our world offers. So here's our goal: fill our stories with fictional characters so enthralling that readers would rather spend time with them than do anything else, even spend time with real people.

Let that sink in for a moment.

Yes, that's right: We want to tell stories so powerful and engaging that our readers will put everything else on hold—even their relationships with other people—to share their time with the characters we've created.

Presumptuous?

Maybe.

Challenging?

Um. Yeah.

Be wary of anyone who tries to sell you a fill-in-the-blanks approach to creating characters. There's no formula to it. You can't just add three parts foibles and two parts quirks, toss in a few cups of backstory and motivation, mix, chill, and serve.

Nope.

Not going to fly.

It's tough work, this storytelling business.

But this book will guide you along the path. There are great kernels of wisdom in here. Writing dialogue? Yes, you'll learn about that. How to come up with character descriptions, habits, and hobbies? Sure. Ways to weave in desires, fears, worries, hopes, and dreams? Yes, of course.

Some of the advice you may have read before, and it'll confirm what you've been thinking. But be ready, because some of it will shatter your assumptions about what makes a story work. However, if you have enough courage to pick up the pieces of your preconceptions, you'll find that you can tell a better narrative than ever before by offering the world more well-rounded, memorable, and addictive characters.

Addictive?

Yes.

Because you don't want your reader to set down your book for anything.

In writing circles, people sometimes talk about the importance of creating three-dimensional characters. The two-dimensional type have no depth. They're bland and shallow and unremarkable, simply taking up space on the page without ever taking up residence in your readers' hearts.

So what about the three-dimensional kind?

Usually that refers to characters who are memorable, who seem real, who "jump off the page," who are intriguing, and whom readers will empathize with or aspire to be like.

But there has to be something else, something more.

After all, a corpse has three dimensions, and yet it's still just a corpse. It needs that intangible breath of life.

And so do the characters you create.

In the biblical story of creation, God speaks the universe into existence and then shapes Adam from the soil. Adam is three-dimensional but isn't yet alive. It's only when God breathes his spirit on him that he actually comes to life.

As world creators, as architects of the impossible, that's our job as well: to shape characters from the soil of our dreams and breathe life into them.

This book will show you how.

The character is in the plot, and the plot is in the character.

And when they come together—in ways you are about to discover—a story with a life of its own is born.

....

STEVEN JAMES is the best-selling author of nine novels that have received wide critical acclaim from *Publishers Weekly, New York Journal of Books, RT Reviews, Booklist, Library Journal,* and many others. He has won three Christy Awards for best suspense and was a finalist for an International Thriller Award for best original paperback. His psychological thriller *The Bishop* (Revell, 2010) was named *Suspense Magazine's* Book of the Year. Steven has a Master's Degree in Storytelling, serves as a contributing editor for *Writer's Digest,* and has taught writing and storytelling principles around the world. He is the author of *Story Trumps Structure: How to Write Unforgettable Fiction by Breaking the Rules* (Writer's Digest Books, 2014).

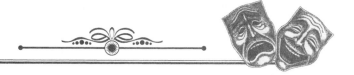

INTRODUCTION

Characters are the lifeblood of your story—whether you're writing a short story, a novel, or even a series. They're intricately tied to every other element of fiction: plot, description, dialogue, and more. Simply put, a strong story is hard to come by without equally powerful characters.

And, as expected, creating compelling characters can be one of the most difficult tasks for any writer. A character must be believable and true to life—not an easy task when you consider how characters develop and change as much as anyone in the real world does.

But that's also why characters are so fascinating. Memorable characters aren't static and tired; they develop before your eyes as the story or series progresses. It is rewarding to see someone rise from nothing, and heartbreaking to watch a life tear apart.

In turning to this book, you've dedicated yourself to creating the kind of characters that every reader yearns for. *Creating Characters* compiles the very best advice from top writers and editors on the different stages of character creation and development. With each chapter, you'll find something new and unique to assist you in this process.

LET THE EXPERTS GUIDE YOU

Each part of this book will walk you through a different, important aspect of creating the strongest characters possible. Using the tips and advice from experts on the craft, you'll learn how to define and shape your characters in compelling and meaningful ways.

- Part 1 has everything you need to get started, from choosing your character's name to bringing him or her onstage for the first time.
- Part 2 guides you in crafting the perfect point of view for your character and story.

- Part 3 helps you develop accurate and believable dialogue.
- Part 4 focuses specifically on creating a protagonist that will carry your story from start to finish.
- Part 5 features methods for bulking up your bad guys and creating a villain to match the strength of your hero.
- Part 6 is about developing a secondary cast of characters that can do a little bit of everything—from supporting the main character to populating the background.
- Part 7 is a guide to creating conflict that will motivate your characters and drive your plot.
- Part 8 builds on the previous section, offering tips on crafting romantic relationships and motivations for your primary characters.
- Part 9 helps you put everything together to develop a captivating character arc.

Each of these sections (including a final chapter on revising for character) will help you develop a full cast of unique story people.

Start with the very first page and work your way through, chapter by chapter, or pick a section and hone a specific part of your craft. With either method, you'll begin to populate your story with characters that will hook your readers from the start and refuse to let them go.

Let the experts of *Creating Characters* guide you in this process. Listen to their advice and take it to heart. In the end, you'll be able to confidently hand the wheel over to your characters and let them drive your story.

PART I

GETTING STARTED

CHAPTER 1

25 THINGS YOU SHOULD KNOW ABOUT CHARACTER

BY CHUCK WENDIG

1. The Character as Fulcrum: All Things Rest Upon Him

Without character, you have nothing. Great plot? Robust story world? Potent themes? Elegant font? Those matter little if your character is a dud. The punch might be delicious but not if someone threw up in it. The character is why we come to the table. The character is our way through all those other things. We engage with stories because we relate to them: They are mirrors. Characters are the mirror-side version of "us" staring back. Twisted, warped, uncertain—but still us through and through.

2. The Cure for All That Ails the Audience

A great character can be the line between narrative life and story death. She's a powerful Band-Aid, a strong swaddling of gauze to staunch the bleeding. Think of the character like duct tape: She can piece the whole thing back together. I will forgive your sins of a so-so plot, of muddy themes, of a *meh-ehhh-enh* story world if you're letting me live for a while with a great character. But don't think character will heal truly grievous injuries. A gaping chest wound—meaning, poor writing, asinine plot, or perhaps a duller-than-two-dead-goats story world—will only swallow your great character into its gory depths.

3. And Yet the Character Must Be Connected

Don't believe that all those other aspects of a story are separate from the character. The character is—or should be—bound inextricably to those other elements. The character is your vehicle through the plot. The character carries the story. Theme, mood, description: Focus them through the prism of character, not vice versa. The character is the DNA in every goddamn cell of your story.

4. You Are the Dealer; the Character Is the Drug

The audience will do anything to spend time with a great character. We're junkies for it. We'll gnaw our own arms off to read just *one more page* with a killer character. It's why sequels and series are so popular—we want to see where the character's going. If you give us a great character, it becomes our only desire to lick him like he's a hallucinogenic toad and take a crazy ride wherever he has to go.

5. Tell Us What She Wants

It is critical to know what a character wants from the start. She may not know what she wants, but the audience must have that information. Maybe she wants her enemies destroyed, freedom from oppression, her child returned to her, true love, the perfect falafel, a pet monkey, the ultimate wedding, or a secret subterranean moon base. She can want many things, and it's of the utmost importance that we know what they are. How else will we know how far she's come? How else can we see the stakes on the table? How else will you frustrate your audience by standing in her way?

6. Not Likability but Rather Livability

It doesn't matter if we "like" your character, or in the parlance of junior high, whether we even "*like*-like" your character. It only matters that we want to live with him. We must see something that makes us want to keep on keeping on, following him into the jaws of Hell and out through the Devil's lava-encrusted keister. For the record, the "Lava Keister" sounds like either a roller coaster or a Starbucks drink.

7. The Care Factor

Ask this up front, as you're crafting the story: *Why will the audience care about this character?* You have unlimited answers to this. Look to the narratives all around us to find reasons to care. We love underdog stories. We love tales of redemption. We love bad boys, good girls, bad girls, and good boys. We want to see characters punished, exalted, triumphant, rewarded, destroyed, stymied, puzzled, and wounded. We gawk at car crashes. We swoon at love. Find a hook. Hang your character upon it.

8. Rub Up Against Remarkability

You must prove this thesis: "This character is worth the audience's time." The character must deserve her own story—or, at least, her own part within it. You prove this thesis by making the character in some way remarkable. This is why you see a lot of stories about doctors, detectives, lawyers, cowboys, bounty hunters, wizards, space rangers, and superheroes ... but you don't see quite so many about copier repairmen, pharmaceutical assistants, piano tuners, or ophthalmologists. The former group is remarkable, in part, by their roles. The latter group can be just as remarkable, however, provided you discover their noteworthiness and put it on the page or the screen. What makes one remarkable can be a secret past, a current attitude, or a future triumph. It can be internal or external. You have infinite options. Choose one.

9. Act Upon the World Rather than Have the World Act Upon Him

Don't let your character be a bump on a log. We tire of characters who do nothing except react to whatever the world flings at their heads. That's not to say that characters shouldn't be forced to deal with unexpected challenges and left-field conflicts—but that doesn't prevent a character from being proactive, either. Passivity fails to be interesting for long. This is why crime fiction has power: The very nature of a crime is about doing. You don't passively rob a bank, kill your lover, or run a street gang. Simply put: *Characters do things.*

Creating Characters

10. Bad Decisions Are a Good Decision

Nobody ever said an active character had to be a smart character. A character can and perhaps should be *badly* proactive, making all the wrong moves and affecting the world with his poor decisions. At some point a character needs to take control, even if it means taking control in the worst possible way. In fact ...

11. This Is Why Suspense Was Created

Tension is created when characters you love make bad decisions. They lie, cheat, steal, break laws, or shatter taboos. They go into the haunted house. They don't run from the serial killer. They betray a friend. Sleep with an enemy. Eat a forbidden fruit. Tension occurs when the character sets free his chickens, and we know full well that those chickens will come home to roost. But the chickens will come home changed. They will have knives. Prison tats. And evil wizard powers. Don't let tension wriggle free, soft and pliable, from external events. Let the character create the circumstances of suspense.

12. How You Succeed Is by Not Having Them Succeed

You as storyteller are a malevolent presence blocking the character's bliss. Imagine that the character is an ant over here and over *there* is a nugget of food, a dollop of honey, and all the ant wants is to trot over to the food so that he may dine upon it. Think of the infinite ways you can stop him from getting to that food. Flick him into the grass. Block his path with twigs, rocks, a line of dish soap, a squeeze of lighter fluid set aflame. Be the wolf to his little piggy, and huff and puff and blow his house down. Pick him up, put him in the cup holder in your car, and drive him a hundred miles in the opposite direction while taunting him with insults. The audience will hate you. But they'll hunger for more. *Will the ant get to the food? Won't he? Will he find his friends again? Can he overcome?* Give him a primal, simple, declarative problem. You are the villain. The character is the hero. The audience thirsts for this most fundamental conflict of storyteller versus character.

13. The Code

Just as a story world is beholden to certain laws, norms, and ways, so too is a character: Every character has an internal compass, an invisible set of morals and beliefs that comprise their "code." The audience senses this. They know when a character betrays his own code and violates the program—it's like a glitch in the Matrix, a disturbance in the dream you've crafted. That's not to say characters can't change. They can and do. But a heroic fireman doesn't one day save a cat from a tree and the next day decide to cook and eat a baby. Changes in a character must come out of the story, not out of thin air.

14. A, B, C, 1, 2, 3

The law of threes. Find three beats for your character—be they physical, social, emotional—with each beat graphing a change in the character over the course of a story. *Selfish boy* to *exiled teen* to *heroic man*. From *maiden* to *mother* to *crone*. Private, lieutenant, general. Knows everything, everything in question, knows nothing. Birth, life, death. Beginning, middle, end.

15. Boom Goes the Dynamite

Screenwriter Blake Snyder calls this the "Save the Cat" moment, but it needn't be that shiny and happy. The point is that every character needs a kick-ass moment, a reason why we all think, "Hell yeah, that's why I'm behind this dude." What moment will you give your character? Why will we pump our fists and hoot for him?

16. Beware the Everyman, Fear the Chosen One

I'm boring. So are you. We don't all make compelling protagonists despite what we feel in our own heads, and so the Everyman threatens to instead become the Eye-Wateringly-Dull-Man, flat as a coat of cheap paint. The Chosen One—arguably the opposite of the Everyman—has, appropriately, the opposite problem: He's too interesting, a preening peacock of special preciousness. Beware either. Both can work, but know the danger. Find complexity. Seek remarkability.

17. Nobody Sees Themselves as a Supporting Character

Your supporting characters shouldn't act like supporting characters. They have full lives in which they are totally invested and where they are the protagonists. They're not puppets for fiction. They don't know they're not the heroes.

18. The Main MC, DJ Protag

That said, they don't call your "main character" the MC for nothing. Your protagonist at the center of the story should still be the most compelling rock star in the room.

19. You Are Not Your Character, Except for When You Are

Your character is not a proxy for you. If you see Mary Sue in the mirror, put your foot through the glass and use that reflection instead. But that old chestnut—"write what you know"—applies. You take the things that have happened to you and you bring them to the character. Look for those things in your memory that affected you: fought a bear, won a surfing competition, lost a fistfight with Dad, eradicated an insectile alien species. Pull out the feelings. Inject them into the face, neck, guts, brain, and heart of the character.

20. Screwed Up

Everybody's a little screwed up inside. Some folks more than that. No character is a saint. Find the darkness inside. Draw their imperfections to the surface like a bead of blood. You don't have to care about Joseph Campbell, but he was right when he said we love people for their imperfections. Same holds true for characters. We love them for their problems.

21. A Tornado Beneath a Cool Breeze

A good character is both simple and complex: Simplicity on the surface eradicates any barrier to entry, and complexity beneath rewards the reader and gives the character both depth and something to do. Complexity on the surface rings hollow and threatens to be confusing, so ease the audience into the character the way you'd get into a claw-foot tub full of steaming hot water—one toe at a time.

22. On the Subject of Archetypes

You can begin with an archetype—or even a stereotype—because people find comfort there. It creates a sense of intimacy even when none exists. But the archetype should be like the leg braces worn by Forrest Gump as a kid—when that kid takes off running, he blasts through the braces and leaves them behind. So too with the "type." This will help the character stand on his own until it's time to shatter 'em when running.

23. Dialogue over Description, Action over Rumination

Don't bludgeon us over the head with description. A line or three about the character is good enough, and it need not be purely about their physical looks. It can be about movement and body language. It can be about what people think, about what goes on in her head. But throw out a couple lines and get out. Dialogue is where a character is revealed. And action. What a character says and does is the sum of her being. It doesn't need to be more than that: A character says something, then does something, then says something about what she just did. In there lurks infinite possibilities—a confluence of atoms that reveals who she is.

24. Take the Test Drive

Write the character before you write the character. Take him on adventures that don't count. Who cares about canon? Here I say, "To Hell with the audience." This isn't for them. This is for you. Joyride the character around some flash fiction, a short script, a blog post, a page of dialogue, a poem, whatever.

25. Get All Up in Them Guts

Know your character. Every square inch. Empathize, don't sympathize. Understand the character, but don't stand with the character. Get in her skin. The closer you get, the better off you are when a story goes sideways. Any rewriting or additional work comes easy when you know which way the character's gonna jump. Know her like you know yourself; when the character does something, you know it comes justified, with purpose, with meaning, with intimate knowledge that the thing she did is the thing she was always supposed to do.

....

CHUCK WENDIG is a novelist, screenwriter, and game designer. He is the author of many novels, including the Miriam Black books (*Blackbirds, Mockingbird, The Cormorant*) and the young adult Heartland series (*Under the Empyrean Sky, Blightborn*). He's recently penned his own writing guide: *The Kick-Ass Writer*, published by Writer's Digest Books (2013). He blogs at www.terribleminds.com, where he speaks frequently on the subjects of writing and publishing.

CHAPTER 2

CHARACTER CONCEPTING

BY JOSEPH BATES

How readers connect with, and relate to, your characters is the true test of effective fiction.

It doesn't matter if your novel takes place in Victorian England or the Old South or Middle-Earth or Mars; when we relate to a character, and see something of ourselves in the character's struggle, then we feel the danger right along with her, feel what's at stake in her quest, feel the same urgency. When the character fails in her quest, we feel the loss as if it were our own. All good fiction, regardless of the genre, is ultimately character-based. And what makes a character real and relatable to us is complexity: The character has the potential for both good and ill, to do the right thing and the wrong thing, to succeed or fail, and it's the character's decision-making along the way that determines the outcome (and the reader's level of interest, hope, and involvement).

But here's the trick: Your characters' ability to develop as rounded, relatable, often-surprising human beings depends first on how you set them up in terms of *motivation*. Complex characters aren't built on competing, conflicted motivations. Rather, complexity emerges when a character's clear-cut wants, goals, or desires come into conflict with, or are otherwise put at risk by, what happens in your story.

This is something beginning novelists, in particular, have a difficult time accepting. They'll believe that motivation should be a kind of psychological maze, the more branches and twists, the better. And rather than real complexity, what emerges is confusion, with a character never grounded enough to know what it is he wants (and as a result, the reader never knows, either).

The other big problem writers run into is the exact opposite: A character who seems to want nothing from the start, who is going through the events of the plot seemingly because there's nothing better to do. The reader gets the feeling the character would be just as happy walking out of the novel to find a bagel.

The events that unfold in your plot are *only* meaningful to the reader if they are, first and foremost, meaningful for your character, and for your plot to be meaningful to your character, the events must come into direct conflict with whatever it is he wants. But just because your character has a simple or clear-cut motivation, that doesn't mean that the *character* will be simple or clear-cut. Do you know what he is *really* willing to do to achieve his goal? Do you know why the goal is important to him in personal—as well as public, professional, or practical—terms? What would the outcome be if he achieved his goal, or if the character failed to achieve it? These are questions you might not know the answer to until your character actually faces the conflict. And the decisions the character makes in such moments not only reveal his full humanity and complexity, but begin to suggest, and to steer, the course of your novel.

CHARACTER: THE HEART OF THE NOVEL

In Cormac McCarthy's *The Road*, an unnamed father and son, survivors of some never-specified apocalyptic event, head south by foot in the hopes of finding some, *any*, more sustainable world than the wasteland around them. "Going south" is thus the stated, *external* goal of the two characters; it's what they hope to accomplish in the most basic sense. And the external conflicts they face along the way—from desperate individuals hoping to steal their few resources to roving gangs of marauders rumbling up the road in diesel trucks to the hostile, unforgiving terrain itself—all stand in the way of that goal.

Does stating and understanding the external goal and conflicts of the story reveal the gripping emotional experience of reading *The Road*? Absolutely not. The external goal and conflict are aspects of pure plot, the general "what happens." And the external motivation and conflict as stated here—characters wanting to get somewhere and being hindered—are familiar to us, forming the basic plotline of everything from *The Odyssey* to *The Wizard of Oz* to Charles Frasier's *Cold Mountain* to the Steve Martin movie *Planes, Trains, and Automobiles*. Reduced to these terms, the external motivation and conflicts of McCarthy's novel seem unremarkable. But *The Road* is a remarkable, even unforgettable, book, and what makes it so is the way the external motivation and conflict parallel, complicate, and deepen our understanding of the characters' *internal* motivation and conflicts.

We find hints at the internal motivation of the characters by looking more closely at the stated external goal: The father and son are heading south in the hopes of finding a more hospitable climate. But the bleak, unrelenting environment McCarthy sets up in the novel's opening pages—with its "ashen daylight" and "cauterized terrain"—makes it clear that there probably isn't any place untouched by the cataclysm; the burnt-out condition of the world seems all-encompassing. If this is the case, and their stated goal of finding a more inhabitable environment is *unattainable*, what's really keeping the characters (and story) moving forward, and why do we care?

If you've read the book, then you know the answer: The father is using the goal of heading south as a way of holding onto the slimmest idea of hope. And the reason he's doing this is simple: He's trying, against all conceivable odds, to keep his young son alive. This is the father's *internal motivation*, the reason the events in the book are meaningful to him and, as a result, meaningful to us.

What would you do to protect the life of the ones you love? Could you steal to keep them alive? Could you take a life? Could you keep one foot moving in front of the other when there is, in fact, nowhere safe on earth you can go? These are all questions of *internal conflict*, questions that, along with the internal motivation, make the *external* motivation and conflict matter. And these are also the questions we find ourselves asking as we read the novel; you need to never have been in a postapocalyptic wasteland to find something relatable, and heartbreaking, in the father and son's journey.

This connection to character and what's personally at risk was a crucial component of McCarthy's initial creative spark, as he revealed in an interview with Oprah Winfrey:

Creating Characters

> My son John and I ... went to El Paso, and we checked into the
> old hotel there, and one night John was asleep, it was ... probably
> about two or three o'clock in the morning, and I went over and I
> just stood and looked out the window at this town. ... I could hear
> the trains going through and that very lonesome sound, and I just
> had this image of what this town might look like in fifty or a hun-
> dred years. I just had this image of these fires up on the hill and
> everything being laid waste, and I thought about my little boy.

What sparked the idea for *The Road* was nothing more than McCarthy's looking out his hotel window at the darkened city, and at that
moment two things converged: First, he imagined the city burnt-out
and decimated. Then he looked at his young son sleeping in bed and
found himself wondering, if the world were in ruins, could he protect
his son? From this seemingly simple wandering thought, *The Road*
was born—an apocalyptic story and vision, and also the story of a
father wondering if he were fully capable of protecting his child from
the harsh world.

This is precisely the way our own novel ideas should start: not just
with an external idea, conflict, and motivation, but with a resonant and
relatable view of who the characters are, what it is they truly want, and
what they would do to achieve it. Without considering your character
in such terms, you run the risk of writing a novel in which things
happen but affect no one, and as a result the events will resonate with
neither your reader nor you as the author. When an understanding of
character informs and is at the heart of your work, you'll find that the
world you've created is one that the reader finds engaging, terrifying,
touching, but above all familiar.

JOSEPH BATES is the author of *The Nighttime Novelist* (Writer's Digest
Books, 2010) and *Tomorrowland: Stories* (Curbside Splendor, 2013). His short
fiction has appeared in such journals as *The Rumpus, New Ohio Review, Identity
Theory, South Carolina Review,* and *InDigest Magazine*. Visit him online at
www.josephbates.net.

CHAPTER 3

CHOOSE A NAME WISELY

BY NANCY KRESS

Juliet was sure she would have loved Romeo even "were he not Romeo called," and perhaps she was right. Still, one has to wonder. If at that masked ball she'd met young Skunkwort Montague, would she really have been so eager to trumpet his name to the night from her balcony?

Names affect our initial impressions of people, and that includes fictional people. This means that you can use the naming of your characters to affect how readers see them. In fact, it's surprising how much information a reader may assume from a simple name, including family background, age, personal relationships, and personality traits. Since these automatic assumptions are going to happen anyway, it's in your best interest as a writer to control them.

FAMILY BACKGROUND

Ethnicity is the most obvious assumption a reader will make from your character's name. The first sentence of Carol Shields' prize-winning novel *The Stone Diaries* is, "My mother's name was Mercy Stone Goodwill." The name immediately suggests an Anglo-Saxon, Fundamentalist woman in a stern milieu, and that's exactly what Mercy is. The name subtly prepares us for what comes next, and the fact that the subsequent story matches the name reinforces our faith in the author. We can trust her. She knows what she's doing.

Similarly, "Karim Abdul" is assumed to be Arab or of Arab extraction, "Angelina Magdalani" to be Italian, "Reuben Goldstein" Jewish. That much is easy, a clear flag to identify the fictional territory. But what is that reader to make of "Karim Goldstein" or "Ethan Washington Magdalani III?"

Something interesting. Immediate questions arise in the mind: Is Karim Goldstein the child of a Jewish-Arab marriage? Are the Magdalanis trying to be more WASP than the Cabots or the Lodges? The answer might be yes or no, but you've definitely aroused interest. Now you can have the pleasure of satisfying it—which, incidentally, you must do. Names follow the general rule in fiction that the further you stray from reader expectation, the more obligated you are to explain how you got there.

Whether you use ethnicity in names for clarity or you play against expectations, remember that in some regional areas, some ethnicities do predominate. This gives your fiction plausibility. The New York Police Department is still dominated by Irish, Italian, Spanish, and African-Americans. Creating an entire Manhattan precinct filled with Russian-named cops will simply undermine readers' faith that you know your territory.

In addition to ethnicity, other aspects of family background can be foreshadowed by names. The family that calls its son John Addams Carrington IV is making a definite statement: "We're proud of our distinguished heritage." In elementary school with young John were twins, Sunshine and Sweetmeadow Smith. This family is making a very different statement, and readers will expect a hippie or New Age background for the twins—especially if they're boys.

In some upper-class circles, female-line family names were preserved by giving them to daughters. Thus McKenzie Wells, a girl born before 1975 (more on this in a minute), comes with a certain amount of family-expectation baggage. If you write her story, that baggage might reasonably be a part of it.

In recent decades, names have migrated much more easily across the gender barrier, in that names once exclusively male have been appropriated for girls: Ashley, McKenzie, Madison. Few names, however, have gone the other way. As with ethnicity, if your male character has a traditionally female name, you need more verbiage to explain why. Johnny Cash wrote an entire song on this phenomenon: "A Boy Named

Sue." A family that calls a boy "Sue" or "Deb" or "Millicent" probably has some interesting dynamics going—and you've foreshadowed them by the simple use of a name.

CHARACTER'S AGE

Names, even "McKenzie" for a girl, are obviously not infallible guides to age. But they can give subtle hints. "Gladys" and "Myrtle," for instance, were popular names a century ago, but you'd be hard put to find a female infant now named "Myrtle." Similarly "Janet" was popular for the generation that came of age during World War II, "Linda" for their daughters, and "Jennifer" for their granddaughters. Boys' names show less variation over time. Still, a character in a contemporary novel named "Tertius" either is very old or has to make constant explanations to classmates.

Generation-appropriate names really matter in historical novels. English Regency belles were simply not first-named "Madison," or even "Linda." "Janet" was still a diminutive of "Jane," not a name in its own right, as was "Nancy" for "Anne." (Boys, however, might well be named "Tertius.") Do careful research on whatever era and locale you're writing. Again, the aim is to create reader confidence in you as a writer.

QUICK TIPS (TO BEST NAME CHARACTERS)

- Choose a name based on what stereotypes you want your audience to automatically assume about your characters, or the stereotypes you want your character to play against expectations.

- A name can show if your character is young—use "generation appropriate" names.

- Create a name with potential to affect how others react to your character.

- In juvenile fiction only, you can get away with names that automatically trigger a basic human emotion.

PERSONAL RELATIONSHIPS

Not everyone in your story needs to address your character the same way. In fact, variations in address can be a subtle and sure way to indicate variations in relationships. Russian novelists were masters of this, so much so that my English translation of Anna Karenina provides a glossary of diminutives for, say, "Nikolai." You probably don't want to go that far, but do consider the fictional implications for all your character's possible names.

For instance a young schoolteacher is named Diane Eugenia Ramsay. Her small pupils call her Ms. Ramsay. Some of their mothers also say "Ms. Ramsay," while others insist on "Miss Ramsay," even when told she prefers "Ms." Her boyfriend calls her Princess Di, which alternately amuses and irritates her. Her mother persists in "Didi," a baby name that definitely irritates Diane (the mother, too, has been corrected numerous times). Her girlfriends call her "Diane" except for those from junior high, when Diane went through a romantic period and was known by her middle name. These buddies still use "Eugenia," or sometimes "Genie." The IRS calls her "Diane Eudora Ramsay," having confused her with somebody else, an error which Diane needs to straighten out immediately.

Look how much you've learned about this woman before she performs a single action in your story.

It's a sad truth of human nature that we're impressed by connections to the rich, famous, and accomplished. This fuels much name-dropping. Do people in your story react differently to your character after they know his name than before they hear it? This phenomenon was the basis for John Guare's successful play *Six Degrees of Separation*, in which a young man falsely claims to be the son of actor Sidney Poitier.

For all your major characters, consider what names others might call them and why. This might even suggest scenes to you. At a minimum, it builds characterization. A contemporary Septimus, poor child, might get called "Septic Tank" at school. What does he do about it? Fight? Brood? Laugh it off? Become scarred for life?

CHARACTER PERSONALITY

The most dangerous use of names is to indicate personality traits. Nineteenth-century writers got away with it. Dickens's "Uriah Heep" sounds oily and unappealing; Bronte's "Heathcliff" suggests that young man's wild, untamed nature. Contemporary audiences, however, tend to dismiss this sort of thing as implausibly ridiculous—unless you're writing comedy or children's books.

The Harry Potter books use names as tip-offs to personality. "Draco Malfoy," with its echoes of dragons and malevolence, sounds like a villain (junior grade). "Neville Longbottom" is destined to be the butt of schoolboy jokes, as is "Luna Lovegood." If you write juveniles—better yet, funny juveniles—you may wish to exploit names as keys to character.

Kids or adults, people's names matter. Choose yours carefully.

....

NANCY KRESS is the author of thirty-three books, including twenty-six novels, four collections of short stories, and three books on writing. Her work has won five Nebulas, two Hugos, a Sturgeon, and the John W. Campbell Memorial Award. Her most recent works are *After the Fall, Before the Fall, During the Fall* (Tachyon, 2012), a novel of apocalypse, and *Yesterday's Kin* (Tachyon, 2014), about genetic inheritance. In addition to writing, Kress often teaches at various venues around the country and abroad; in 2008, she was the Picador visiting lecturer at the University of Leipzig.

Creating Characters

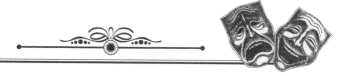

CHAPTER 4

NAME-DROPPING

BY ELIZABETH SIMS

The auditorium was dark except for a pool of light at the center of the stage. One of my all-time heroes, Joyce Carol Oates, was giving a guest lecture at my school, Michigan State University. As her book jacket photos suggested, she was a waif, standing there so pale behind the microphone, with a voice like a small stringed instrument.

I was an intense young writer of short stories, and to this day I remember part of her lecture word for word.

She spoke about her deep feeling for her characters, and her commitment to creating just the right name for each one. I thought of how her characters stuck into me like darts, and I realized that some of their power came from their names: the creepy Arnold Friend in "Where Are You Going, Where Have You Been?" The doomed Buchanan in "Wild Saturday." The primeval Sweet Gum and Jeremiah in "The Death of Mrs. Sheer."

Getting the names right requires patience, she said, and sometimes it's hard. She said that occasionally in her sleep a character she had invented but not named would appear before her and stand in silence. Oates extended her thin white arm, hand cupped. "And I ask, 'What is your *name*? Tell me your name!'"

Since then, I've taken character naming very seriously. It's something far too many writers neglect. The best authors know that a fitting name for a character is a precious gift to readers. Some names resonate as miniature poems, whether masculine or feminine:

- Dracula (*Dracula*, Bram Stoker)
- Holly Golightly (*Breakfast at Tiffany's*, Truman Capote)
- Atticus Finch (*To Kill a Mockingbird*, Harper Lee)
- Becky Sharp (*Vanity Fair*, William Makepeace Thackeray)
- James Bond (*Dr. No* and others, Ian Fleming)
- Scarlett O'Hara (*Gone With the Wind*, Margaret Mitchell)
- Mr. Skimpole (*Bleak House*, Charles Dickens)
- Mrs. Gummidge (*David Copperfield*, ditto)
- Little Toot (*Little Toot*, Hardie Gramatky)
- Cinderella (folktale, timeless)

Like Oates, you're rarely going to come up with that terrific name instantly; you'll have a character who demands to be born, and you'll have to start writing him or her (or it) without a name. In such cases I use "Evil Cutie" or "Brother A" until I can really work on a name.

I'm against using nonsense names as some authors do for ease of typing during their draft phase. "Jiji," for instance, uses just the first two fingers on your right hand, in the central part of the keyboard, and it could definitely save you keystrokes during the course of a long novel, especially if your character ends up being "Charlotte Summerington." However, there is more to writing fiction than saving keystrokes. Every character's name interacts with you as you write, melding with your ideas and feelings for the character. You don't want to stay dissociated from your characters' names for any longer than necessary.

Dickens is great to study for character names. He wrote most of his novels as long magazine serials; their character-packed success depended on every name being quickly and easily distinguished in the reader's mind—and held there from one month to the next. Contemporary British authors must have inherited some of his DNA, because they tend to be terrific namers too (more on them in a moment).

If you think about it, character names come in two basic breeds: those with carefully crafted meanings, and those that simply fit your players like a silk suit, inexplicably perfect. We'll look at both kinds, along with strategies for creating them.

Creating Characters

TYPE 1: LAYERED NAMES

First up are the "meaningful" names, which pull back the skin of your characters and can be analyzed quite like literature itself.

Ironic Names

Large chunks of Alexander McCall Smith's best-selling 44 Scotland Street series concern the difficult life of Bertie Pollock, an Edinburgh schoolboy. Two of his schoolmates are lads named Larch and Tofu. Though minor characters, they're there for a distinct purpose.

The names interact with a savory irony. Tofu and Larch's names obviously have been bestowed by parents with finely tuned ideals. Political correctness abounds: One boy's name is a legume paste, the other a tree. Yet the characters, we learn from their actions and words, are as shallow and phony-hearted as their names are sophisticated.

Smith gives us, by contrast, the simple, direct, honest Bertie. He is worth more than both Tofu and Larch put together. His is an ordinary, unpretentious name; his surname, Pollock, is a common fish. Bertie, then, is the humble everyman who must endure everybody else's idiotic, self-serving vanities.

But for pure triumphal irony, can anything top the Veneering family, of Dickens' classic *Our Mutual Friend*? Such a vaguely grand-seeming name for a vaguely grand family. Simultaneously, of course, their name clues us in that they are nothing but surface. And we enjoy watching them try—and fail—to live up to their banal aspirations.

Ironic names are easy to create: Just think of your character's opposite qualities and brainstorm liberally. Let's say you've got a clumsy guy who lives with his parents and aspires merely to avoid work and download porn. You could give him an ironic name like Thor or Victor or Christian or even Pilgrim. Or you could give him a first name that's a family surname, like Powers or Strong.

Authors who want to use ironic character names should strictly limit themselves to one per story or novel.

Symbolic Names

We love symbolic names—sometimes. Carson McCullers, in *The Heart Is a Lonely Hunter*, manages a good one with John Singer, a deaf-mute who essentially acts as the prophet in the story. Harry Angstrom, the hero of John Updike's Rabbit books, has, I think, a particularly good symbolic name. First of all, we have angst right in there. Then, as you'll remember from science class, an angstrom is a teeny-tiny unit of length. An allegory for a man who feels his life is too small—and who by his actions shows that he might also be a bit insecure about a certain part of his anatomy?

Be warned, though: Symbolic names are treacherous shoals for authors. Way too many novels (first or otherwise) feature bad guys named Grimes and heroes with some form of *truth* or *justice* incorporated into their names. Also, we have too many heroines with the word *sun* in their names, more detectives called Hunter or Archer or Wolf than we can count, and multitudes of good guys with the initials J.C. (Jesus Christ).

Here's the key: Symbolic names work only if they're not heavy-handed. Challenge any symbolic name with the question: Would a twelve-year-old get it during a first reading? If yes, trash it! Keep looking for something subtle, based on your character's deepest traits, or use another approach.

Connotative Names

A connotative name suggests without being explicit.

For instance, in Ernest Hemingway's short story "The Short Happy Life of Francis Macomber," the handsome hunting guide is straightfor-wardly named Richard Wilson, while the client he cuckolds has the fussy name of Francis Macomber. (For some reason in Western culture, Francis sounds sissy-ish, perhaps because it's similar to the feminine form, Frances. A fair number of spoiled pantywaists in literature bear that name; Scout's nauseating cousin in *To Kill a Mockingbird* springs to mind.) In the end, however, Macomber achieves true heroism (albeit briefly!), while Wilson is stuck with Macomber's sexy, monstrous widow, Margot.

You can make up connotative names by asking yourself questions like these as you brainstorm your characters: What expression is on his face when he looks in the mirror in the morning? If she were an animal, what

Creating Characters

would she be? If this character were a building or a political party or a piece of furniture, what would he be? How is her self-image at odds with reality?

Phonetically Suggestive Names

Dickens again. In his masterpiece *Bleak House*, he tells the story of the mother of all lawsuits, "Jarndyce and Jarndyce." And the suit drags on, and your flesh creeps as that name hammers at you throughout the book: *jaundice, jaundice, jaundice.*

Ayn Rand's despicable character Wesley Mouch (weasly mooch) from *Atlas Shrugged* is a pretty good example of a name that sounds like an epithet.

Let's make up a phonetic name that fits a character. What if we had a coach who gambled on his basketball team? Well, it's about winning and losing, and it doesn't matter which if you can make money betting either way. Winning, Winton, Win, Lose, Fail, Failer.

How about Winton Fayhler (win failer)?

TYPE 2: PLAIN NAMES

What of names that have no hidden meaning, but just play off the ear like powerful verse?

- Howard Roark (*The Fountainhead*, Rand)
- Anna Karenina (*Anna Karenina*, Leo Tolstoy)
- Frankenstein (*Frankenstein*, Mary Shelley)
- Blanche DuBois (*A Streetcar Named Desire*, Tennessee Williams)

Such names are the holy grail of authors. You know them when you see them—the rhythm, the grace, the style!—but defining them is almost impossible. Fortunately, it's also irrelevant. What we need are ways to generate those lovely combinations of consonants and vowels.

Judging by successful character names, it seems a strong first syllable in both first and last names works well, regardless of the number of syllables. (Harry Potter, Jo March, Robinson Crusoe.)

Here's how you can generate pure plain good names:

Collar Them in Your Dreams

Awaiting inspiration is perhaps the most organic way to name your characters, though it could take some time. Seriously, though, often you'll be working with a character and his name—complete, perfect, incontrovertible—will simply pop into your head. It can happen while you're writing, or weighing plums at the grocery, or drifting in dreamland. Accept these pieces of luck as your due. Expect them.

Get Bookish

Remember phone books? Leaf through yours, and try putting different first and last names together. Phone books, however, are usually limited regionally. If you live in a small town in Minnesota, for instance, you're going to find a whole lot of Johnsons and Olsons but not many Garciaparras and Hoxhas. I keep a couple of baby-name books handy when I'm in the early stages of an outline or draft. I also save commencement programs.

Surf the Web

You can go online and find helpful reference sites that list first names and surnames by national origin, and you'll find sites that tell you name meanings, etc. You'll also find assorted sites that simply generate names. Browse around.

Surf the Original Web

For real inspiration I suggest a trip to your local library, where you'll be amazed at the wealth of name stuff you'll find in the reference department. Besides general encyclopedias, which are rife with names from all eras, you'll find encyclopedias on every specialized subject from military history to music, sports, radio and television, steamships and railroads, law enforcement, crime and more. All of these books are crammed with names. The real pay dirt in your library is in the genealogy section. Here you'll find books packed with names from all over the world, along with dates, cities, and other location names, too. You might even get ideas for characters right out of those books—or whole plots, for that matter. That's the serendipity of browsing, the fostering of which physical libraries are still unsurpassed.

Creating Characters

THE MAKINGS OF ANY GOOD MONIKER

No matter what sort of character name you're pursuing, heed common sense and do the following.

Check Root Meanings

It's better to call a character Caleb, which means "faithful" or "faithful dog," than to overkill it by naming him Loyal or Goodman—unless you want that for comic/ironic purposes. Some readers will know the name's root meaning, but those who don't might sense it.

Get Your Era Right

If you need a name for an eighteen-year-old shopgirl in a corset store in 1930s Atlanta, you know enough not to choose Sierra or Courtney, unless such an unusual name is part of your story. Browse for names in the era you're writing. A Depression-era shopgirl who needs a quick name could go by Myrtle or Jane; it will feel right to the reader. Small public libraries will often have decades' worth of local high school yearbooks on the shelves. Those things are gold for finding name combinations from the proper era.

Speak Them Out Loud

Your novel might become an audiobook or an e-book with text-to-speech enabled. A perfectly good name on paper, such as Adam Messina, may sound unclear aloud: Adam Essina? Adah Messina?

Manage Your Crew Appropriately

Distinguish your large cast of characters by using different first initials, of course, and vary your number of syllables and places of emphasis. Grace Metalious (a great name right there) demonstrates this in her blockbuster *Peyton Place*, as do any of the successful epic writers like James Michener and Larry McMurtry.

Use Alliterative Initials

Employ this strategy to call special attention to a character: Daniel Deronda, Bilbo Baggins, Ratso Rizzo, Severus Snape.

Think It Through

You might notice that in most crime fiction the murderer rarely has a middle name or initial. Why? Because the more you explicate the name, the more likely there's a real person out there with it. And reading your story they might become upset and try to sue you or come after you some night with a bayonet.

Check 'Em Again

When writing my novel *The Actress*, I needed a name for a Japanese-American criminal defense attorney, and the name Gary Kwan burst upon me. I loved the name and used it in the book. Only thing was, as soon as the thousands of copies of hardcovers were printed and shipped to stores, I heard from a reader who pointed out the simple fact that Kwan is a *Chinese* surname. I cursed loudly and decided: a) that I would ALWAYS check name origins, and b) that Gary Kwan had a Chinese grandfather who adopted a Japanese orphan who became Gary's father. Or something like that.

Naming characters just right is a challenge, but give it some time and thought, and you'll start to find the fun in it. Study the names great authors have come up with, let your mind loose to play, do your research, and above all, trust your ear.

....

ELIZABETH SIMS (elizabethsims.com) is a contributing editor to *Writer's Digest* magazine, a prize-winning novelist, and author of the bestseller *You've Got a Book in You: A Stress-Free Guide to Writing the Book of Your Dreams* (Writer's Digest Books, 2013).

Creating Characters

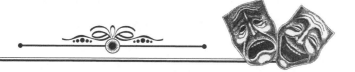

CHAPTER 5

INTRODUCING YOUR CHARACTER FOR THE FIRST TIME

BY JEFF GERKE

Many novelists give little thought to how they're going to lift the curtain on their main character. They begin with the character in a conversation or doing something uncharacteristic of him. Often this is because they're trying to engage the reader with action while also introducing the main character.

In fiction, as in life, first impressions are crucial. The first time the reader sees your protagonist, you want her doing the perfect thing, something that instantly typifies her and shows what's wonderful about her.

It's no mistake that every James Bond film begins with 007 doing something incredible to take down the bad guys or get the information he needs. There's usually a beautiful woman involved in the event as well. We get a perfect sense of who this character is (and what kind of story this is going to be) before anything else has happened.

That's what you should be going for with your book. So let your mind hover over your character and your "story stew" a bit while you think about ways you could reveal her essence in an introductory scene.

The best example I know of a great character introduction is the opening sequence from the movie *Raiders of the Lost Ark*. Remember the iconic jungle scenes? With very few words uttered, we get to see exactly what this Indiana Jones person is like. We see that he's a tough hombre who knows his way around not only a gun but a whip. We learn he knows a lot about ancient traps and treasures. We see his grit and daring. We feel like he could punch our lights out. We see his resourcefulness. We also see his limits, his vanity (the hat), and a taste of his fears (the snake). We even meet his nemesis.

By the end of that sequence, when he's swinging through the trees and escaping in the get-away plane, we know not only who this person is but what kind of movie this is going to be.

If it had to, this sequence could stand alone as a short film. It is a self-contained unit in and of itself, with a great story arc. The fact that it's the beginning of the movie sets the viewers' expectations. They know it's going to be a very special ride.

To bring your main character onstage the first time, write a short story. Pretend this is a cameo, the only time she's going to be in the story, but you want to give her an unforgettable moment of glory.

Begin with what you have identified as the essence, the core, of this person, and craft an episode around that. Keep the Indiana Jones and James Bond examples in mind, and see what you can come up with.

Of course it doesn't have to be an action scene. If your story is a romantic comedy, an action scene would be all wrong. Just think about what kind of book yours is going to be and write a fun little scene or sequence that allows your main character to reveal who she is at heart.

This introduction is the perfect opportunity to reveal what your character is wanting or trying to achieve *and* what's likable about her. Your reader is thinking of committing days or even months to your book, and if she's going to spend three hundred-plus pages with this character, she'd better not be a jerk. Even if she *is* a jerk and that's the whole point of her inner journey (eradicating her unpleasantness), you still have to show us something sympathetic about her in these opening moments.

Your protagonist isn't the only character you should craft a special introduction for. If you have an antagonist, that person ought to have a wonderful intro, too—perhaps in the prologue. If there is a romantic interest in your book, that person should be brought on with a carefully crafted scene to give us—and the main character—the right first impression. Sidekicks, henchmen, possible suspects, and anyone else you want to feature should get his or her own well-chosen walk-on scene.

Creating Characters

Lesser characters should get less-developed introductory scenes, of course. Maybe it's just a moment, like a character stumbling into a room and dropping a box of doughnuts or a fabulous quick scene of a singing telegram at the door. Who can forget Dickens' introduction in *A Tale of Two Cities* to Marquis Evrémonde, who runs down a plebian child in his carriage and then curses peasants for getting in his way?

Barliman Butterburr has a small part in The Lord of the Rings, but it's memorable. The first time we see him, he's doing exactly what he does: tending to his tavern guests. But he's kind and affable, and Tolkien created a scene that revealed these characteristics, and his forgetfulness, which becomes important later.

Use that model as you're constructing introductory scenes for your featured minor characters. Give thought to how you can raise the curtain on them in their essence and doing what characterizes them.

As we come to the end of this chapter, I'd like to spend a minute on the topic of the prologue-free novel. A story that doesn't begin with a prologue still needs to begin well, right? It still needs to engage the reader and get the energy flowing. If you choose to go sans prologue, your opening scene will need to do triple duty. Not only do you need to kick off the book in a way that gives the story the right tone, you also need to introduce the main character (because any opening scene that doesn't introduce the main character is a prologue!). So you have to find a method for giving the hero the perfect entrance *and* engage the reader *and* set the right flavor for the book.

It can be done, certainly, and done well. The James Bond and Indiana Jones movies do it every time. Go for it.

....

JEFF GERKE is the author of three books from Writer's Digest: *Plot Versus Character* (2010), *The First 50 Pages* (2011), and *Write Your Novel in a Month* (2013). He is the founder of Marcher Lord Press, the premier publisher of Christian speculative fiction. He currently freelances for clients: editing, creating book cover designs, and typesetting (at www.jeffgerke.com). He lives in Colorado Springs with his wife and three children.

PART II

POINT OF VIEW

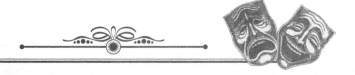

CHAPTER 6

WHOSE EMOTIONS
ARE WE SHARING?

BY NANCY KRESS

Since we lack telepathy, we humans are imprisoned in our own skulls. As Joseph Conrad wrote, "We live, as we dream, alone"—at least alone within our heads. The only thoughts, plans, dreams, and feelings we can directly experience are our own. It's because this one-viewpoint reality is hardwired in us that fiction is so fascinating. It lets us experience the world from inside someone else's head.

This is the definition of point of view: whose eyes we view the action through, whose head we're inside of, whose feelings we experience as that character feels them. As such, your choice of point-of-view character or characters is critical to your story. It will determine what you tell, how you tell it, and, often what the action means.

PROTAGONIST VS. POV CHARACTER:
IF I'M NOT THE STAR, WHO IS?

The protagonist of your story is the "star," the person we're most interested in, the one with the interesting action. Usually, but not inevitably, your protagonist will also be a POV character. Thus we see the events of John Grisham's best-selling *The King of Torts* through the eyes of its major character, Clay Carter. Carter is both the star and a POV character.

However, you can obtain some interesting effects by having your POV character be someone other than the protagonist. Two classics that do this are F. Scott Fitzgerald's *The Great Gatsby* and W. Somerset

Maugham's *The Moon and Sixpence*. *Gatsby* is told through the eyes of Nick Carraway, who is only peripherally involved in the main action, mostly as a standby friend and go-between. The real protagonists are the illicit lovers, Jay Gatsby and Daisy Buchanan, particularly Gatsby. Maugham goes farther yet. The protagonist of *The Moon and Sixpence* is Charles Strickland, who abandons his middle-class London existence to travel to the South Seas and become a painter; Strickland is based loosely on Paul Gauguin. The unnamed narrator of the novel, the sole POV character, knows Strickland only slightly, as the friend of a friend. The narrator has several casual encounters with Strickland, first in England and then in Tahiti. At no time does the narrator ever affect Strickland's life or Strickland affect the narrator's. Much of Strickland's later life is told to the narrator by other people, after the artist is dead.

The disadvantages of this convoluted structure are obvious; it lacks immediacy. Everything important that Strickland does, or that is done to him, occurs offstage. The narrator is told about events later, and he tells us about them. Maugham sacrifices a great deal of drama this way. So why did he do it?

Because separating your POV character from your protagonist also confers certain advantages:

- The POV character can continue the story after the protagonist dies, which both Charles Strickland and Jay Gatsby do during their respective novels. Maugham's POV character traces the fates of Strickland's widow, children, and paintings.
- The protagonist can be portrayed as much more secretive if he is not also a POV character. No one learns about Jay Gatsby's real past until he is dead; he has invented for himself a much more glamorous background than his actual one. Had Gatsby been a POV character, we readers would have known from the beginning, since we would have been "inside his head." Protagonists who are not also POV characters can preserve their mysteries. As Maugham's narrator says, "I felt that Strickland had kept his secrets to the grave."
- The POV character can make observations that would never in a million years occur to the protagonist. Thus Nick Carraway

comes to see Daisy Buchanan as a careless lightweight and Jay Gatsby as a touching idealist, views neither character (nor anyone else in the book) would have shared.

The first questions you should ask yourself about your use of POV are: Will my protagonist and POV character(s) be the same? If not, do I have good reason for the split? Will I gain more than I lose?

Once you know whether your protagonist will be a POV character, the next step is to determine who else will occupy that critical role.

CHOOSING POV CHARACTERS: THROUGH YOUR EYES ONLY

It's a good idea, before you write anything at all, to consider all the choices for POV characters. The first choice to come to mind may not be the best pick.

Consider, for instance, Harper Lee's *To Kill a Mockingbird*, which takes place in pre-World War II Alabama. The main plotline concerns the framing of a black man, Tom Robinson, for the beating of a white woman, a crime he did not commit. His lawyer is the respected Atticus Finch, father of two children. Finch forces the identification of the true assailant, the victim's father, who then attempts revenge by attacking Finch's kids. Harper Lee could have told her story from any of these points of view. Instead she embeds her main plot in a coming-of-age story and makes her first-person narrator one of the children, Finch's eight-year-old daughter, Scout. As a result, she ends up with a far different story than if the POV character had been Atticus Finch, Tom Robinson, or the true assailant. A better story? A worse one? No one can say; we didn't see the alternate versions.

But certainly Scout is an effective choice. She meets the general criteria you should consider when choosing your POV character:

- **WHO WILL BE HURT BY THE ACTION?** Someone strongly affected emotionally usually makes the best POV character (although Maugham, as we have seen, chooses to sacrifice emotional immediacy for other goals). Scout is the victim of attempted murder by the disgruntled woman-beater and thus is in danger. Pick for your POV character someone with a strong stake in the outcome, including pain if the outcome will be negative.

This criteria, incidentally, is why detective novels often work very hard to create a personal connection between the murderer and the detective. It raises the pain possibilities, which in turn increases narrative tension.

- **WHO CAN BE PRESENT AT THE CLIMAX?** In *To Kill a Mockingbird*, Scout is there. So is Nick Carraway in *The Great Gatsby*. Your POV character should be, too, or else we'll have to be told secondhand about the most important event of your story. This almost never works.
- **WHO GETS MOST OF THE GOOD SCENES?** We want to be present at those, too. Scout sneaks into the courtroom to witness her father's defense of Tom Robinson.
- **WHO WILL PROVIDE AN INTERESTING OUTLOOK ON THE STORY?** Scout brings to Harper Lee's novel an innocent, fresh view of the racism that no adult could. Nick Carraway similarly views the action of *The Great Gatsby* from a more idealistic, simpler vantage point than do its other characters, mostly New York sophisticates. What kind of observations about life do you want to make in your novel? Who is fit to make them? Do you want that character as your "eyes" and "heart"?
- **WHOSE HEAD ARE YOU MOST INTERESTED IN INHABITING DURING THIS STORY?** Don't underestimate this criterion; it's key.

DIFFERENT EYES, DIFFERENT STORY

You may think you already know who your POV character will be. Perhaps you're right. But take a few moments to imagine what your story might be like if you chose differently.

Let us suppose, for instance, that you are writing a novel about the abduction of a child. Major characters are the father, the mother, the child, the abductor, a suspicious-but-innocent neighbor, and the lead detective on the case. The child will be recovered, but the family will never be the same again. There are at least six potential novels here, all vastly different.

If the mother or father (or both) is your viewpoint, you will have a novel of anguish (which might be what you want). These are good points of view if the couple will eventually divorce, unable to incorporate the strain of the abduction into an already fragile marriage. Perhaps one of them has an extramarital affair. Perhaps one mounts an independent investigation. Perhaps one hires someone to murder the neighbor, who turns out to be innocent.

If the child is the POV character, you have a novel of bewilderment, fear, maybe eventual escape. You will, of course, lose all scenes of the investigation and of parental interaction, because the kid won't see them. You'll gain a lot of scenes between the abductor and abducted.

If the neighbor is the POV character, you will have a novel of injustice. This could be quite interesting; stories of people wrongly accused always make for strong reader identification. Everyone loves an innocent underdog.

If the abductor is the POV character, you probably have a novel of either evil or madness. What is his motivation? Do you want to explore that? If so, he's your man.

If the police officer or FBI agent is the POV character, you have a mystery novel. What's his stake in this, beyond professional competence? Do you want to focus on how an investigation looks from the inside?

I want to emphasize that none of these POV choices are inherently better or worse than any other. It all depends on which suits the version of the story you want to tell. But if you don't at least consider points of view other than the one that first occurs to you, you may be cutting yourself off from some very exciting possibilities.

Even existing stories, if they are not protected by copyright, are sometimes retold from another POV. The results can be fascinating. Jean Rhys retold Charlotte Bronte's *Jane Eyre* from the viewpoint of the first Mrs. Rochester, the madwoman imprisoned in the attic, in her novel *Wide Sargasso Sea*. Valerie Martin retold Robert Louis Stevenson's *The Strange Case of Dr. Jekyll and Mr. Hyde* as seen through the eyes of a housemaid in her novel *Mary Reilly*. And Susan Meddaugh produced the delightful *Cinderella's Rat*, which retells the familiar tale from the POV of one with a tail.

Who among your assembled cast might be an interesting POV character, with a more original outlook on the plot than your first choice? If you were not the writer but the reader, who might be the most satisfying POV character?

CAST OF THOUSANDS: HOW MANY POINTS OF VIEW ARE YOU ALLOWED?

There is no one correct answer to this. A general rule of thumb is to have as few points of view as you can get away with and still tell the story you want to tell.

The reason for this is the aforementioned entrapment in our own skulls. We're used to experiencing reality from one POV. Each time you switch from one fictional viewpoint to another, the reader must make a mental adjustment. If there are too many of these, the story feels increasingly fragmented and unreal.

On the other hand (there is always "another hand" in writing fiction), you may gain more than you lose. If you want to show how a romance feels to both parties, then you need two points of view. If one character simply cannot be present at every important scene you need to present, then you need more than one POV. You may need three, or even more, especially for a complicated or epic plot.

Figure out the least number you can have and still cover all major scenes and internal dialogues that your story requires. The point is to lessen the demands on the reader as much as possible so he can concentrate on the story and its implications, rather than try to remember what that eighth POV character was doing the last time we saw him, which was two hundred pages ago because it takes a while to cycle through eight points of view and do justice to each. Too many points of view are hard on the reader.

And, I might add, it's not easy on the writer, either.

Once you know your POV, the next step is to make a choice among first person, third person, or omniscient.

FIRST PERSON: THE GREAT I AM

First person means the story is told as "I." Everything is seen through the eyes of that one person, and we readers exist right there in his head for the duration of the story. Here is an effective example of first person; it is the opening of Michael Frayn's novel *Spies*:

> The third week of June and there it is again: the same almost embarrassingly familiar breath of sweetness that comes every year about this time. I catch it on the warm evening air as I walk past the well-ordered gardens on my quiet street, and for a moment I'm a child again and everything's before me—all the frightening, half-understood promises of life.

This passage illustrates the other advantages of first person, in addition to one-head verisimilitude:

- **IMMEDIACY.** We are inside the character's head, so our experience of his sensations, such as the scent on the evening air, feels natural and plausible. Such is the power of pronoun that when something happens to a fictional "I," it feels as if it's happening to the reader "I."
- **LANGUAGE.** This character thinks in fairly formal phrases ("almost embarrassingly familiar breath of sweetness"). This tells us a great deal about him, in terms of class and education, before we have so much as one fact. Contrast this with an opening such as this hypothetical one:

> I never did get none of that preacher talk. Heaven? Don't make no sense to have a whole other world in the sky when this one's already here.

- **RANGE.** Frayn's character's thoughts range easily over memory, opinion, and impressions because they're his *thoughts*. We're already inside his head, and these are things that people naturally think about. Introducing thoughts in third person can feel more artificial and even awkward ("His thoughts wandered back to earlier Junes…").

These are strong advantages, but first person also has strong disadvantages:

- You cannot include any scene at which your POV character is not present.
- You cannot include any information that your POV character would not naturally have.
- You must include all information the POV character does have; to do otherwise is usually considered cheating. For example, if your POV detective notices a key clue, you cannot withhold it because "it would give the plot away." If he knows it, we know it.
- You are limited to your POV character's view of the world. This is why some writers consider first person "claustrophobic." If your POV character is naturally suspicious, then all the other characters must be described in suspicious terms. You can *show* that another person is actually honorable, but you cannot *tell* us that because no matter what she does, the POV character will interpret it suspiciously. You will have to dramatize the other character's honorableness strongly and repeatedly in order to counteract the POV character's viewpoint.
- Perhaps the largest danger of first person is that you already have an "I" in your head—yourself. The temptation, especially for beginning writers, is to assume that because you feel a certain way, so will your fictional "I"—and that this congruence of thought is automatically clear to the reader. It's not. In other words, first-person POV demands, even more than other choices, that the writer be objective enough to "become the reader" in judging what is actually on the page, not merely intended in the author's mind. This structure is why many writers consider first person the hardest POV to do well.

THIRD PERSON: HE, SHE, OR IT

Third-person POV means that the story is told in terms of "he did this" or "she thought this." We can go inside the head of the third-person POV character, but we can also see him from the outside. Third person that goes into only one character's head is called limited third-person viewpoint. Third person that goes into more than one POV is called multiple third-person viewpoint.

Here is a third-person scene opening from Ken Follett's best-selling *Triple*:

> Al Cortone knocked and waited in the hall for a dead man to open the door.
>
> The suspicion that his friend was dead had grown to a conviction in the past three years. First, Cortone had heard that Nat Dickstein had been taken prisoner. Toward the end of the war, stories began to circulate about what was happening to Jews in the Nazi Camps. Then, at the end, the grim truth came out.
>
> On the other side of the door, a ghost scraped a chair on the floor and padded across the room.
>
> Cortone felt suddenly nervous. What if Dickstein were disabled, deformed? Suppose he had come unhinged? Cortone had never known how to deal with cripples or crazy men.

This could have been written in first person, in which case it would look like this:

> I knocked and waited in the hall for a dead man to open the door.
>
> The suspicion that my friend was dead had grown to a conviction in the past three years. First, I'd heard that Nat Dickstein had been taken prisoner. Toward the end of the war, stories began to circulate about what was happening to Jews in the Nazi Camps. Then, at the end, the grim truth came out.
>
> On the other side of the door, a ghost scraped a chair on the floor and padded across the room.
>
> I felt suddenly nervous. What if Dickstein were disabled, deformed? Suppose he had come unhinged? I'd never known how to deal with cripples or crazy men.

So does that mean that there's no real difference between first person and third person? No. That this particular passage could be transformed so easily only points up that Follett writes in what is called "transparent prose style." This means that he writes plain, straightforward prose more interested in advancing the plot than creating an individual style. Limited sections of transparent prose can often be changed easily from third person to first person, or vice versa—but that doesn't mean the whole story can be or that all stories can be so transposed. For many, you'd lose too much.

Like what? Let's start with the advantages of third person over first person:

- You can describe the POV characters from the outside, what they're doing and what they look like, which you cannot in first person because people don't think about themselves that way.
- You are not limited to the narrator's worldview. You can present objective facts, such as the last two sentences of the second paragraph in the above passage, without filtering them through one person's individual, often quirky, lens on the world. Third person "opens up the story," making it feel less claustrophobic.
- You can include more than one POV in third person. In fact, much contemporary popular fiction is written in multiviewpoint third person because it allows the author to roam freely over his plot, and to include everything major that happens to all POV characters instead of just one character.
- You can withhold crucial information. Simply do not put those characters who possess the information among your POV characters.
- You may gain more objectivity about the characters when you do not write "I," thus more fully imagining them and also becoming more capable of evaluating the results on the page.

The disadvantages of third person are:

- More distance between the character and the reader (although this can be controlled by varying distance).
- Less distinctive language patterns.
- Greater awkwardness in using memory, flashback, and opinion, unless very skillfully handled.

CHOOSING BETWEEN FIRST PERSON AND THIRD PERSON

So which POV is best for *your* story? Obviously there's no right answer; it's an individual decision based on how you want to present your material. But there are a few guidelines.

If your story is epic in scope, covering many people in many places (as is Follett's *Triple*), you need multiple third person.

If you want flexibility to pull back from the character and include brief blocks of objective information, you need third person, either limited or multiple.

If you want to describe the character extensively from the outside, as do many romance novels, you definitely want third person.

If you want readers to identify strongly with your POV character, seeing the world as she does, you want either first person or limited third person, but first person may end up more vivid.

If your character's thoughts are quirky, far-ranging, and stylistically interesting, you can use either first person or third person, but first person will bring us closer to that quirkiness. On the other hand, if your character is really bizarre, first person may not give you enough flexibility to tell us things about him that will help us make sense of his weirdness.

OMNISCIENT POV: I SEE ALL AND KNOW ALL

Omniscient, a POV universal in the nineteenth century and much less so now, has two hallmarks. First, it goes into the mind of any character the author chooses, sometimes repeatedly and sometimes only once. Second, the author himself comments freely on the action, sometimes addressing the reader directly with his comments and interpretations.

Howards End is written in omniscient POV, and at a tense point in the novel, E.M. Forster takes full advantage of its flexibility:

> "How do you do, Mr. Bast?" said Margaret, trying to control her
> voice. "This is an odd business. What view do you take of it?"

> "There is Mrs. Bast, too," prompted Helen.
> Jacky also shook hands. She, like her husband, was shy, and
> so bestially stupid that she could not grasp what was happening.

In just fifty-four words, we have dipped into three minds: Margaret's, who is "trying to control her voice;" Jacky Bast's, who "could not grasp what was happening;" and the author's, who tells us that Mrs. Bast is "bestially stupid." Certainly this is neither Jacky's opinion of herself nor Margaret's of Jacky (the two women have just met). Forster is editorializing here, a hallmark of omniscient POV.

Its unlimited flexibility would seem to make omniscient POV the easiest of all viewpoints for the writer. In fact, it is the most difficult.

....

NANCY KRESS is the author of thirty-three books, including twenty-six novels, four collections of short stories, and three books on writing. Her work has won five Nebulas, two Hugos, a Sturgeon, and the John W. Campbell Memorial Award. Her most recent works are *After the Fall, Before the Fall, During the Fall* (Tachyon, 2012), a novel of apocalypse, and *Yesterday's Kin* (Tachyon, 2014), about genetic inheritance. In addition to writing, Kress often teaches at various venues around the country and abroad; in 2008, she was the Picador visiting lecturer at the University of Leipzig.

CHAPTER 7

WHAT POV COMMUNICATES ABOUT YOUR STORY

BY ALICIA RASLEY

You don't choose POV; it chooses you. Well, not exactly. But rather than conceiving a story with a desire to write in a particular POV ("I'm just dying to write in omniscient!"), think instead about the story you want to write and then determine which POV will help you best tell this story.

You are important here. The sort of novels you like to read and want to write is probably reflective of some aspect of your character, and that's going to affect which POV you find most comfortable for your story. I have a theory that visually oriented people tend to prefer multiple POV over third-person limited or first-person POV. They might "see" a story as the braiding of the lives of several different characters. Someone kinesthetically oriented, however, might prefer to tell this same set of events in the more directly active first person. If you can't imagine writing in first person, don't chose that POV just because you admire other first-person books similar to your project in style, tone, or theme. First and foremost, know yourself and get to know your story. Make your manner of writing the best way to tell that particular story.

POV APPROACHES AND THEMES

Each POV approach reflects a particular concern that has preoccupied fiction writers since the dawn of storytelling. These themes, if recognized, can deepen your story's own themes.

- First-person POV explores questions of persona and identity: What of myself do I reveal the world? What do I conceal? (Multiple–first person, by the way, adds the dimension of contrasting views both of the world and of the self.)
- Second-person POV explores the nature of identity construction: How does *you* compare to *I*?
- Objective POV explores whether there is, apart from each of our own interpretations, an objective reality.
- Classical omniscient explores human society: How do we interact and why?
- Contemporary omniscient explores the conflict between our need for society and our need for freedom.
- Third-person limited explores the issue of the interior life: How do internal needs and conflicts drive an individual's external actions?
- Third-person omniscient explores the issue of perspective: What we see is very much dependent on where we stand.

These themes are not mutually exclusive. For example, if you use a contemporary-omniscient opening to a scene and then slide into third-person limited or third-person omniscient POV, the combination can help you explore the tension or balance between self and society.

This does not mean that these POV themes are the only ones that can be examined in your story. Rather POV approaches evolved, in part, to explore these issues; your attraction to any particular method probably reflects your subconscious interest in the issues it brings up. For example, if you are writing about a woman whose life is still being affected by her parents' early deaths, you might decide that third-person limited POV will help you delve more deeply into her internal reality. Then again, if you are more interested in how a cold-case police unit investigates her parents' deaths, a single-POV focus might unnecessarily limit the narrative and action. A multiple-POV account could show the action from the characters who are most involved, while contrasting their different versions of reality.

As you build your own story, keep the central issues provided by POV in mind and let them enhance your own work. At the very least, make sure the POV approach you choose doesn't undercut the themes you are trying to develop.

Creating Characters

Does Your Story Focus on the Group or Individual?

In addition to thinking about central themes, you should also consider whether yours is more of a "social novel" or a "personal novel." The social novel focuses on the interaction of a group or community, while the personal novel tightly addresses the experience of a central protagonist. As always with fiction, these are not hard and fast categories. Charles Frazier's *Cold Mountain* involves both the exploration of a Civil War town and the personal journey of a soldier trying to find his way home.

Social novels are more likely to use omniscient or multiple POV, so that we are privy to the understanding of several characters and their interactions. Personal novels are more likely to use a tightly focused single POV, whether third person or first person, so we can share the internal experience of the character.

Social and personal novels both appear in most genres. For example, the thriller genre encompasses both Robert Ludlum's *The Bourne Identity*, which follows an amnesiac spy's attempt to discover his past (personal), and Ian Caldwell and Dustin Thomason's *The Rule of Four*, which solves an ancient mystery while exploring the friendships and rivalries within an Ivy League academy (social).

It helps to consider whether you are more interested in the journey of one (or two) main characters or in the actions and interactions of a larger group. Since most genres allow both types of novels, make sure you're not undermining your own purpose by, for example, using too many viewpoints in what is meant to be a deeply personal psychological thriller, or, conversely, sticking too tightly to one POV in a novel that's meant to describe the workings of an entire culture.

WHO'S HEADLINING?

Your POV choice can also affect the name of your story, as the focus of the story is often reflected in the title: *David Copperfield* promises a much more personally focused Dickens novel than *A Tale of Two Cities*. Two books in Stephen King's The Dark Tower series provide another good contrast. The first is called *The Gunslinger*, and it's very much concerned with a man who fights alone and ends up alone. The second book, however,

---

is called *The Drawing of the Three*, which suggests the protagonist's new recognition of his need for allies and the building of his little army. Before you title your story, ask yourself: Is it the character or group that deserves top billing?

One or More Than One? Genre Considerations and POV

Your choice of genre will greatly affect your POV, and your approach to POV may influence an editor's opinion about how to market your work (as a particular genre, as general fiction, or as literary fiction). The boundaries between genres might vary depending on historical period—a "romance" today doesn't mean what it did to Chaucer—but most contemporary fiction falls into one of these genres: mystery, detective, suspense, science fiction, fantasy, romance, horror, Western, thriller (legal and medical), adventure, or literary.

POV is infinitely variable, and you must choose the approach that works best for your story. Some books do stick very close to a single-protagonist POV, but most novels are filtered through more than one character's viewpoint. There's no rule that dictates you must use only one POV, even in first-person narratives. But while there's no real "formula" for writing popular fiction, each genre has a distinct purpose, set of conventions, and boundaries that readers understand and expect. These genre expectations, which are based in the experience readers want from these novels, may affect whether you use only one POV in your book or many.

For example, many mysteries are told entirely in the POV of the "sleuth" (using first person or a very close third-person limited) so that the readers get only the information available to the sleuth. Part of the reason readers like mysteries is because they can compete with the sleuth in solving the crime; as a result, they don't want to know anything extra that might "leak" through another POV character. On the other hand, in romance novels, most readers would feel cheated if they didn't get into the heads of both the hero and heroine, as a romance requires both of these viewpoints in order to get the "full" story of how the couple comes together.

Creating Characters

Usually literary and historical first-person novels are told through only one POV, but authors have also experimented with sequential multiple first person, where one character might have his say for a hundred pages, then another character might have her say, or narrators might alternate chapters. Susan Howatch's multigenerational family saga, *Cashelmara*, is a good example of sequential-multiple first-person POV, and William Faulkner alternated narrators in *As I Lay Dying*, the story of the Bundren family's pilgrimage to bury their deceased matriarch.

If you're writing popular fiction or using any of the traditional storytelling structures (like quest or Gothic or romance), you'll need to understand tradition, particularly when it comes to approaching POV. As always, if you're writing a particular type of novel, read widely in that genre and figure out what's conventional, what is unusual, and what is rarely, if ever, done. It's helpful to study novels in your chosen genre to see the variety of choices and how each choice might fulfill the author's purpose in the novel. But you might also look for the elements that don't work: when a glimpse into the twisted mind of the villain provides laughs rather than thrills, when you figure out the mystery too early because the author let too many clues drop in that secondary character's POV, or when time travel is explained by a twenty-third-century engineer who can't possibly know how ignorant we twenty-first centurians are.

You don't have to stick with what's conventional if you sincerely feel your approach is better for the story, but think it through before you do something groundbreaking in that type of work—say, second person in the traditionally first-person detective novel. Readers and editors are willing to experiment, but they also have an appreciation for the conventions of the story type, which have proven their effectiveness for many years. Because POV has such a comprehensive effect on how the story is experienced, always consider the influence on the readers as you make choices.

The following is a breakdown of the major story types and some challenges and conventions you should consider before choosing a POV for your novel.

Crime Novels: Private Eyes, Mysteries, and Thrillers

The *private-eye/detective novel* has traditionally been told entirely in the first-person voice of the detective. The purpose of the tightly focused POV is to allow the reader to follow one person's interpretation and investigation of a case. The first-person approach also lets the protagonist's voice convey the narrative, and private-eye voices are usually intriguing, another genre tradition. In fact, ever since Raymond Chandler's sardonic and cynical Philip Marlowe solved his cases out loud, readers have expected detective novels to offer not only satisfying plots but also compelling P.I. characters.

I suspect the private-eye first-person POV convention is one of the most rigid in popular fiction today, although variations occasionally emerge. For example, Robert Crais will intersperse third-person secondary-character scenes with the more traditional first-person scenes of detective Elvis Cole. That allows him to reveal events and motivations that his detective doesn't know. Other authors have written most of the story in first-person narration by the private eye but used third person (or another first-person perspective) to offer a glimpse into the villain's head. But readers still enjoy private-eye novels as much for the private investigator's voice and personality as for the mystery; so if you're interested in writing detective fiction, work on getting to know the central character's POV and developing his unique voice.

There are alternatives for crime-fiction writers who prefer the third-person POV. The *mystery novel* has traditionally used a tightly focused third-person narrative, concentrating on the viewpoint of the "sleuth." But the sleuth's voice isn't as central to the experience of a mystery novel, which focuses on plot, as it is in a detective novel, which asks the reader to focus both on the crime and the person solving it. (Notice that even the names of the subgenres—*detective* and *mystery*—suggest what their relative focus is: the puzzle solver or the puzzle.)

The essential element of the mystery genre, the one most important to the author, is that both reader and sleuth have access to the same essential information, and this is ensured by POV control. Some mysteries offer occasional omniscient passages (such as a scene when the body is discovered), but with the assumption that the sleuth also has access to the information revealed to the reader in those passages. Additionally, I have read mysteries with passages in the POV of a minor character, but where the information provided isn't essential to figuring out the puzzle (such as the victim's last moments before the murder). The author's most important task in a mystery novel is to use the sleuth's perspective to create the puzzle while leaving enough distance for the reader to jockey for the solution.

Cozy mysteries, however, which feature an amateur sleuth, often use a first-person narration. *Cozy* makes these books sound very sweet, but there's a paradoxical form of sociopathology in cozies that you seldom get in third-person POV. The sleuth is usually only peripherally involved with the victim and therefore has a less emotional response to the death. (Indeed the victim is often unlikable, the town bully or gossip.) First-person narration might be the only way to draw the reader close to a sleuth who thinks of murder as a game and murderers as competitors.

The *thriller or suspense novel*, on the other hand, has the purpose of not only providing a puzzle but also a vicariously scary experience. To achieve this sort of thrill, these books usually focus on the "victim," the person being stalked or threatened. But they'll also often provide a glimpse into the villain's mind in order to give more sense of her psychology. These passages in the villain's POV can sometimes reveal her identity or at least give clues that allow the reader to guess. In other books, the author will go to some lengths to disguise the villain's identity even while using that POV; you'll see a lot of first-person villain passages, as that avoids telling if this person is a *he* or *she*. Occasionally, an investigator's POV will reveal the process of tracking down the villain (though notice in a thriller, the investigator often fails or ends up dead, and the potential victim actually resolves the problem). The author's primary POV challenge in a thriller is to use the victim's perspective to create a growing sense of menace and terror, and to portray the villain without diminishing the threat with too much familiarity. Third-person (often multiple) POV is common in thrillers, especially in stories that have several settings and simultaneous action.

Legal and medical thrillers are also concerned with crime, but they are more likely to examine the intersection of individuals within the greater society (in the court system or the medical establishment). Often these stories use the viewpoints of several characters—for example, a nurse, a doctor, and a patient; or a victim, a defendant, a prosecutor, and a defense attorney. The multiple POV approach gives a more expansive and comprehensive perspective that reflects the institutional conflict of law or medicine. The author's primary POV task in these books is to identify and stick close to a central protagonist while fleshing out the narrative with other perspectives.

Emotion Novels: Horror and Romance

Crime stories usually provide an intellectual experience, pitting the reader against the villain to discover the solution to the crime. But another type of novel aims to create an emotional experience, which is facilitated by POV. *Horror novels* create both a sense of personal terror and an overall awareness of evil. Stephen King often uses a contemporary-omniscient POV, tightly focusing on a single character once the scene is launched. He has also used a single–first-person narrator for an entire book, creating a bond with the victim. Dean Koontz is known for his tight, almost claustrophobic passages from the viewpoint of either a terrified victim or a deranged villain. At the same time, horror is the genre most likely to use some form of omniscient to help replicate the looming dread of a supernatural entity and the foreboding atmosphere that hangs over the characters themselves.

Romances provide a different sort of emotional experience that allows the reader to participate in a couple's journey to love. These books typically have two protagonists, the hero and the heroine, and the narrative is usually told entirely or almost entirely in these two viewpoints. Occasionally, especially in historical romances, there will be an omniscient narrator at the beginning of scenes, but it's unusual these days to see an entire romance in that distant viewpoint. Both multiple POV (more than one per scene) and single POV (one per scene) are common in romance. Since the romantic plotline follows the growing compatibility between these two people, crosscutting from one POV to the other is often used to compare and contrast their understanding and interpretation of events. Romances sometimes have an external plot that might take the form of a mystery or a quest, but the focal plot will probably guide you to a tighter focus on the POVs of the hero and the heroine. The major challenge in writing a romance is creating distinctive POVs so that both the hero and heroine come across as intriguing, sympathetic individuals.

Romance is an element of the large category of novels marketed as *women's fiction*, a niche that is hard to define but includes novels that are more likely to appeal to female readers. They can have male protagonists (like Susan Howatch's books) and violence and murder (like Tess Gerritsen's thrillers), but generally the authors place more emphasis on relationships and personal journeys than they would in books targeted at men. The more character-focused women's novels generally use a tightly limited third-person or first-person POV. But many works of women's fiction, like those written by Jan Karon and Debbie Macomber, are more community-based and use multiple or contemporary-omniscient POV to show a small group's interaction. These community-based novels are often shelved as general fiction rather than romance.

Men's Fiction: Western and Action-Adventure

Just as there's a category of novels made to appeal specifically to women, there are two genres written for men. (Of course, women read men's fiction and vice versa; I'm talking about target markets here.)

Western is an American genre (though it has become popular in Europe) that mythologizes the ethos and events of the Old West. Even before the Old West was "old," authors were writing dime novels featuring cowboys and ranchers, and the grand vistas of the Great Plains and Upper Rockies. These earliest Westerns treated cowboys as emblems of manly virtues, rather like medieval knights, but the great author Zane Grey focused more on the unique American geography and experience. He often used a contemporary-omniscient POV to emphasize the epic scope of the frontier and the themes it inspires—nature, God, and human heroism. Louis L'Amour continued the exploration of the frontier but focused more on the Western man in interaction with his environment and community, moving closer to third-person limited. New Westerns, such as those by Mike Jameson, use a deep third to create an even tighter focus on the individual in conflict with the land and its people. But some Western authors (like Tabor Evans) have returned to omniscient for a more ironic view of the Western myths.

Action-adventure, like the Western, has in some ways been co-opted by Hollywood. Where horror and romance stories, for example, seem best embodied in words and books, the vast vistas of the West and the explosive clashes of action plots might have been designed for cinematography. But, as with the Western, the action-adventure still has a novel market. There are two basic kinds: the big techno-thrillers (like Tom Clancy's novels) and the shorter "special-ops" books that are either stand alone or belong to a series (like Warren Murphy and Richard Sapir's The Destroyer or John F. Mullins's Men of Valor). The action-adventure genre might seem to be a successor to the Western (both deal heavily in guns), but the Western—traditional and contemporary—is inextricably tied to the setting and themes of the American frontier, and so follows the slower rhythms of an earlier time. The action-adventure genre is, in contrast, hypermodern, often concerned with state-of-the-art technology and tomorrow's headline news. These novels are usually fast paced and detail oriented, with a greater emphasis on narrating *what* and *how* rather than *why*.

Techno-thrillers appeal to an audience that values precision and detail (often military enthusiasts), and the POV approach, therefore, is usually more traditional. These books tend toward a comprehensive, even exhaustive approach to describing and explaining technology and processes, and, as a result, most are in a contemporary-omniscient POV that facilitates the narration of a large cast over several central settings. The special-ops books, which are shorter in length, usually focus on one adventurer or a small team, and the POV is tightly focused on one character at a time. Because these stories appeal to a technologically savvy, mostly male audience, often the prose is edgy and clipped. The narration means to create the visceral experience of danger and excitement, so the POV, though deep into one character, is more physical

Creating Characters

than emotional. The POV challenge in these books is to give the narrator such an authentic voice and perspective that he can explain complex technology and intricate plots while still propelling the action forward.

Speculative Fiction

Science fiction and *fantasy* have an eclectic mix of POV approaches. Although they often get lumped together as "science fiction and fantasy," they are two very different genres, and the POV purposes vary because of that. Science fiction might employ faster-than-light travel, but otherwise the genre tends toward realism or even naturalism, often focusing on the scientific or social aspects of life in the future. (Science fiction is one of the few genres, by the way, with a thriving short-story market.) There is third-person limited POV (sometimes throughout the entire novel) for the novels that follow one character, and multiple POVs for the more epic novels with several settings and a large cast. First person is rare, though recently it has become less so.

Science fiction writers face a challenge in explaining an alien world or as-yet-uninvented technology to readers, using the POV of characters for whom all this exotica is nothing new. This is also a genre where many readers are Web savvy and have come to expect more innovation than is generally found in print, such as hypertext novels with elaborate graphics and maps. This is the popular fiction genre where you're most likely to see experimental narration, such as Robert Silverberg's *Sundance*, which starts in second-person POV (itself very experimental), moves into third person, and then shifts into first person. The thriving science fiction short-story market allows more experimentation than seen in most novel-oriented genres do.

In some ways, fantasy resembles the historical novel more than it does science fiction. Both fantasies and historical novels require a lot of "world building"; that is, explaining this setting to the reader who lives in a different world. Most fantasies are set in a world that technologically resembles the Middle Ages, however advanced the culture is socially. (You seldom see a hero in a fantasy novel attacking the dragon with a tank, after all.) The common POV approach for fantasy also resembles that of historical novels, a mix of omniscient and third person (limited or omniscient), which allows both a comprehensive worldview and a tight character focus. The challenge of fantasy novels is to create identification with characters who might have gifts few readers share, like magical powers or telepathy.

General Fiction

This is a generic description, just as indistinct as the category itself. *General fiction*, also called *mainstream* or *contemporary fiction*, is a marketing term, not a literary term. Basically it refers to those novels that appeal to the broadest possible audience and are often shelved in bookstores and libraries apart from genre novels or literary fiction. They may contain elements of one or more genres, but they do not adhere as strictly to any set of genre conventions. Also, they may contain themes or characters that publishers and booksellers feel could appeal to more readers than any single genre audience. Some novels with a genre structure are considered general fiction because they are "bigger"—longer in length and more epic in scope. They often span a greater period of time than the more tightly plotted genre novels. Examples would be the mysteries of P.D. James and the romances of Nora Roberts. In this category, you'll find most bestsellers, many of the earlier "Oprah books," and many women's fiction novels.

General fiction can be tragic or comic, a family saga or a war drama, an old man's reminiscences or a young mother's diary. So the POV approaches in these novels will vary according to the author's judgment of which method will work the best. You'll seldom see experimental POV (like second person) in general fiction, as that choice would put the emphasis not on the story but on how the story is told, and with general fiction, story is more important. Multiple POV is also relatively rare, but first person is very common, as is third-person limited. Omniscient is more common in general fiction than in genre fiction because general fiction follows a more classical form and tone.

The purpose of general fiction is a well-told story, without strict genre conventions. So if you're writing general fiction, your guideline is only that: Choose the POV that best suits the story. The primary consideration is the relative tightness of focus. Personal novels like Marek Halter's *Sarah* would probably benefit from the intimacy of third-person limited or first-person POV. Social novels like *The Bookseller of Kabul* by Asne Seierstad will convey more about the featured culture through an omniscient approach.

The challenge in writing general fiction is choosing from a wide variety of POV options for the one that best suits this story. Since there are no conventions to adhere to, it's not unusual for writers of general fiction to learn by trial and error. This is a large and varied category of fiction, but that doesn't mean anything goes. General fiction is all about story, and POV is the most important way to enhance readability.

Literary Fiction

Literary novels defy an easy definition, but generally speaking, they don't fit into the traditional storytelling genres, and they get creative with language or style and may be narratively experimental. Their plots often seem secondary, but this might be by design, as they frequently focus on how seemingly trivial events transform the characters in unpredictable ways. Some literary fiction, like Vladimir Nabokov's *Lolita*, uses the journey motif to show the deadening or maddening effect of modern life on the ability of characters to grow and change.

The term *literary fiction*, incidentally, is usually used only to define post-WWI fiction. Anything from an earlier period is simply considered "literature"—Dickens, Austen, et al—even though the themes and structures these authors instilled in their work are more likely to be found now in popular fiction. It's the experimental nature of literary fiction that breaks away from its influences, while popular fiction follows the traditions of earlier eras. Most literary novels, following the modernist custom (à la James Joyce), have a tightly focused POV, either first person or third. But they seldom stop there: Good literary novels use POV to explore hidden aspects of story and character, to innovate in prose passages, and to cast doubt on the veracity of the narrative itself. Narrative experimentation often involves experimenting with POV. Joyce told his stories through a third-person POV so internal it replicated the chaos of a troubled man's thoughts. This type of narration even warranted its own name: stream of consciousness.

While the stories in this category vary widely, some factors remain constant. You will catch a literary editor's attention with more experimental ways of telling your story, deeper immersion into the internal workings of a character, or strikingly inventive prose and imagery. All of these unique aspects of the novel require a particular attention to how you use POV as a narrative element, so as you draft, think about *how* you can tell this story in an innovative way.

Postmodernism: "This Book Isn't True"

Postmodern novels, a subgenre of literary fiction, are even more experimental than their parent genre. While the aim of most traditional novelists is to make you forget you're reading a book, to subsume you into the reading experience with a "suspension of disbelief," postmodern novels keep reminding you that this story is an invented experience. They use metafictional techniques to undermine the traditional logic of the narrative by juxtaposing events, providing ambiguous endings (John Fowles's *The French Lieutenant's Woman* has three alternate endings, one of which features the author as a character), inserting seemingly irrelevant details (Thomas Pynchon's speculation on JFK's excrement in *Gravity's Rainbow*), and using academic devices such as footnotes and professorial commentary (David Foster Wallace's extensive footnotes in *Infinite Jest*).

You might think anything goes as far as POV in a postmodernist novel, but, in fact, postmodern POV, like the other narrative elements, should serve the purpose of the experiment. That might even mean casting doubt on the value or truth of the story. A more traditional novelist might juxtapose two characters' versions of the same event to challenge the reader to determine for herself what the truth is. But a postmodernist might jumble up POV passages to assert that there is no objective truth at all and indeed the search for truth is futile (as in Robert Coover's famous short story "The Babysitter").

The postmodernist tradition is difficult for most writers to work within; we actually believe, naïfs that we are, that truth can be found

Creating Characters

in fiction if not in reality. But if you're more skeptical of the fictional experience, if you distrust eternal verities and feel more comfortable with artistic relativism, then go for it. Just remember that your motto should be "This book is a lie," so your POV approach should cast doubt on the credibility of your story—just the opposite of the usual POV task.

When in Doubt, Read

While I have broken down and summarized the major fiction categories for you, there is no substitute for reading other works in your target genre and seeing what they do and how they do it. Your book will be individual, but its impact will depend in part on how it connects with and reacts against other books the reader has read.

....

ALICIA RASLEY is an award-winning author of women's fiction, romance, and mystery. Her book *The Year She Fell* (Bell Bridge Books, 2010) was an Amazon Kindle bestseller. She teaches and advises writers at two universities and leads writing workshops around the country and online.

CHAPTER 8

DEALING WITH MULTIPLE POINTS OF VIEW

BY JORDAN E. ROSENFELD

In fiction, point of view is the camera through which the reader enters your protagonist's world, sees what he sees, and shares in his feelings and perceptions. POV has a direct influence on the tone, mood, energy, and pace of a scene (not to mention your overall narrative).

In order to master POV from one scene to the next, you must use it with integrity and consistency, by which I mean that the reader should feel expertly guided at all times throughout your scenes, never confused about whose POV is being presented. If you've shown the scene of a murder through a shocked widow's eyes, for example, you don't want to suddenly leap, without legitimate reason and careful transition, into the point of view of the vigilante detective who is hunting the murderer down. Otherwise you'll leave the reader feeling a little whiplashed and out of sync with your story.

In this chapter, we'll talk about how to make POV leaps and transitions inside scenes, and from scene to scene, so that whatever POV you choose to use works for your scenes, not against them.

THE STORY ARC OF MULTIPLE PROTAGONISTS

Once you've decided on each protagonist's POV, and whether you will use multiple scenes per chapter or let each chapter be a stand-alone scene, you must remember one final element: When you have multiple protagonists who each get POV scenes and chapters, you have a burden to give each character a narrative arc—each must undergo change and be connected to the significant situation, and their plotlines must also merge. Co-protagonists must share a journey and come together in the end for the narrative to work.

This means that each character has an imperative to:

- Respond to the significant situation (your work will be a lot more cohesive if they all share the same significant situation)
- Engage in consequences stemming from the significant situation
- Change as a result of the significant situation
- Merge his individual storyline with those of the other protagonists by narrative's end

Ultimately you want to select points of view that will convey the appropriate intimacy or distance levels you aim to achieve, offer consistency to the reader so that there is no confusion over whose point of view you are in, and devote equal stage time to every protagonist who stars in your narrative.

Books that successfully merge two or more protagonists' storylines: *A Thousand Splendid Suns* by Khaled Hosseini; *My Sister's Keeper* by Jodi Picoult; *Fall on Your Knees* by Ann-Marie MacDonald; *Case Histories* by Kate Atkinson.

USING MULTIPLE POINTS OF VIEW IN SCENES

In order to discuss multiple POVs in scenes, we need to quickly refresh the concept of a scene (at its most distilled): a container of significant action in which a protagonist acts on a scene intention, and in which conflict ensues, leading toward climax and change. POV is the camera through which you choose to show the events in the scene to the reader. If you have one protagonist only, then that is the character who gets the camera. Use the POV descriptions in this chapter to decide what kind of effect you want to achieve and to choose your POV accordingly.

Choosing POV gets trickier when you have multiple protagonists, or simply multiple points of view that you want to show in a given scene. If you elect to use a limited POV, you will never have to worry about jumping from head to head within a given scene. Your biggest concern will be when and where to switch from narrator to narrator. But if you *do* want to be able to pan the camera through the thoughts of characters *A*, *B*, and *C* as event *X* unfolds, you will want to pay attention to this next part.

Changing POV Within a Scene

If you have more than one character within a scene whose points of view are relevant, then you'll need to use the omniscient POV. When your narrative tackles large issues: war, culture, race, identity—in which a complex or comprehensive look at a situation is required, omniscient POV is a good choice. Omniscient allows you to go beyond the personal—beyond the intimate experience of a small handful of characters—to include more history, cultural details, or perspectives that will add up to a more cohesive look at a subject.

An omniscient POV is also useful when you need to show more than one side of a story and therefore need to be able to jump back and forth between characters to offer alternate takes on events as they're happening, rather than later on in reflection.

However, you must make omniscient clear right away from the first paragraph in the first scene. If the reader believes that he has *only* been able to see inside character *A*'s head, and then you suddenly leap into character *B*'s head, the reader will feel confused and possibly irritated. And a word of warning: Too much jumping back and forth—or between more than three or four people in a given scene—*will* create confusion.

Here's an example of omniscient POV from the novel *Rosie*, by Anne Lamott—the story of a single mother raising her daughter after her husband's death. From the first scene in the book, Lamott shows the reader that she is in the omniscient by providing information that comes as if from a god-like source, a source that knows all:

> There were many things about Elizabeth that the people of Bayview disliked. They thought her tall, too thin, too aloof. Her neck was too long and her breasts were too big. The men, who could have lived with the size of her breasts, found her unwilling to flirt

and labeled her cold. The women were jealous of how well her clothes hung on her.

Since this information is not being delivered directly through the camera of any one character, the reader is signaled immediately that it is omniscient—the camera can move wherever it needs to go. Lamott maintains this POV throughout all the scenes, dancing effortlessly into the thoughts and feelings of her protagonists, Elizabeth and Rosie. In one paragraph she is in Rosie's POV:

> Rosie Ferguson was four when her father died. As she sat on her mother's lap at the crowded Episcopal service, she knew that her father was dead but kept waiting for him to join them in the first pew, wondering what he would bring her.

Then in the next paragraph in the same scene, we're in Elizabeth's POV:

> Elizabeth held Rosie on her lap, dimly aware that her daughter was trying to take care of her—Rosie kept patting her and smiling bravely—but Elizabeth couldn't concentrate on what was happening. It was too surreal. ...

Once you choose omniscient, you have to commit to it—you can't back down from it within the scene. Notice, too, that Lamott lets each character have an entire paragraph of her own—the minimum amount of headspace I recommend you give each character if you're going to hop from head to head. Starting a new paragraph is a good way to signal to the reader that you're moving the camera again. Along those same lines, keep in mind:

- To keep a sense of cohesiveness, change POV at the end of action, not in the middle
- Change POV at the end of a line of dialogue—do not try to weave one character's thoughts into another character's speech
- Change POV when you want to offer another character's reaction to an event in the scene

A word of warning: When you're in the omniscient and can move into any character's head, be selective. The reader doesn't need to hear the thoughts or know the opinions of all minor characters. Stick to the point of view of characters who can contribute to plot information or deepen the reader's understanding of your protagonists.

Changing POV from Scene to Scene

Remember that a scene should largely take place in one location (unless the characters are on a moving vehicle or taking a stroll). Therefore, if you've got a chapter-long scene—that is, you're writing one scene per chapter—you automatically limit the physical location of the chapter.

When you have multiple scenes within a chapter, try to think of each scene within the chapter as a separate square of a quilt or a piece of a puzzle that must add up to some sort of goal or understanding within the chapter. It's best to use multiple scenes in a given chapter when you want to:

- Look at one issue or topic from multiple angles
- Switch to multiple physical locations or in and out of present time
- Build up new plot information that the current scene won't allow but that needs to come at that juncture in the story
- Introduce another character within the chapter

Author Jodi Picoult includes multiple scenes per chapter in her books because she writes about subjects that can be viewed from many different angles: suicide, rape, motherhood. Therefore, in a given chapter, when addressing a specific plot angle, she'll often give multiple characters a scene of their own, thereby shedding numerous different kinds of perspective on a plot element.

For instance, her novel *Second Glance* is about Comtosook, a Vermont town where paranormal events occur when a developer threatens to build on sacred land. A long-hidden eugenics program designed to weed out unwanted genes is revealed to have been conducted there in the early 1920s. The novel features multiple viewpoints. Each chapter is broken into a series of short scenes told from the points of view of as many as ten different characters who are affected by the strange events. Note that although there are multiple scenes per chapter, each scene has only one point of view. To show that she's beginning a new scene,

Picoult uses a visual cue—a break of four lines (sometimes called a soft hiatus) or a symbol like Ï or * * *—and identifies the point-of-view character within the first couple of lines. These scenes offer different pieces of insight into the plot that is being explored at that particular juncture. Here are three samples of scene launches that all appear within *Second Glance*'s chapter two, in which people are trying to determine whether Angel Quarry is haunted or someone is pulling a prank:

> Ross didn't know whom he blamed more: Ethan, for planting this seed in his mind; or himself, for bothering to listen. Angel Quarry is haunted, his nephew had said, everyone says so. ...
>
> "What do you make of it?" Winks Smiling Fox asked, grunting as he moved the drum a few feet to the left. Where they'd been sitting, the ground beneath their feet was icy. Yet over here, there were dandelions growing. ...
>
> "Ethan?"
> From his vantage point beneath the blackout shades, Ethan froze at the sound of his mother's voice. He whipped his body back so that it wasn't pressed against the warm glass windowpane. ...

Each scene may be its own unit, but the three to six scenes within the chapter all play off each other and add up details for the reader. By the end of the chapter, the reader is pretty sure that, yes, Angel Quarry is haunted.

Using multiple scenes within a given chapter is a common and effective way to allow for a mosaic feeling—a feeling of little parts adding up to a larger, more comprehensive whole. But it comes with a caveat: When you have multiple scenes within a chapter, you will serve the reader best if each of those scenes has only one viewpoint—and not an omniscient one—since you're already forcing the reader to move around.

Changing POV from Chapter to Chapter

In many narratives, one chapter can be its own long scene. The benefit of this construction is that you don't have to get complex with your POV structure. One scene per chapter is undoubtedly the simplest and clearest structure to work with, and if you are new to writing, I recommend that you use this structure until you've mastered scenes and can move on to more complex structures. When your whole chapter is just one long scene, you can focus on the protagonist's scene intention, decide what kind of scene it's going to be, and use your core elements one chapter at a time. This structure requires less work of you, and it also allows the reader to stay in one place and time per chapter. This structure will feel more straightforward to the reader, and perhaps also less textured or layered, but you can guarantee that you will tell a simple, clear story by using this method. One scene per chapter is an ideal structure when:

- You want to keep your characters in a unified time and place
- You're writing a dialogue scene, as dialogue takes up a lot of room
- You're writing a suspense scene, as it requires more time to draw out actions
- Your narrative has a linear chronology—it doesn't flashback in time
- You want to switch to a different type of point of view to achieve a different effect for another protagonist—for instance, protagonist A is narrated in the first person, but protagonist B is better served by third-person limited

Consider that when a chapter is one long scene, you have time to devote to a particular protagonist, and you may consider using a limited point of view because, by nature of the length of a chapter, you have more page time to delve into one protagonist's experience and reveal it to the reader.

DEVOTING EQUAL TIME TO POV CHARACTERS

Now that you fully understand the idea of using multiple points of view, it's important to discuss how to let your protagonists share the time on the page. The most definitive way to tell the reader that you have more than one protagonist is to give each protagonist equal time in your narrative. You may devote an equal number of scenes, or give individual chapters to your protagonists, but you should also be egalitarian if you're going to have multiple narrators.

A lot of authors adopt a simple formula such as this: Each point-of-view character narrates one chapter or scene, taking turns in order. Character *A* goes first, then *B*, then *C*. Then you repeat that pattern: *ABC, ABC, ABC*. In other words, you give each character a chance to narrate, then you start all over again. You might give each character a chance to narrate within a given chapter, so you have three scenes for every chapter, or you may devote whole chapters to one character each. You may find the need to do variations on this: AAA, BBB, CCC, for instance, or AA, BB, CC, so long as the time each protagonist gets is as close to equal as you can make it.

....

JORDAN E. ROSENFELD (www.jordanrosenfeld.net) is author of the suspense novels *Night Oracle* and *Forged in Grace*, and the writing guides *Make a Scene* (Writer's Digest Books, 2008) and *Write Free*, with Rebecca Lawton (Kulupi Press, 2008). Her two forthcoming books from Writer's Digest Books are *A Writer's Guide to Persistence* and *Deep Scenes*, with Martha Alderson.

PART III

DIALOGUE

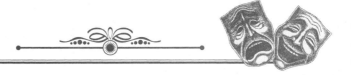

CHAPTER 9

WRITING DIALOGUE

BY HALLIE EPHRON

Most authors have an Achilles' heel, something they need to work at. Mine is dialogue. I have to work to make each character's dialogue feel authentic, individual, and natural. It's probably related to the fact that I can never remember anyone's exact words. After a party, for example, ask me what was on the walls, what people wore, what food was served, and I can give you chapter and verse. But ask me what anyone said and I can only paraphrase. Paraphrasing isn't dialogue. If you paraphrase, everyone else's speech sounds like your own or, even worse, like no one's in particular.

WRITING CONVINCING DIALOGUE

The guy who wrote the book on convincing dialogue is Elmore Leonard. Just about everything you need to know is illustrated in this brief, two-part excerpt from *LaBrava*:

> Cundo Rey said to Nobles, "Let me ask you something, okay? You ever see a snake eat a bat? Here is a wing sticking out of the snake's mouth, the wing, it's still moving, this little movement, like is trying to fly. The snake, he don't care. You know why? Because the other end of the bat is down in the snake turning to juice, man. Sure, the snake, he don't even have to move, just lay there and keep swallowing as long as it takes. He don't even have to chew," Cundo Rey said, watching Richard Nobles eating his

Big Mac and poking fries in his mouth a few at a time, dipped in
ketchup. "Mmmmmm, nice juicy bat."

...

He [Nobles] said, mouth full of hamburger, "I ate a snake.
I've ate a few different kinds. You flour 'em, deep-fry 'em in some
Crisco so the meat crackles, they're pretty good. But I never ate
a bat. Time you skin it, what would you have?"

There—if the Cuban was trying to make him sick he was
wasting his time.

Use these same techniques to give your characters authentic, unique voices:

- **CONTENT AND TONE.** *You ever see a snake eat a bat?* What your
  character talks about and how he says it—that's the fundamental
  choice you make when you write dialogue. Here there's something sinister, weird, and confrontational about Cundo Rey's
  little monologue about how a snake eats a bat. There's a not-so-
  veiled threat, and we get the sense of a ruthless, cold individual
  who gets his jollies watching another creature tortured.
- **GRAMMAR AND WORD CHOICES.** *The snake, he don't care.* Use
  grammar to show the character's personality and background.
  Here the grammatical error suggests a character who is tough
  and uneducated, perhaps not a native English speaker. You might
  choose other words to convey casual and hip ("That snake, he
  could care less") or painstakingly formal and correct ("From the
  snake's perspective, it matters not").
- **A LITTLE DIALECT OR NONE AT ALL.** *You flour 'em, deep fry 'em*
  … Characters mispronounce words and speak with accents. Do
  you have to render what's said phonetically in order to make
  the character sound real? You can, but more than a touch of
  phonetically rendered dialect can be distracting and difficult
  to decipher. Not only that, dialect can turn character into
  caricature. Use the occasional phonetic version of a phrase
  to give the reader the flavor of how a character sounds, but
  do so sparingly. Trust the reader to mentally apply what you
  suggest to the remaining dialogue.

- **SIMPLE ATTRIBUTION OR NONE AT ALL.** *Cundo Rey said ...* New writers think they need to vary their choice of a verb to express speaking (*chimed, chirped, responded, hissed, retorted, bellowed, queried*). Equally egregious is when an author writes something like, *"Thanks," he grinned.* As if grinning had anything to do with speaking. (It's fine to say: *"Thanks," he said, grinning.* Or *"Thanks." He grinned.*) Yes, you can occasionally use *whispered* or *shouted*, if that's what the character did. But *said* and *asked* are perfectly sufficient 98 percent of the time. In fact, often you can get away without any attribution at all, if you make it clear to the reader who's talking.
- **HOLD THE ADVERBS.** *Cundo Rey said coldly ... icily ... scornfully.* You rarely find an adverb with *said* in Lenoard's prose: nor should one show up in yours. Using adverbs in this way is a clunky way to tell the reader what's better shown through the dialogue itself and the character's behavior.
- **DIALOGUE/ACTION COMBO.** *... watching Richard Nobles eating his Big Mac and poking fries in his mouth a few at a time, dipped in ketchup. "Mmmmmm. Nice juicy bat."* How do you convey the tenor of dialogue to the reader? Pack emotion into the words and the physical gestures and body language that accompany it. Combine dialogue with the right action, and the result is more than the sum of the parts—as the example shows with the combination of eating French fries with *"Mmmmmm. Nice juicy bat."*
- **BRING THE CHARACTERS' RELATIONSHIP TO LIFE.** *I ate a snake.* The thrust and parry of dialogue shows the relationship between the characters talking. When Nobles responds, the reader sees that these two guys are evenly matched for bravado.
- **SPRINKLE LIGHTLY WITH INTERNAL DIALOGUE.** *There—if the Cuban was trying to make him sick he was wasting his time.* During an exchange of dialogue, use internal dialogue to show your reader what's going on in the point-of-view character's head and to add a dimension to the interaction. Notice the internal dialogue need not sound or look like dialogue. Here Nobles's thoughts are more grammatically correct, with less

swagger and without the staccato sentences of this character's spoken dialogue. Notice also that internal dialogue doesn't require quotes, italics, or even *he thought* to cue the reader that these words are thoughts. Leonard maintains tense and point of view (here it's first person, past tense) and just writes the thought.

MAKING DIALOGUE SOUND AUTHENTIC

Good dialogue is not realistic conversation. People digress, pause, use the wrong words, repeat themselves, fail to clearly express themselves, or go on and on, boring everyone around them. If you write dialogue that's too realistic, your book will be a great sleeping aid but little else.

So how do you write authentic-sounding dialogue without making it too real? Take a cue from how real people talk. They speak in sentence fragments. They drop nouns and verbs. They use jargon, vernacular, and sometimes profanity. Edit out the meanderings, the repetitions, the digressions, get rid of the irrelevancies, and you've got something that approaches good dialogue. Remember, dialogue shouldn't call attention to itself. If it's too clever, get rid of it.

Here's an example. In this dialogue from S.J. Rozan's *Absent Friends*, notice how Zannoni drops words, uses sentence fragments, profanity, and police jargon, and comes off sounding like the tough, jaded, retired homicide detective he's supposed to be.

> "I was a detective at the 124 then," he said. "Later got transferred to the Bronx. Christ what a schlep. Those days, right after the Knapp Commission—you heard of that?—they didn't have this community policing thing like now. They wanted you to live outside your precinct. Keep down graft. Pile of crap. Cops running all around the goddamn city, damn waste of time. I retired eight years ago."

To check whether your dialogue is working, read it aloud to yourself. Wooden dialogue jumps out at you when you hear it, more so than when you read it.

Creating Characters

SHOWING EMOTIONS

Presencing is a term that a wonderful writing teacher, Arthur Edelstein, used when urging his students to write characters that seem physically present. For example, when a character is talking or listening, a bit of physical action gives the reader insight into the character's inner state.

This is why authors give characters props. What a character does with a drink while she's talking, for example, can alter how the reader perceives the dialogue delivered.

Here are two examples with identical dialogue:

> "Did you know him long?" I asked.
>
> She stirred her drink and stared into it. "Too long, and not long enough."

***

> "Did you know him long?" I asked.
>
> She knocked back her drink and slammed the empty glass down on the table. "Too long, and not long enough."

Just about anything in a scene—a cigarette, a tissue, a strand of hair, a necktie, a belt, shirt buttons, and so on—can be used, in combination with dialogue, to show different mental states. You don't even need props. A character can wring his hands, crack his knuckles, pick at a pimple, or take a quick intake of breath. Choose the actions carefully and you effectively nuance the dialogue the character delivers.

WHEN TO SUMMARIZE INSTEAD

Not everything your characters would say in a given situation belongs to dialogue. It's better to summarize and fast-forward through the necessary but unexciting bits than risk bogging down your story with trivial talk.

For instance, *He introduced himself and we shook hands* is fine instead of a lot of hello-and-how-are-you-ing—unless you're using the greetings to show the relationship between the two characters. If your character has to tell his partner about a visit to Nina's house, and that visit was dramatized a chapter earlier, then *told him about my visit to Nina's house* is all you need.

Use dialogue only when it's dramatic, when it moves your story along, or when it develops characters and their relationships. Never force a character to deliver a speech about himself or another character, or to explain why something is happening.

HALLIE EPHRON is the best-selling, award-winning author of nine novels and *Writing and Selling Your Mystery Novel: How to Knock 'Em Dead With Style* (Writer's Digest Books, 2005).

Creating Characters

CHAPTER 10

DIALOGUE THAT PROPELS THE STORY FORWARD

BY GLORIA KEMPTON

I sighed and put the novel manuscript down. How could this fiction writer really think she was engaging the reader? The two characters were simply sitting at the breakfast table, chatting about their daily to-do lists while eating bowls of cereal. The viewpoint character was crunching her corn flakes and staring out into the field behind her house while saying such profound things as, "I wonder if we should take Ginger in for her distemper shot," and "Do you think *Law &Order* will be a rerun tonight?" Crunch, crunch. How would I nicely tell this writer that her dialogue needed a bit of help?

I decided to ask the students in my weekly novel class what would make this dialogue spark.

"Well, if while the lady is staring into the backyard, a spaceship lands," one student suggested.

"If the lady is rambling on and on about nothing and the husband calmly tells her he's having an affair or wants a divorce or is a cross-dresser. She keeps talking and doesn't even hear him."

"If the lady is talking, taking the day for granted, and doesn't notice that her husband's face is in his breakfast cereal. He's just died of a heart attack."

These were pretty good ideas. I was proud of my class. They understood that dialogue should be *about* something. The dialogue needs to move the plot forward in some way or it's useless.

As a writing coach, I see pointless and useless dialogue all the time. It feels harsh to continually point it out, and writers don't always *understand* why their dialogue doesn't work, but unless it connects to the theme and plot and includes tension and suspense while moving the story forward (a tall order), why bother? Why write a story at all?

DIALOGUE THAT MOVES

Writing a story that stands still will risk your reputation as a writer of artistic fiction. I can't overemphasize the importance of making sure your dialogue moves the plot forward. Dialogue is only a means to an end—it's not the end itself. Dialogue, in and of itself, is simply a fiction element, a tool to be used to move the story forward. That means engaging your characters in conflict and using dialogue to increase their struggle.

As you will see in the examples in this chapter, your characters' struggles are revealed through both your theme and your plot. The first is internal and the second is external. Writers in my classes will often say to me, "Why do I have to have a theme? Can't I just write a nice little story?" Sometimes they even ask that question about plot. "Plot? Why do we need a plot?"

Woe be it unto me to try to convince you that stories need both a theme and a plot. Sure, you can just skip these two elements of fiction—if you want to write stories for yourself, that is. I could be wrong, but I'm going to take a wild guess and assume that if you're reading this book, you most likely are thinking about submitting your short stories and novels for publication at some point. If that's true, then you need both a theme and a plot in your stories.

Dialogue is one of the fiction elements you can use to propel your plot forward and integrate your theme into each scene. The way you do this is to set your characters up in an animated discussion that does any one of a number of things: provides new information to the characters about the conflict, reveals new obstacles that the viewpoint character must overcome to achieve his goal, creates the kind of dynamic between the characters that furthers the story's theme, intro-

Creating Characters

duces a pivotal moment in the plot that transforms the character(s), sets up the discussion so the character (and reader) are reminded of his scene and story goals, and accelerates the emotion and story movement to increase the suspense and make the situation more urgent for the characters.

Yes, this sounds like a tall order—how can you possibly use dialogue to do all of this, and in every single scene? It's not that difficult once you become aware of all of the purposes of dialogue and keep reminding yourself that your dialogue scenes must accomplish something and keep the story moving.

FIXING YOUR OWN STORY

What's the criterion for dialogue that moves a plot forward? How do you know whether your dialogue is or isn't propelling the story onward? Ask yourself the following questions to find out:

- If I remove the passage of dialogue that I'm suspecting isn't moving the story, will it be missed? Does the story work just as well without it?
- Does the dialogue cause the exclusion of the other important scene elements, like story movement?
- How does the dialogue passage further the story's theme?
- How does the passage of dialogue increase the suspense for what's to come, raising the stakes for the protagonist?
- How does the dialogue make it clearer what the protagonist wants in the story?
- What kind of external and internal obstacles does the passage of dialogue surface for the protagonist?
- What new information about the plot and theme does the dialogue reveal?
- How is the dialogue pivotal in changing the characters—making them more desperate for what they want, causing them to want to give up, bringing them to a place of new determination?

The answers to these questions will help you gauge whether your dialogue passages are pulling their weight when it comes to story movement. Every single scene of dialogue should in some way change the situation for the characters so they are either closer or farther away from their individual goals. When you're clear about your theme, your characters will be discussing only what matters in the immediate story action so the theme can come through a clear and focused channel.

It Provides New Information

Recently I called up a couple of friends of twelve years to thank them for a birthday gift and to ask them when they might like to get together, but before the words were barely out of my mouth, Ellen was saying, "We won't be able to get together. We're breaking up."

Have you ever found yourself relaxed and talking to someone and then suddenly that person inserted something into the conversation that completely threw you, maybe even changed your life in some way?

This is the kind of opening you want to look for in your dialogue passages, those seemingly innocuous moments when you can throw a zinger into the dialogue and completely take the plot in another direction. The viewpoint character receives some new information that causes him to see all of the other characters in a new light or to get a different perspective of the story situation. In Albert Zuckerman's book *Writing the Blockbuster Novel,* he calls this a pivotal scene and says we need at least twelve of them in an average novel. They don't all have to be dialogue scenes, but making a dialogue scene pivotal will ensure that the dialogue is moving the story forward.

In John Grisham's *The Chamber,* the author includes a pivotal passage of dialogue that momentarily upends the protagonist's world. Adam is a young, inexperienced, naïve lawyer who is just learning the ropes, and in his inexperience he's always doing things that threaten the older, more experienced lawyers in his firm. In this passage of dialogue, Adam receives a bit of new information that definitely moves the story forward, creating a crisis that could be a serious obstacle thwarting his goal to get his grandfather a reprieve from his scheduled execution.

"Come in, come in," Goodman said, closing the door as he invited Adam into his own office. He hadn't smiled yet.

"What are you doing here?" Adam asked, throwing his briefcase on the floor and walking to his desk. They faced each other.

Goodman stroked his neat gray beard, then adjusted his bow tie. "There's a bit of an emergency, I'm afraid. Could be bad news."

"What?"

"Sit down, sit down. This might take a minute."

"No, I'm fine. What is it?" It had to be horrible if he needed to take it sitting down.

Goodman tinkered with his bow tie, rubbed his beard, then said, "Well, it happened at nine this morning. You see, the Personnel Committee is made up of fifteen partners, almost all are younger guys. The full committee has several subcommittees, of course, one for recruiting, hiring, one for discipline, one for disputes and on and on. And as you might guess, there's one for terminations. The Termination Subcommittee met this morning and guess who was there to orchestrate everything."

"Daniel Rosen."

"Daniel Rosen. Evidently, he's been working the Termination Subcommittee for ten days trying to line up enough votes for your dismissal."

One character has just announced something to another character that has the potential to short circuit everything he has been working so hard for, and this announcement moves the story forward. If his firm terminates him, he loses his power to do anything to save his grandfather's life. It literally is a matter of life and death.

Grisham excels at this kind of thing—throwing obstacles at protagonists in the middle of scenes of dialogue to make their goals more difficult to achieve. If you haven't already, you might want to read some of his novels and study how he does this.

It Reveals New Obstacles

In dialogue, an obstacle to a character's goal works the same as new information by stopping the viewpoint character in his tracks and creating immediate conflict for him. He may express his discomfort verbally, he may not, but he has to *do something*, so the story is moved forward. If he chooses to express his discomfort verbally, you can create immediate conflict in the scene with the other character who presented him with the obstacle. Whether or not the viewpoint character likes the other character doesn't really matter—he won't like that the other character has presented him with an obstacle to his goal.

In the scene from *The Chamber,* Grisham decides to develop a conflict right in the middle of the dialogue. Adam grows more upset as the scene continues, and his perception of the obstacles begins to increase. Goodman is the voice of reason. When presenting a protagonist with obstacles in the middle of a scene, it's his perception of them that's important. The obstacles may or may not be insurmountable, but if the protagonist *thinks* they're insurmountable, they are, at least momentarily. This is where you want to keep your protagonist much of the time he's in dialogue with other characters because it creates suspense and tension and moves the story forward.

Now, every character will react differently when presented with an obstacle. One character will burst into tears while another character will see the obstacle as a challenge, roll up her sleeves, and get to work solving the problem. Another character will start delegating and another conniving. Another will start considering the options right out loud in the middle of the dialogue and then look at them forever. Still another character will get scared and want to run away from the problem while still another will get discouraged and give up. Then there's always the character who will get mad and start blaming his mother and father and anyone else who was around when he was being potty trained. As you can see, this is why it's absolutely crucial that you know your characters. It's only in knowing your characters that you'll know how each one will react when presented with an obstacle in a scene of dialogue, which then determines the direction the story will move.

It Increases Suspense

As your story is moving forward, you need to keep increasing the suspense for the reader by making everything look worse for the characters. Dialogue works well for this because the characters are in the immediate moment and are suddenly hanging suspended in time while the reader watches the stakes being raised right before the characters' eyes. Raising the stakes is clear to us, and sometimes it's clear to the characters.

Margaret Atwood does this well all through her novel *The Robber Bride*. The main character is Tony, and the antagonist, Zenia, is a very bright and manipulative character who is always catching the other characters off guard with her conniving and scheming. She's always up to something, and it's never good. This is a very character-driven story, and the reader is able to closely watch Zenia's every move. The other characters are only mildly aware of it, as this type of person always acts like she's your best friend, and you don't want to believe you've been taken for a very long ride and she's your worst enemy. Here's one passage of dialogue, which is very typical for Zenia, as she moves forward in her manipulative ways.

> "What would cause you to kill yourself?" says Zenia.
>
> "Kill myself?" says Tony wonderingly, as if she's never thought of such a thing. "I don't know. I don't think I would."
>
> "What if you had cancer?" Zenia says. "What if you knew you were going to die slowly, in unbearable pain? What if you knew where the microfilm was, and the other side knew you knew, and they were going to torture you to get it out of you and then kill you anyway? What if you had a cyanide tooth? Would you use it?"

When Tony finally realizes that Zenia has just stolen her boyfriend out from under her nose, she remembers another conversation she had with her "friend."

> She recalls a conversation she had with Zenia, early on, in the days when they were drinking coffee at Christie's and Zenia was such a friend.

"Which would you rather have?" said Zenia. "From other people. Love, respect or fear?"

"Respect," said Tony. "No. Love."

"Not me," said Zenia. "I'd choose fear."

"Why?" said Tony.

"It works better," said Zenia. "It's the only thing that works."

Look at how much is accomplished in a brief flashback scene. What Zenia is saying is that she wants others to fear her, and if she can get others to fear her she'll be able to manipulate them to get what she wants. This is really what the story is about, how one person is able to do this to many other people and have power over all of them. As long as they don't wake up to what she's doing, she's queen. Because this is a character-driven story, Atwood uses dialogue scenes over and over to create the kind of suspense that shows Zenia's increasing realm of power, moving the story forward with each of these scenes. Tony will eventually wake up, but not until Zenia has done some incredible damage. What I like about the way Atwood does this is that Tony doesn't analyze Zenia after every scene, which would dilute the creepiness of it. She just observes it, wonders about it a bit, feels uneasy, and goes on—until Zenia's next weird question.

Suspense is achieved in dialogue when the viewpoint character gets "that feeling" about the other character in the scene. Or suddenly realizes that things are not as they seem. Or gets some new information that suggests he isn't going to get what he wants. He may learn that someone else's agenda is different than what he originally thought. He may make a decision right in the middle of the scene that lets us know the plot is now going to turn in a different direction. He may think something in the middle of a dialogue scene that he knows he can't say out loud. Suspense is created in a scene whenever characters are surprised, feel threatened or attacked (it doesn't even matter if the threat is real, as long as they feel it is real), lose something, interpret events to be unjust—there are a hundred ways to create suspense. As long as the moment of suspense is intricately connected to the plot and theme, you're moving the story forward with the dialogue.

It Furthers the Tension

"Sometimes the right course demands an act of piracy." These are the words spoken by Geoffrey Rush's character in the movie *Pirates of the Caribbean: The Curse of the Black Pearl*.

It's not that I amuse myself by going to movies looking for themes and boring my friends by pointing them out in the middle of a crowded movie theater, but I get kind of excited when I hear a character speak a line that is clearly the movie's theme. As a storyteller myself, I get a kick out of observing how other writers do it, whether a novelist or a screenwriter.

When a character announces the story's theme in the middle of a passage of dialogue, it gives the other characters the opportunity to respond and move the action in one direction or another. This can be very effective, because while the reader may not necessarily be able to recognize the theme as the "a-ha" moment in the story as I did in *Pirates of the Caribbean*, subconsciously it registers as a pivotal moment and the reader holds her breath, waiting to see how the other characters will respond.

In Nicholas Sparks' novel *The Notebook*, the author uses a minor character to bring home the theme of enduring love in a character's twilight years. These characters are living in a home for the elderly, and Noah's wife, Allie, has Alzheimer's. Even though his beloved no longer even recognizes him, he keeps going to sit with her. The last time he did, she freaked out and started screaming at him to leave. Immediately the staff appeared and let him know that the visits to his wife are now over. Here the night nurse catches him sneaking down the hall to Allie's room.

> "Noah," she says, "what are you doing?"
>
> "I'm taking a walk," I say. "I can't sleep."
>
> "You know you're not supposed to do this."
>
> "I know."
>
> I don't move, though. I am determined.
>
> "You're not really going for a walk, are you? You're going to see Allie."
>
> "Yes," I answer.

"Noah, you know what happened the last time you saw her at night."

"I remember."

"Then you know you shouldn't be doing this."

I don't answer directly. Instead I say, "I miss her."

"I know you do, but I can't let you see her."

"It's our anniversary," I say. This is true. It is one year before gold. Forty-nine years today.

"I see."

"Then I can go?"

She looks away for a moment, and her voice changes. Her voice is softer now, and I am surprised. She has never struck me as the sentimental type.

"Noah, I've worked here for five years and I worked at another home before that. I've seen hundreds of couples struggle with grief and sadness, but I've never seen anyone handle it like you do. No one around here, not the doctors, not the nurses, has ever seen anything like it."

She pauses for just a moment, and strangely, her eyes begin to fill with tears. She wipes them with her finger and goes on:

"I try to think what it's like for you, how you keep going day after day, but I can't even imagine it. I don't know how you do it. You even beat her disease sometimes. Even though the doctors don't understand it, we nurses do. It's love, it's as simple as that. It's the most incredible thing I've ever seen."

How does this dialogue move the story forward? It's not terribly profound, but this minor character, a nurse, has observed in Noah his deep abiding love for his wife of forty-nine years, and this scene brings it home to the reader. The novel ends only a few pages later. We've seen this before, certainly, but the nurse puts words to it and is able to turn her back while Noah goes to his wife. The dialogue is a brief summation of the theme—enduring love—and moves the scene and story forward to its final conclusion.

It Shows Character Transformation

Our characters should be changing, at least in subtle ways, all the way through the story. This is one reason we write fiction—to show how characters become better people. Or worse. I don't think it's particularly easy to create a scene of dialogue that is so transformative that our characters are changed forever and our reader knows it. Our characters have to speak some profound words to each other to make this happen. In the following scene in *The Great Santini* by Pat Conroy, it's more the action rather than the dialogue that really changes Ben Meecham, but the dialogue that follows the action reveals just how big the transformation is. It has truly changed all of the characters in the Meecham family, not just Ben. In this scene, Bull Meecham challenges his son to a game of basketball, planning to easily beat and humiliate Ben in front of the other family members. This is a typical way Bull keeps himself amused on a daily basis, by humiliating others; there's nothing unusual here. What *is* unusual is that this time Bull doesn't win, causing all of the characters, especially his wife Lillian, to stand up to him. And we know that he will never have the same power over any of them ever again.

> Then Bull shouted at Ben, "Hey, jocko, you gotta win by two baskets."
>
> The backyard became quiet again. Ben looked at his father and said, "You said by one."
>
> "I changed my mind; let's go," Bull said, picking up the basketball.
>
> "Oh, no, Bull," Lillian said, marching toward her husband. "You're not going to cheat the boy out of his victory."
>
> "Who in the hell asked you anything?" Bull said, glaring at his wife.
>
> "I don't care if anybody asked me or not. He beat your fair and square and I'm not going to let you take that away from him."
>
> "Get over here, mama's boy," Bull said, motioning to Ben, "and let's you and me finish this game."

Ben moved forward until he heard his mother shout at him, "You stay right there, Ben Meecham. Don't you dare move."

"Why don't you go hide under your mother's skirts, mama's boy?" Bull said.

He was gaining control of the situation again and was entering a phase of malevolent calm that Lillian was having difficulty translating.

"Mama, I'm gonna play him," Ben said.

"No, you're not," his mother answered harshly, with finality, then speaking to her husband, she said, "He beat you, Big Marine. He beat the Big Marine where everybody could see it, right out in the open, and it was beautiful. It was just beautiful. Big Marine can't take it that his baby boy just beat him to death on the basketball court."

"Get in the house, Lillian, before I kick you into the house."

"Don't threaten me, Big Tough Marine. Does Big Tough Marine have to pick on his family the day his son becomes the better man?"

This novel's theme is about a man growing smaller and his family growing larger. Ultimately it's about forgiveness. It's painful to watch, but something inside of the reader cheers when Bull missteps and Ben and the others are given the glorious opportunity to emerge as bigger people. In this basketball scene, Bull continues to taunt Ben, but we know something is different. We can feel it. This is a pivotal scene in the story and Conroy executes the character transformation so well, I think it's my favorite story scene of all time.

It Reveals and Reminds Goals

The most important element of each scene that you create in a story is to know what your protagonist wants and to be able to *show* it through the action and dialogue. The protagonist wants something in the overall story that in each scene he takes steps to achieve. You're moving the story forward in each scene by challenging the protagonist, throwing an obstacle at him, thereby reminding us of his goal and intention in the scene and in the story.

Creating Characters

In the following excerpt from *Saint Maybe* by Anne Tyler, Ian, the main character, is trying to confess a perceived horrible sin to his parents. His mother, however, is just not hearing him, choosing instead to focus on her role as a victim. Ian believes he is responsible for his brother Danny's suicide because of something Danny told him shortly before smashing his car against a concrete wall and killing himself. Now Ian has decided to drop out of college and to learn to build furniture so he can help his mother with his brother's stepchildren after their mother also dies. He feels he needs to in some way pay for his sin. In this scene, we're reminded of Ian's goal, his intention—penance and forgiveness—and the story moves forward as we see once again what he's really all about.

His mother said, "I don't believe this. I do not believe it. No matter how long I've been a mother, it seems my children can still come up with something new and unexpected to do to me."

"I'm not doing this to you! Why does everything have to relate to you all the time? It's for me, can't you get that into your head? It's something I have to do for myself, to be forgiven."

"Forgiven what, Ian?" his father asked.

Ian swallowed.

"You're nineteen years old, son. You're a fine, considerate, upstanding human being. What sin could you possibly be guilty of that would require you to uproot your whole existence?"

Reverend Emmett had said Ian would have to tell them. He'd said that was the only way. Ian had tried to explain how much it would hurt them, but Reverend Emmett had held firm. Sometimes a wound must be scraped out before it can heal, he had said.

Ian said, "I'm the only one who caused Danny to die. He drove into that wall on purpose."

Nobody spoke. His mother's face was white, almost flinty.

"I told him Lucy was, um, not faithful," he said.

He had thought there would be questions. He had assumed they would ask for details, pull the single strand he'd handed them till the whole ugly story came tumbling out. But they just sat silent, staring at him.

"I'm sorry!" he cried. "I'm *really sorry!*"

His mother moved her lips, which seemed unusually wrinkled. No sound emerged.

After a while, he rose awkwardly and left the table. He paused in the dining room doorway, just in case they wanted to call him back. But they didn't. He crossed the hall and started up the stairs.

This is a pivotal scene as Ian unburdens his soul to his parents and gets no response whatsoever. We're reminded of his intention in the story when he says, "It's something I have to do for myself to be forgiven." This is what the story is about, Ian working hard to get forgiveness for his "sin." In every scene, you want to remind your reader of the main character's intention, as this is the way you engage your reader and keep engaging her as the story progresses. Using dialogue for this purpose is especially effective because the character is stating his goal out loud. It's coming right from his mouth.

Your protagonist can sit around and think about his intention or you can create a scene of dialogue and action and show his passion about his intention in a scene with other characters. Dialogue shows.

KEEPING YOUR CHARACTERS IN SOCIAL SETTINGS

Dialogue can only keep the story moving when you put more than one character in a scene. When you isolate your characters, there's no one for them to talk to. There's no dialogue. Of course, there is no way to get around putting your characters in scenes by themselves once in a while. But if an isolated character scene goes on too long, the story starts to dry up.

This seems to be a problem with many mainstream and literary stories; the protagonist is too often alone in scene after scene, engaged in self-analysis. The reader will hang in there for a while, but rambling self-analysis slows the story way down, and if it goes on too long, you risk losing the reader. So, when thinking through the scenes you want to create, remember that, for the most part, your reader most enjoys those scenes where two or more characters are engaged in some degree of dialogue and action.

A scene of dialogue must always move the story forward in some way. No exceptions. If you ever find yourself creating dialogue that fails in this purpose, you'll just have to throw it out later, no matter how creative, clever, funny, or brilliant.

....

GLORIA KEMPTON is the author of ten books, including *Write Great Fiction: Dialogue* (Writer's Digest Books, 2004) and *The Outlaw's Journey: A Mythological Approach to Storytelling for Writers Behind Bars* (Third Place Press, 2013). Gloria teaches her Outlaw's Journey course in correctional facilities and writers conferences around the country.

CHAPTER 11

USING PROFANITY AND OTHER RAW TALK IN YOUR FICTION

BY ELIZABETH SIMS

The expletive known in polite circles as "the f-word" was most famously used in a major novel, Norman Mailer's *The Naked and the Dead*, published in 1948.

Except it wasn't.

Mailer's publisher prevailed upon him to change the common but crass four-letter description of sex to "fug," so as not to offend readers. Given the fact that the book was about men at war, the word occurred a lot. This resulted in a cluster-fug of criticism and discussion in literary circles, and gave rise to the anecdote about Tallulah Bankhead (or in some versions, Dorothy Parker) meeting Mailer and saying, "Oh, you're the man who can't spell that word."

Times change.

These days, the f-word has lost some of its shock value, and most people—though by no means all—are not deeply offended by it. Still, authors often debate the role of racy talk in contemporary literature.

How much is too much? How do you know when you've gone too far, or not far enough?

First, let's consider the rich palette of risqué words available to us and clarify their technical differences, so we know what's what. Once you can differentiate among profanities, curses, obscenities, and the like, you'll be better equipped to determine how, why, and if you should use them.

Profanity

Although it is often used to denote any objectionable word, *profanity* literally means words that are considered profane—that is, words proscribed by religious doctrine. (*Proscribed* generally means forbidden by written order.) In the Judeo-Christian tradition, this primarily means taking the Lord's name in vain (that is, not in prayer).

For the love of God, stop complaining.

Jesus Christ, look at the size of that thing!

Curses

A *curse* calls upon a deity, or fate, to visit harm on someone or something.

Mild curse: Damn this zipper!

Strong curse: Goddamn her!

To be "damned" is to be condemned to hell. (See the common root lurking in con*demned*/*damned*?)
"Hell" can also be used as a curse—

Go to hell!

—or as mild profanity—

Oh, hell, the Potomac's polluted again!

Swears

To *swear* literally means to take an oath or to proclaim an oath. (An *oath* is a resolution or promise, usually calling on the deity's assistance in carrying it out.)

As God is my witness, I'll never go hungry again!

By God, I'll show you!

Swearing can also be used to bear witness:

I swear, you're the best cook in Memphis!

Obscenities

Obscene means something disgusting or morally abhorrent, often connoting sex. The f-word is considered the most objectionable of these. (Adding "mother" as a prefix ups the ante.)

Non-objectionable variants of the present participle form of the word—besides "fugging"—include "fecking," "freaking," "flipping" and "fricking." (To be honest, I really don't know why that "u" is so important.)

"Screw" is a milder word. Notice that both the f-word and "screw" are used not just to literally describe the act of intercourse, but to connote "taking advantage of":

> Don't go to that repair shop—they screwed me out of $500 for
> a brake job I didn't need.

Words referring to the pelvic area, male and female, are also considered obscenities.

Vulgarisms

Vulgarism is a great word that covers a lot of bases. If it's crude and objectionable and falls outside the aforementioned categories, you've got yourself a vulgarism.

Casting aspersions on the circumstances of a person's birth qualifies as a vulgarism. "Bitch," "son of a bitch" and "bastard" can be termed vulgarisms. Ditto for "jackass," which is often used as a substitute for another two-syllable word that starts with "ass."

Excretory acts and their results fall under this rubric as well. "Crap" seems to be the only one that's acceptable virtually everywhere.

TO USE OR NOT TO USE

Authors are divided about spicy talk, which is not surprising because readers are divided about it. Some really popular tough-guy authors—Lee Child comes to mind—use no profanity in their books, and lots of readers don't even notice. Why? Because Child, for instance, doesn't even write the watered-down "dammit," which would call attention to the fact that he's not using "Goddamn it." For the same reason he's certainly not going to have his characters, who blow one another's brains out at the drop of a hat, say "darn it." On the other hand, Tom Clancy, another leader in the same genre, uses lots of profanity, and he sure sells books.

Some readers are turned off by even a single curse word, whereas nobody will buy your book simply *because* you use raw language. So the safest path is to use zero raw language, right?

Well, writing is a journey, and journeys involve risks. I'm certain there are authors who have been successful in part because they shun propriety. I remember being happily shocked by Holden Caulfield's speech in *The Catcher in the Rye* when I was a teenager.

As you write, look for a balance involving what you feel comfortable writing, what suits the characters and story you are creating, and what might please or displease your hoped-for readers.

WHY TO USE

Humans get angry. They crave precise expression. There's something about cursing or using vulgar language that acts as a release valve. Most of us have experienced a moment when a good old rule-breaking bad word just feels sublime rolling off the tongue, and so it is for fictional characters. Be true and honest to the voices of those characters. Moreover, if you want to write realistically about certain milieus, such as wharves, mines and battlefields, well-written raw talk can make your characters seem lifelike and more authentic.

HOW TO USE

Spicy language generally works best when it's used sparingly, or at least in moderation. That way, you preserve the element of the unexpected, which can be a pressure reliever for both character and reader. Aside from conveying anger or frustration, raw talk can also be humorous, in that it reveals how a character truly feels about something. For instance:

> I ate another doughnut.

Versus:

> I ate another goddamned doughnut.

You instantly get a clue about this character and her relationship with doughnuts.

You can also have a character who habitually uses profanity in contrast to others who don't. That, in itself, is a good individualizer.

In the case of the wharf workers, miners and soldiers, here's a caveat to remember: You shouldn't just throw in spicy talk willy-nilly. You have to make it sound real. Go and listen to the people who populate the worlds you're writing about. Read about them, experiment, read their words aloud.

But even if real cliff-blasting miners use a vulgarism every other word, it's unnecessary for you to make your characters talk exactly that way. Just as with dialect and accents, using raw talk wisely serves to keep the reader grounded in your imaginary world while avoiding the potential fatigue of overdoing it.

Consider your characters and employ common sense. A suburban matron wearing a linen dress and pearls might never swear in public, but she might let loose in the principal's office over a dispute between her kid and a teacher or when she breaks a nail opening her prescription amphetamines.

HOW NOT TO USE

Shakespeare knew that raw talk is the spice of writing.

He wrote the mother of all literary cuss outs (*cuss* is simply a variant of *curse*) in *King Lear*, but interestingly there is no profanity or obscenity as we know it, merely terrifically imaginative vulgarisms, delivered with passion. Here it is, the Earl of Kent preparing to thrash the crap out of Goneril's loathsome lackey, Oswald:

> KENT (TO OSWALD): A knave; a rascal; an eater of broken
> meats; a base, proud, shallow, beggarly, three-suited, hundred-
> pound, filthy, worsted-stocking knave; a lily-liver'd, action-taking,
> whoreson, glass-gazing, superserviceable, finical rogue; one-

trunk-inheriting slave; one that wouldst be a bawd in way of good
service, and art nothing but the composition of a knave, beggar,
coward, pander, and the son and heir of a mongrel bitch, one
whom I will beat into clamorous whining if thou deniest the least
syllable of thy addition.

Knowing the historical references helps; for example, "broken meats" means leftover table scraps. But even without that, we can luxuriate in the rant. This is a beautiful speech for many reasons: It's forceful, it's unique, it covers many aspects of insult, it clearly communicates one character's contempt of another, and—important for many in Shakespeare's audience—it avoids serious curses and obscenities.

It's a shining example of how a writer can invent insults far more entertaining than those found in the standard lexicon.

You can do it by brainstorming aspects of your characters and their circumstances:

He was as appealing as a baboon's butt.

You are the worst thing to happen to the world since call-waiting.

May you be condemned to an eternity of weak coffee, warm gin,
and a driveway paved with roofing nails.

By now, I think you'll agree that it's useful to explore—and perhaps even challenge—your own comfort zone. Certainly if it's not you, it won't ring true. But whether you decide to write common curses and vulgarisms into your work or not, your characters do need a verbal pressure valve. Don't use tacky asterisks to replace vowels. Just have fun with the process and remember that a fug by any other name might sound remarkably original.

....
ELIZABETH SIMS (elizabethsims.com) is a contributing editor to *Writer's Digest* magazine, a prize-winning novelist, and author of the bestseller *You've Got a Book in You: A Stress-Free Guide to Writing the Book of Your Dreams* (Writer's Digest Books, 2013).

CHAPTER 12

THE UHS, ANDS, AND ERS OF DIALOGUE

BY GLORIA KEMPTON

I once had a Marine boyfriend with a bit of a speech problem. I was attracted to his dark looks and muscular build the moment I met him at a friend's party, but then he spoke.

"Would you like to go for a walk?" he asked. "To the thore? Ith's cold outthide, but you can wear my jacket."

"Okay..."

"Let me thee if Richard needsth anything at the thore."

Aaargh! How could this good-looking guy have such a horrible lisp? As much as I tried to get over it, every time he came home on leave and showed up on my doorstep, I just couldn't cope. As I reflect on that time in my life now, of course, I feel terrible that it even mattered to me. But I was seventeen and needed a perfect boyfriend to show off to my friends. The point is, as much as I hate to admit it, and though I wasn't aware of it at the time, the lisp was a deal breaker for me as far as feeling attracted to this man. That's how important speech can be in a story, too. It can make or break relationships and business deals, and it certainly affects how seriously we take a character.

Most people speak fairly normally—if there is such a thing as normal. But every now and then, someone opens his mouth and something distinctive comes out. It could turn us off or it could turn us on, but what it does do is mark that person. In the 1980s television show *The Nanny*, the main character had this nasal voice and really, really nasal laugh. It was horrible. No matter what she said, we were laughing, just because of her voice.

The quirkiness of a character's speech should be something we think consciously about. It should rise organically out of who the character is and what his purpose is in the story. You don't want to just have a character stuttering or talking ninety miles an hour for no reason. Remember—with dialogue you're not just trying to find something to use to characterize your cast, you're creating a story that needs to hang together and connect on all levels to communicate your theme to the reader.

With that in mind, let's look at a few ways of speaking that will distinguish your character from the rest of the cast in your story while at the same time *show* us who he is and how his way of speaking will enhance his role. The challenge for us as writers is to find a way to *show* our characters' speech on the printed page. Sometimes we can do it by formatting our words and sentences in a certain way; other times we need to use tags to indicate that the dialogue is being said in a certain way. For the sake of example, let's use my boyfriend's sentence above, "Let me thee if Richard needsth anything at the thore."

THE TWISTED TONGUE

Let's start with this one—which would include my boyfriend's lisping problem. But there's also the stutterer, which in real life can be painful to listen to because you keep wanting to help the speaker get the words out. "L-l-let me see if R-R-R-R-Richard needs anything at the s-s-store."

This is something you don't want to overdo. When a character has a speech impediment, you want to just show it once in a while, throwing in a line or two of lisping or stuttering so we remember how this character talks. Use it too much and the reader begins to find reading the story a rather annoying task. And remember, there needs to be a good reason for giving a character a speech impediment. Characterization isn't enough; it needs to have something to do with the plot so it's part of the piece of art that eventually becomes your novel.

THE ROCKET

This character is off like a rocket every time he gets a chance to talk.

"LetmeseeifRichardneedsanythingatthestore." This could be one way of showing the speed at which this character talks. Of course, if this is a major character in your story, it could be annoying to read much of his dialogue. Also, this could simply indicate not necessarily speed but that this character runs all of his words together.

You could simply describe the pace at which he speaks the first time he appears and then just allude to it occasionally after that. This is sometimes the most effective way to work with speech patterns of all kinds—make sure the reader gets it the first few times, then simply indicate it here and there after that so it doesn't take over the story or become so difficult to read that the reader puts your story down.

What's important with all speech patterns is what's underneath. In some cases, like a stutter or lisp, it could be something physical, though I've learned that these particular disabilities can be corrected through therapy because they are often acquired in childhood when a person is traumatized.

But most often, the way we talk emerges out of who we are. I can personally speak about the "rocket" because this is me a lot of the time. Unless I'm consciously trying to talk slowly, I'm off like a rocket. I just get so excited about whatever it is I'm saying. It doesn't do any good for someone to tell me to slow down. I can't seem to do that for long.

I don't just talk fast. I move fast. I think fast. I drive fast. If I could find a way to sleep faster, I would, because I'm always afraid I'm missing something. Keep your character's entire personality in mind when giving him a distinctive speech pattern.

THE TURTLE

"Let ... me see ... if ... Richard needs ... anything ... at ... the store."

This is the opposite of the rocket. My best friend happens to be a slow talker, and again, this is because of who she *is*. She moves slowly, thinks slowly, and drives so slowly that it's often painful for me to ride in the car with her, given who I am.

Are there other ways you can indicate a character's slow pattern of speech? Be creative. Practicing will give you the opportunity to be

Creating Characters

creative with each of these speech patterns and consider how you might *show* each one in a page of dialogue.

This character in your story is in no hurry and can't be made to move or talk faster, no matter what. I think it might even be physically impossible for her.

You could indicate her slow pace in narrative that describes her dialogue.

> Sue meandered from subject to subject while my soup grew cold. "You're ..." yawn ... "not ... eating ..." she looked around the restaurant... "your soup."

THE BABY DOLL

This character talks in a high-pitched voice, like a little girl who's never grown up, but who is grown up. I don't know of any males who talk like this—well, Michael Jackson did. That doesn't mean there aren't others out there who do. I just think it's rare.

This character comes from an unsure place inside of herself, perceiving the world through a not-quite-grown-up view. Her voice squeaks, like a vocalist hitting the high notes and her voice cracking. That might be one way you could *show* it. "Let me see"—squeak—"if Richard needs anything at the store"—giggle. Since you can't really *show* a tone because it's a sound, you have to be creative and think how you might let the reader in on how this character's voice *sounds*.

THE BASS DRUM

This character sounds like Tom Brokaw. Again, because this speech pattern has more to do with sound than it does the *way* the speech is said, you might have to describe the voice rather than *show* it in the actual dialogue. You can simply use narrative, something like:

> Whenever he spoke, it sounded like he was inside the chamber of a bass drum, hollow and deep.

Sometimes you can use famous people to help the reader key into how a character speaks. You might just use the famous newsman to show how a character sounds:

Every time he spoke, I found myself looking toward the television to see if Tom Brokaw was broadcasting the news.

THE CALCULATOR

This character is constantly weighing his words, speaking very carefully and methodically. There is any number of reasons for this. Sometimes this character is concerned about his image, wanting to come off well to others, so he chooses every word. It could be that he wants power over another character and is weighing every word to make sure he's manipulating the situation to his advantage. He could simply be scared and being careful not say anything that would put him in danger or bring on a threat of any kind.

He seemed deep in thought, then finally spoke. "Let me see if … Richard," he paused then continued, "needs anything at the … store."

Put yourself inside of your character's head in order to get to the motivation behind the patterns of speech you give her. Being inside her head will help you determine what she says and how she says it. Sometimes a speech pattern is a permanent part of a character's speech; other times it's momentary and temporary because of the situation in which she finds herself.

THE ACE

The ace simply doesn't talk much at all and when he does, he gives one-word answers. Or he grunts. He probably wouldn't even complete the sentence about Richard. "Let me see if …" His words may trail off. "Let me see if … Richard … needs …" You can't always understand the ace because he usually doesn't want to be talking to you anyway. A conversation with him might go something like:

> "So, Joe, how's it going?"
>> "It's goin'."
>> "You have enough work to do?"
>> "Yep." (Or a nod.)
>> "How's your family? June, the boys?"

Creating Characters

"Fine."

"You have a vacation planned this year? You taking your family anywhere?"

"Camping."

Somehow you'll have to characterize this guy, and while the one-word answers help do this, you're going to have to find other ways: his clothes, his mannerisms, and his demeanor. This character just doesn't have a lot to tell you about himself.

THE APOLOGIZER

This character is basically apologizing for being alive. No matter what the subject of conversation, she's saying she's sorry. This dialogue is easy to write, simply being characterized by "I'm sorry" thrown in at regular intervals. Since she's sorry for everything, this is a character who is often full of shame and doesn't like to be seen. She wishes she were invisible, so she talks in low tones and might mumble a lot. You can show this in narrative or you could be creative and use a smaller font for her speech. In dialogue with others, she's easily manipulated and controlled, thinking she's responsible for everything that happens.

THE SHIELD

Have you ever talked to someone who, no matter what you're talking about, is defending himself or whomever you're talking about? His tone of voice shows this. It's like he feels that he's always under attack and has to ward off the next blow, so he's always standing at the ready. To get into this character's mind-set, you have to imagine what it would feel like to think that everyone is against you, trying to pin something on you, and working constantly to find the gap in your armor where they can zoom in and get you. This character's face is often pinched as he waits for the next zinger he needs to deflect. He's quick on the draw, as he has a lot of experience deflecting verbal blows and is used to verbal sparring. His answers in conversation are fast and his goal is to keep others away from him.

"Do you think—"

"No, of course not," Earl quickly said. "I didn't know anything about it. How could I have been there?" His voice was rising, growing shriller, then, "Let me see if Richard needs anything at the store."

Here Earl is deflecting what he thinks is coming before it can hit him and then quickly changing the subject. He has many strategies to keep others as far away from him as possible.

THE CHANNEL CHANGER

The channel changer speaks in sentence fragments.

"See if Richard needs anything. At the store, you know."

This character is distracted and may not be altogether focused on the conversation she's having. Or she may be thinking about another conversation she'd like to be having. Or many other conversations she'd like to be having.

The channel changer talks in circles, so have to do mental cartwheels to make any sense of what he's saying. This type of character may suffer from a mental illness that causes him to jump around a lot in his speech. Those with attention deficit disorder often use sentence fragments as do geniuses in social settings. This could be a character on drugs or alcohol, just saying whatever comes into his mind at any moment. Those who find themselves in a state of terror can begin to speak like this.

This character may complete a thought but then make a gigantic leap to the next subject without waiting for a response. This is what marks the nonsensical speaker. He's simply all over the map in conversation. He's disconnected from himself and his own thoughts and isn't often tuned in to those around him, at least not in a rational way. So you want to show his disjointed thoughts by showing his disjointed speech.

"I'll see if Richard, you know, I was thinking that you and I should hook up—I wonder if Richard's even here, I'm going to the store and, hey, he might need something." This character simply changes frequency more often than the other characters may be able to keep up with her. You might want to use this character to keep all of the other characters in the story a little off balance. She comes in handy when the other characters are trying to accomplish something verbally and you want to stop them. She may interrupt and take everyone in a completely new direction in which they had no intention of going. Once there, the channel changer is probably either on to a new subject or out of the room altogether.

THE DIALECT

This is one of the most difficult types of speech to do well just because if you use too much of it for any one character, the reader finds it tough going as far as getting through the story. And if it's a novel, it's a lot of pages of dialect. Every once in a while the author gets away with it, of course. Alice Walker's *The Color Purple* is an example of a dialect we all worked through because the story was so compelling. But I wouldn't try that if I were you, unless you have an equally compelling story. And there hasn't been a *The Color Purple* since, well, *The Color Purple*.

The best way to handle dialect is to just sprinkle a few words of the foreign language or slang into the dialogue here and there. For example, if it's a speaker who's deep into hip-hop, you can throw a "yo" into the dialogue once in a while to characterize the speaker and make the dialect sound authentic. But you don't want to write the dialogue exactly like a rapper would talk, as it just becomes too tedious to read.

"Yo, let me see if my man, Richard, needs anything at the store."

Sometimes dialect requires that the writer change the spelling of words here and there to show the character's nationality and/or background. Again, don't go overboard with this in the dialogue. A subtle change of spelling once in a while will remind the reader of this character's background.

THE CANNON

In John Irving's novel *A Prayer for Owen Meany*, I would call the protagonist a cannon because of the loudness of his speech.

"DO YOU THINK I CARE WHAT THEY DO TO ME? "he shouted; he stamped his little foot on the drive-shaft hump. "DO

YOU THINK I CARE IF THEY START AN AVALANCHE
WITH ME?" he screamed. "WHEN DO I GET TO GO ANY-
WHERE? IF I DIDN'T GO TO SCHOOL OR TO CHURCH
OR TO EIGHTY FRONT STREET, I'D NEVER GET OUT
OF MY HOUSE!" he cried. "IF YOUR MOTHER DIDN'T
TAKE ME TO THE BEACH, I'D NEVER GET OUT OF
TOWN. AND I'VE NEVER BEEN TO THE MOUNTAINS,"
he said. "I'VE NEVER EVEN BEEN ON A TRAIN! DON'T
YOU THINK I MIGHT LIKE GOING ON A TRAIN—TO THE
MOUNTAINS?" he yelled.

And this is the way Irving indicates it—in all caps. It's very effective, and it's not annoying for the reader, as unlike dialect, the words are all easily pronounced—they're just loud. What a delightful characterization device that immediately signals to the reader when Owen is speaking.

"LET ME SEE IF RICHARD NEEDS ANYTHING AT THE
STORE."

THE SWITCHBLADE

"Let me see if that punk, Richard, needs anything at the store." This character might punch whoever he's speaking on the shoulder as he asks him this question. He's a tough guy and his voice reflects that. He likes the power he has over others and knows how to use it, physically and in conversation.

Thinking from inside of this character means putting on a tough-guy persona and talking out of that to the other characters. His voice has an edge to it. He needs to be the one in charge at all times, and so much of his speech consists of directives, telling others what to do and how to do it. This is his goal, what he sees as his purpose when relating to others. Sometimes a switchblade's toughness expresses itself more indirectly, and that can be effective, too. In the book *Scene & Structure*, Jack Bickham offers a tip about this that is especially helpful if the switchblade happens to be the antagonist, and he usually is:

Creating Characters

Don't hesitate to use dialogue at cross-purposes once in a while as a scene-building device. Such dialogue can be defined as story conversation in which the conflict is not overt, but where the antagonist either doesn't understand what's really at issue, or is purposely nonresponsive to what the lead character keeps trying to talk about. Dialogue at cross-purposes, or nonresponsive behavior by an antagonist, will be experienced by both the lead character and the reader as conflictual. After all, in such a situation the lead character feels thwarted in some way, and so struggles harder. If the opposing character does not start responding quite directly, the viewpoint character will fight harder.

You can probably think of some ways of speaking that we haven't covered in this chapter. That's okay. Be creative and consider how you might show a particular speech pattern without overwhelming the reader or having it come off corny. Giving your character a particular manner of speech can go a long way in characterizing him and helping your reader recognize him when he appears onstage. It distinguishes him from the other characters, setting him apart. If you have a specific role for a character to play and need to set him apart, then consider giving him a distinct speech pattern.

GLORIA KEMPTON is the author of ten books, including *Write Great Fiction: Dialogue* (Writer's Digest Books, 2004) and *The Outlaw's Journey: A Mythological Approach to Storytelling for Writers Behind Bars* (Third Place Press, 2013). Gloria teaches her Outlaw's Journey course in correctional facilities and writers conferences around the country.

PART IV

PROTAGONISTS

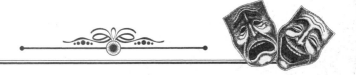

CHAPTER 13

THE HERO AND THE COMMON MAN

BY ORSON SCOTT CARD

When the ancient Greeks and Romans told a serious story, the characters were kings and queens, great warriors and heroes, the sort of people who expected to receive visitations from the gods—heck, the gods were often their aunts and cousins anyway. But when the Greeks and Romans set out to tell a story about common, everyday people, the result was comedy, in which the characters were lewd and foolish and corrupt.

It was long believed that great poetry could never be written about low characters—magnificent art demanded magnificent subject matter. The rules have changed since then. The invention of the novel—with such landmarks in English as *Pamela, Tom Jones, Robinson Crusoe,* and *Tristram Shandy*—proved that wonderful stories could take common people seriously.

Oddly enough, however, storytelling keeps drifting toward extraordinary heroes, so that the common people have to be rediscovered every few decades or so. Noted critic Northrop Frye examined this pattern and came up with the idea that our preference in fictional heroes swings back and forth like a pendulum. Frye used the words *Realistic* and *Romantic* in a special way, as the two ends of a descriptive spectrum. Romantic, in this context, doesn't have anything to do with whether or not a character is in love. At first heroes become more and more Romantic (idealized, extraordinary, exotic, magnificent) until finally they become so overblown and so clichéd that we cease to believe in or care about them. In reaction, the pendulum swings back the other way, and our fictional heroes become Realistic—common, plain people, living lives that are well within the experience of the readers. However, these Realistic heroes quickly become boring, because people who live lives no different from our own are not terribly interesting to read about—or to write about. So storytellers almost immediately begin making their heroes just a little out of the ordinary, so that readers will again be fascinated—until the Romantic hero is in the saddle again.

In creating characters, we don't have to worry about pendulums. What concerns us is that our main characters must be at once believable and interesting—simultaneously Realistic and Romantic. Each of us, however, finds a different balance between the two. How extraordinary or exotic or "elevated" do characters need to be for you to want to read or write about them? How much detail, how much commonness, how much familiarity must characters have before you believe in them? Your answer will be different from mine and from every other writer's; your audience will consist of readers who agree with your answer.

Look at the fiction market today, and you'll see what I mean. Do you want Roman characters? Thrillers deal with people who are on the cutting edge of power in the world—spies, diplomats, heads of state—and their lives are never ordinary; even shopping for groceries, they have to watch out for the enemy. Historical romances deal with characters in exotic times and places, and usually people of high station in an era when class distinctions meant all the difference in the world. Glitter romances deal with the very rich, jetting between assignations in Rio, Paris, and Singapore. Mysteries offer us the detective as avenging angel, tracking down the guilty despite their best efforts to escape retribution. Fantasy, the true heir of the Romantic tradition, still shows us kings and queens wielding the power of magic. Science fiction takes us to worlds that have never been, to show us new kinds of magic, new kinds of nobility, new kinds of humanity.

Yet every single one of these genres includes stories that rebel against Romantic excess, that insist on realism. John LeCarre's spy thrillers achieved great note in large part because his characters were *not* Romantic, James Bond-like heroes, but instead ordinary people who got sick, confused, tired, old; people who made mistakes and had to bear the consequences. Yet is George Smiley *really* ordinary? Of course note. He is only one of the "common people" by comparison with the extravagance that went before. We still look at George Smiley with admiration and awe; we still expect him to achieve great things. He still moves through an exotic world. He is still a true hero, no matter how much shine has been taken off his armor.

The same pattern can be found among mystery novels. John Mortimer's wonderful hero Rumpole is an English barrister who will never achieve recognition, who isn't terribly successful and loses a lot of cases, and who certainly isn't rich. His home life is deplorable, as he endures a testy relationship with his shrewish wife whom he calls "She-who-must-be-obeyed." His very ordinariness is endearing—we read of him and feel that he is One Of Us. Yet Rumpole is really not ordinary at all, or we wouldn't like reading about him. After the realism has won our belief, we still see him solving cases through remarkable persistence and clever insights, and we come to believe that in fact he *deserves* great recognition and a place on the bench. Others may think he's ordinary, but *we* know he's a truly remarkable, admirable man. The same pattern is followed by other "ordinary" mystery heroes—Ruth Rendell's Inspector Wexford, Robert Parker's Spenser, and of course all the heroes of the American hard-boiled detective tradition.

Just when the fantasy genre seemed likely to lose its last connection with reality, Stephen R. Donaldson made a bitter-hearted leper named Thomas Covenant the reluctant hero of his stories; and Megan Lindholm's *Wizard of the Pigeons* found magic in a Vietnam veteran living among the street people of Seattle. A large part of Stephen King's appeal as a writer of horror, fantasy, and science fiction has been his insistence on using heroes from the American middle class, living in the familiar world of fast food, shopping malls, and television. Yet even as we recognize people and details from the real life around us, all of these stories would have been pointless had their heroes not been extraordinary in one way or another, though their uniqueness was hidden even from themselves.

Readers tend to like a character who is at least superficially like themselves. But they quickly lose interest unless this particular character is somehow out of the ordinary. The character may wear the mask of the common man, but underneath his true face must always be the face of the hero.

Why? Because we don't read stories to duplicate real life. In our own diaries and journals we tend to write down only what was out of the ordinary, skipping the dull parts of the day. Why should we read the dull parts in the life of a made-up character?

We read stories to get experiences we've never known firsthand or to gain a clearer understanding of experiences we *have* had. In the process, we follow one or more characters the way we follow our "self" in our dreams; we assimilate the story as if what happened to the main characters had happened to us. We identify with heroes. As they move through the story, what happens to them happens to us.

In comedy, heroes go through all the terrible things that we fear or face in our own lives—but they teach us to look at disaster with enough distance that we can laugh at it. In non-comic fiction, the hero shows us what matters, what has value, what has meaning among the random and meaningless events of life. In all stories, the hero is our teacher-by-example, and if we are to be that hero's disciple for the duration of the tale, we must have *awe*: We must know that the hero has some insight, some knowledge that we ourselves do not understand, some value or power that we do not yet have.

This is true even in that great bastion of extreme realism, the academic/literary genre (those who refer to their genre as "serious literature"—as if the rest of us are just kidding). One reason why the academic/literary genre usually reaches such a small fragment of the reading public is because in the pursuit of seriousness, they have beaten down the Romantic impulse wherever it rears its head. But the Romantic impulse is still there. Even in the endless stories about college professors or advertising writers or housewives entering midlife crises and trying to make sense of their senseless lives, the heroes always seem to face some uncommon problems, always seem to be extraordinarily contemplative and perceptive, always seem to reach a moment of epiphany in which they pass along a key insight to the reader. Despite their seeming ordinariness, these heroes always turn out to be extraordinary, once we truly understand them.

Arthur Miller may have meant Willy Loman to be a nonhero in *Death of a Salesman*—he was named "low man" to make sure we got the point—but by the end Miller has shown us that Loman dreamed of greatness for himself and his children, and his failure to achieve it destroyed him. The fact that Loman reached such a point of despair that he killed himself moves him out of the ordinary—but what really makes Loman a figure of awe is that he *expected* himself and his sons to be great, that he measured himself against such high standards that, by trying to meet them, he became exactly the Romantic hero that Arthur Miller was trying to avoid. He was one of the knights of the round table who failed to find the Holy Grail—but he was nobly searching for it nonetheless.

The writers in the Realistic tradition—for instance, Updike, Bellow, and Fowles—still give their characters heroic proportion; only it's more restrained, used less boldly, better disguised. By the end of Bellow's novel *Humboldt's Gift*, Humboldt is definitely bigger than life; he is, in his own way, as romantically "enlarged" as Captain Blood or Rhett Butler. The difference is that Captain Blood was involved in jeopardy on page one and bigger than life by page thirty, while Humboldt didn't really become recognizably heroic in size until near the end of the book.

Without giving the audience some reason to feel in awe of the hero, there would be no story. Eliminate the usual sources of awe, the usual ways of making a character larger than life, and the storyteller will either find another or lose interest in the tale.

More recently, many academic/literary writers have striven to avoid "naïve identification" by creating "aesthetic distance"—but these writers have merely replaced the character-hero with the author-as-hero, so that the admiration that used to be directed toward a character is now directed toward the artist who created the exquisite, extraordinary text.

If there is no awe, there is no audience. In every successful story—every story that is loved and admired by at least one reader who is not a close friend or blood relative of the author—the author has created characters who somehow inspire enough admiration, respect, or awe that readers are willing to identify with them, to become their disciples for the duration of the tale.

I'm not for a moment advocating that you artificially juice up your characters to make them more Romantic. That's no more likely to result in good characterization than overwhelming your heroes with humdrum details. You'll do much better if you trust your own instincts to choose the balance between Romance and Realism that's right for you and for your natural audience.

What you need is not a specific recipe but rather a general awareness: It's vital that along with making a character seem exciting and wonderful, you also help your readers understand and believe in her, so they can connect her with their own lives. Along with making another character seem understandable and believable, you should also show your readers why he is important enough and admirable enough to deserve a place in their memories, to be a worthy exemplar of the meanings of life.

Often when you find yourself blocked—when you can't bring yourself to start or continue a story—the reason is that you have forgotten or have not yet discovered what is extraordinary about your main character. Go back over your notes, over the part of the story you've already told, and ask yourself: What's so special about this woman that people should hear the story of her life? Or, more to the point, ask yourself: Why does her story matter to *me*?

You've got a story going. Pete's just an ordinary twenty-three-year-old man, just finishing college after a three-year stint in the army, degree in business administration with good-enough but not spectacular grades, a few failed romances just like everybody else's failed romances. He's hired by a major corporation and put in charge of a department. After a year on the job, others are getting promoted—but not him. He just isn't doing all that good a job. He keeps getting distracted.

Then you don't know what to do. You sit down to write, and what you say doesn't seem to make any difference, it's all lousy. You're blocked. So you take a look at Pete's character. There's no reason to notice him, nothing obviously special about him. You realize that until you find—or invent—something extraordinary about him, you don't have a story.

So you look for what it is that makes him not just different, but *better* or more admirable than the others. Why *isn't* he succeeding? What is it about the others that gets them promoted? You search through what you've written so far and you haven't answered that question. You did a great job of making him ordinary and common. But there *is* something different about him: He isn't getting promoted on the normal track. Why?

It's not that he's unambitious—he read *Iacocca* just like everybody else in the M.B.A. program, and he dreams of seven-figure salaries and million-dollar bonuses, of heading a company with a budget larger than Brazil's. So maybe his "lack" is that he can't bring himself to have the attitude toward his underlings that most other managers in his company seem to have. He doesn't regard them as machines that must run at maximum efficiency or be replaced; he can't bring himself to judge their worth according to the bottom line. Pete just can't stop caring about them as human beings.

If this is what makes Pete special, how does that affect your story? Consider what you have to work with. You've already got a character, an office manager named Nora. In the present draft you had Pete try to joke with her, but she took it as flirting and shut him down with a nasty little speech about sexual harassment. You never meant that relationship to go anywhere—you were just using Nora as a minor character to show Pete making an ordinary dumb mistake. But now that you have keyed in on Pete's extraordinary tendency to care about people even when it's bad for his company and his career, why not use Nora to develop that trait? Pete has good reasons to think she's a jerk—if he could fire anybody, he could surely fire her, right?

So when Nora starts having problems, the solution is obvious: Get rid of her. She's inattentive. She makes mistakes. She isn't assigning work to her staff—one of her typists has even gone around *asking* for work because Nora hasn't assigned her anything in a week. Some of your other people are beginning to complain that Nora's office is slow in returning paperwork. Nora has been snapping at anyone who dares to ask about late or missing work, and morale in her office is awful.

But Pete just can't fire her. For one thing, he's afraid that she'll think he's firing her because she rejected his "sexual advances," even though *he* didn't think his joking had any sexual overtones. For another thing, she used to do terrific work—something must be wrong. So he calls her in and finds out that Nora is having a terrible time with her six-year-old in school and her three-year-old's day-care situation is awful; her ex-husband is trying to get custody, and the school and day-care problems play right into his hands. In other words, her life's a mess—and the very worst thing that could happen right now is to lose her job.

He talks about Nora to a friend from school who has a managerial job in the same city. The friend tells him to fire her—she isn't doing the work, and Pete doesn't have the right to turn the company into a charitable organization for people with screwed-up lives. He was hired as a manager, not a clergyman. But Pete can't bring himself to fire her. Instead he works late, going over Nora's workload and finding ways to redistribute it, to take up the slack—in essence, he ends up doing her job.

If this were a love story, you'd develop a romance between Pete and Nora. But that idea bores you. So you have Nora react nastily to Pete's "intrusions" into her office domain, not realizing that he's saving her bacon; she even complains about Pete to the people above *him*. He can't even tell them what he's doing—they'd be appalled if they knew he had done her job for her instead of playing the role of a manager. After five months of Nora sniping at Pete while he covers for her, she finally gets her kids' problems straightened out, her husband off her back, and her life back in gear. Naturally Pete reassigns to Nora all the work he had removed from her during her hard times. Nora, however, is outraged at a sudden doubling of her workload with no commensurate rise in salary. She quits—after writing nasty letters complaining about Pete to the people over him.

Maybe that's the end of your story; maybe it's just one incident along the way, with other plot threads weaving through the story. What

Creating Characters

matters is that it establishes that, while Pete is definitely a common man, there is also something uncommon about him—even heroic. He is able to empathize with people who aren't even nice to him. He is, in fact, a noble figure.

Sure, he gets so furious at Nora that he writes out her dismissal notice a half-dozen times before she finally quits. When she's gone, after doing real damage to his career when his only "crime" was helping hold her life together, he vows that he'll never be such a sucker again. These are all common, natural, ordinary reactions. But the audience knows that when it comes right down to it, Pete *will* do it again, over and over. He won't have a Lee Iacocca career—but the audience is in awe of him for a virtue he doesn't even value himself.

Searching for the extraordinary in your characters can help you write your story. More important, though, it will help your readers find what they're looking for in fiction. You won't please everybody. Some readers will reject your story because your hero isn't heroic enough for them to bother with; others because you made him too heroic for them to believe. That will always happen, and there's nothing you can do about it.

What you *can* do is search for what is "larger than life" in your characters and then make sure that your story reveals their nobility, their grandeur, however subtle and well-disguised it may be amid realistic and common details.

....

ORSON SCOTT CARD is the author of the novels *Ender's Game* (Tor Books, 1985), *Ender's Shadow* (Tor Books, 1999), and *Speaker for the Dead* (Tor Books, 1986), which are widely read by adults and younger readers, and are increasingly used in schools. His most recent series, the young adult Pathfinder series and the fantasy Mithermages series, are taking readers in new directions. Besides these and other science fiction novels, Card writes contemporary fiction, biblical novels, the American frontier fantasy series The Tales of Alvin Maker, poetry, and many plays and scripts.

CHAPTER 14

FROM ZERO TO HERO

BY DAWN WILSON

A true friend will tell you if your outfit makes you look heavy or if you have something between your teeth.

A true friend will also dare to ask, "What did you see in him?" Most important, though, a true friend will tell you if your main character is annoying.

Such was the case when a friend of mine volunteered to proofread my second novel. The story's hero was a little unsure of himself, somewhat naïve and still recovering from an unhappy love affair. I meant for him to be unassuming. My friend, however, thought he needed a few sessions with Dr. Phil.

"Is this character supposed to be this pathetic?" she asked. "Because he's really pathetic."

I thought he was humble, but evidently he'd left humble behind several chapters ago. Why did I spend more time describing his love handles than his beautiful green eyes? Why hadn't I given him the good lines and witty remarks?

I didn't allow my hero these things because, truth be told, he was getting on my nerves.

If I found him annoying, how would the readers react? Would they put up with him through 60,000 words?

No one's saying your protagonist has to be a warm and fuzzy tree-hugger, but if you find the dialogue drags when he enters the scene and his chapters become a chore, your hero may have worn out his welcome.

Here are some tips to help you tame any annoying character traits.

IDENTIFY WITH THE PROTAGONIST—AND ELIMINATE EXTREMES

Few characters are 100 percent virtuous. A completely benevolent character may come across as more of a goody-two-shoes than a heroine (unless you're writing a farce). On the same note, even the most vicious antiheroes have some good qualities. Darth Vader had the deep, soothing voice of James Earl Jones, and the Artful Dodger was, well, charming.

In Charlotte Brontë's *Wuthering Heights*, Heathcliff and Catherine are immortalized as passionate, tormented lovers of mythical proportions. Despite everything, many readers want them to live happily ever after.

But let's face it: As far as lovers go, Heathcliff leaves something to be desired. He destroys personal relationships with his bitterness and jealousy, and is reduced to a Gothic misanthrope lurking around his estate. A true friend would've told Catherine to get therapy and get over him.

So why do so many readers want to see Catherine and Heathcliff as lovers? For all his rough edges, Heathcliff does have a few good qualities. He's survived a tormented childhood and, despite humble beginnings, he eventually becomes a landlord (even if he uses his power for spite). Most important, he has an intense love for Catherine.

Who hasn't felt the pain of unrequited love? Who hasn't had some childhood memories direct us to the therapist's couch? Anyone who had trouble finding a prom date can relate to Heathcliff—even if only in a small way.

Assign your hero characteristics you can relate to or admire. He could, for example, generously tip an overworked waitress. And even malicious characters may love animals. And how's this for relatable: Eventually all heroes think about what to eat for dinner. You might want to explore ways in which such details can be used to move the story.

Perhaps your heroine is wishy-washy, but she loves cats. Suppose she saves the life of an injured kitten that belongs to a neighbor who'll become her love interest a few chapters later. While these characteristics don't have to necessitate major plot twists, they can be used to drive plot subtleties.

DON'T ASSOCIATE NEGATIVE EXPERIENCES WITH YOUR CHARACTER

Whether you realize it or not, our characters have associations based on personal experience. Even a name can lead to character traits that weigh down your hero. When I was in fifth grade, a boy named Travis used to terrorize me on the trench ball court (it's like dodge ball, only more sadistic). I can't call a character Travis without picturing a large, red ball coming at my head. If I named a character Travis, I'm sure that, at least subconsciously, I might try to avoid writing about him.

ARGUE WITH YOUR HERO

Picture yourself talking with your main character about why he's so annoying and driving you nuts. It helps me if I imagine myself at a place my main character frequents.

For example, I envision sitting in my protagonist's office and asking, "Why don't you get a life? Why don't you just do something—build up your nerve; ask her out!? Why are you such a wimp?"

The strange thing is that at first, he just avoided my stare, shuffled papers and even twiddled his thumbs. But as I gave his character more edge and doubled his dose of confidence, he responded: "You made me this way, so maybe that's something you need to ask yourself. You're the one who sits at a computer all day."

Another exercise might be to picture yourself in a restaurant with your protagonist. Perhaps you're upset when she sends her steak back even though it's cooked to perfection. Or maybe your hero professes that meat is murder but wears a leather jacket. What does your hero say to you? How does she respond?

If you can picture the character in your imagination, take a close look at her body language. Even the slightest twitch and tap can reveal new aspects of your character that you might have overlooked.

GET FEEDBACK

Whether it's from a writing group, teacher, or true friend, feedback helps, so run your writing by others. Note that I said "true" friend. You don't want the type of person who thinks everything you do is fantastic.

If you're not sure, just stick a piece of lettuce between your teeth before you meet with him and see if he tells you.

You want that friend to be brutally honest. Granted you don't have to agree with her on everything, but you do need to know she has your best interests at heart.

The bottom line is this: You have to develop a tough skin. This is a time to seek opinions, not to debate why your work doesn't need a rewrite (and by the way, if Lord Byron did rewrites, you need to do rewrites).

Finally, realize this is a fine-tuning exercise and not an extreme makeover. We're not trying to make your character likeable at the cost of doing something uncharacteristic. But a few human characteristics now and then will go a long way toward making your protagonist palatable.

....

DAWN WILSON is a freelance writer and author of the novel *Saint Jude* (Tudor Publishers, 2001).

CHAPTER 15

HOW TO CHALLENGE YOUR PROTAGONIST

BY LARRY BROOKS

The enlightened writer understands that plot and character, at their most effective, are separate yet interdependent essences, both driven by story physics. Plot is the stage upon which character is allowed to unfold, where dramatic tension is launched, escalated through pace, and ultimately resolved. Character is the means by which plot becomes relevant and meaningful, the realm of empathy and vicarious experience.

The search for optimal story physics seeks to create harmony and balance across these two critical story elements, without a myopic focus on either.

CHARACTERIZATION IS COMPLEX

If you can grasp the nuance of subtext and *inner dialogue*, if your concept becomes a tension-driven stage upon which this plays, then you'll have the chops to make your characters more vivid and visceral than you thought possible. Characters are almost always more interesting and transparent when they're doing something, rather than thinking about something or waxing eloquent in a vacuum. Or worse, being written *about*.

Just look deeper at your life and relationships and you'll notice all manner of dialogue going on everywhere. People are constantly engaged in conversations with their most deeply hidden, most despised, and most coveted inner *selves*. The "self" that is actually in charge is usually up for debate, and in our fiction, that's the fun of it. It's not a verbal thing, per se: Folks aren't going around muttering quietly to themselves, nor should your characters, unless that's part of their deal. Often there is a very clear, sometimes palpable gap between one's inner thoughts and his exterior behavior and attitude. That gap is something most people are dealing with right beneath the surface, sometimes 24-7.

The shy person who must contrive an air of confidence and warmth in a crowd.

The insecure person who walks through the world with a cloak of bluster.

The person who conforms to fit in, even when he realizes this isn't who he is.

The person faking it in a marriage. At work. In church.

The self-absorbed person sitting with friends at dinner in a nice restaurant, uttering not a single word, totally checked out or waiting until the conversation circles around to his favorite topic—himself.

The seething person hiding hate, resentment, bitterness, and fear behind a mask of calm.

Moods, both good and bad, are part of an inner dialogue. But sometimes the inner noise isn't obvious.

The extent to which someone—including your hero *and* your villain—*recognizes* the gap between her true thoughts, beliefs, preferences, and comfort zones, and the way she chooses to behave or appear in spite of them ... is *inner dialogue*. A constant tug-of-war within the psyche. A devil on one shoulder, an angel on the other. Or at least, the voice of reason, whose hat is borrowed from either of the former.

Inner dialogue is also something readers will relate to, and when they can relate, it jacks the element of *empathy*.

If a character has no idea how conflicted he or she is, well, that's a dialogue of another sort. The person can't see it, though everybody else can. Don't kid yourself, though, most of us (even those who aren't in therapy) usually *know*. The façade, or the vacancy, is a *choice*.

So what to do with this?

Before you square off with this dramatic can of worms, think about it. Go through a roster of people you know, and suddenly you'll realize how transparent the wall behind which this inner dialogue plays can be. The better you know the person, the more aware *you* are of what's going on inside *him*.

He thinks he's fooling everybody ... but not so much.

Scary, isn't it?

Chances are that, because you are human, *you* are among these inner conversationalists. All the better to put this to use in your fiction.

Now imagine you're casting this person—or you—in your story. Consider the possibilities of revealing that inner tension, the inherent contradiction as narrated by an inner dialogue, in a dramatic moment.

Walking into a crowded room. Lying about what you did last night. Asking a girl out for the first time. Feigning joy while considering suicide.

This faux existence is too often the human experience. When depicted artfully in your story, it will evoke empathy from readers on both sides of the hero-villain proposition. In recognizing this, you now have another arrow in your quiver of character-building weapons. Go as deep as you like, picking your moments to maximize revelation, tension, and complexity.

First-person narrative invites this, but you can pull it off in third person, too. Start to look for inner dialogue and character layering in the work of folks like Stephen King, Dennis Lehane, Jonathan Franzen, John Irving, and probably your favorite writer.

Heroes are obvious candidates for inner dialogue. But if you can bring this complexity to your antagonists, as well—who may or may not be human, so write accordingly—you'll have achieved a new level of depth there, too. This depth will set your story apart.

THE MAGIC PILL OF COMPELLING CHARACTERIZATION

Just like a writer's discovery of story architecture (for some, an epiphany), the sudden recognition and understanding of what you're seeing on the inside of your characters, and how that relates to what they

Creating Characters

do on the outside, can change everything about your ability to write compelling characters.

This is huge. Get ready to go to the next level the moment this sinks in.

This is as much about recognizing and verbalizing the *essence* of something that resists description as it is about leaving it to literary instinct or experiential happenstance. The same case can be made for structure and, perhaps, the story physics that drive it.

Let There Be Characterization

The nuances of characterization cannot be fully appreciated until one first grasps the fundamentals, which are unto themselves eternally challenging. You can't negotiate the order of that evolution.

But where compelling character excellence is concerned, you must dig deeper than just the basic facets of characterization technique (such as backstory, inner conflict versus exterior conflict, character arc, etc.). Like concept, it's best to begin crafting character with something compelling in mind.

The most compelling way to suck us into a story and have us immediately understand and root for a character (or hate her, your call), the best way to give your story a shot at *huge* success, is to show us *how the character feels about* and *responds* to the journey you've set before her.

This means character surfaces *in the here and now*, and along the path to come. This is the hero's humanity, for better or worse: her opinions, fears, feelings, judgments, and *inner response to the moment*. Too often writers depend on backstory to show character landscape, but that's only one opportunity. The more effective window into character is having her act out and respond.

And *that* goes far beyond showing us what she says and does.

The writer who commands this advanced technique of characterization isn't just showing us what *happens*. He's allowing us *into the head* of the character *as it happens*, and in a way that allows us to interpret (or misinterpret), emotionally respond to, assess, fear, plan against, flee from, or otherwise form opinions about all that is being processed in a given moment or situation.

This is, at a simplistic level, called *point of view*. This is where the power of hero empathy kicks in.

But it is an *informed* point of view, because we are made aware of how the world in any given moment *feels* and how it is *interpreted* by the character. And in doing so, we immediately empathize.

The key word here is *interpreted*. It's beyond simple characterization. It's mind-melding the hero with the reader from an emotional, analytical, and sociological point of view.

When done well, it's the magic pill of characterization. Empathy, leading to *rooting for*, is the most empowering thing a writer can achieve in the relationship between hero and reader.

It is the whole point.

....

LARRY BROOKS is the *USA Today* best-selling author of six novels, all psychological thrillers. His latest novel, *Deadly Faux*, was published in October 2013 by Turner Publishing, along with new trade paperback editions of his entire backlist. He is the author of *Story Engineering* (Writer's Digest Books, 2011) and *Story Physics* (Writer's Digest Books, 2013), and the creator of Storyfix.com, named one of the "101 Best Websites for Writers" by *Writer's Digest* magazine.

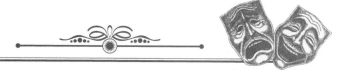

CHAPTER 16

RELATE TO READERS WITH A LEAD CHARACTER

BY JAMES SCOTT BELL

Before I started to sell my fiction, I had a major weakness with characters. I would come up with a plot or situation, but I'd stock it with cardboard story people, characters who seemed to be on the page just because I stuck them there.

Then I happened across Lajos Egri's advice about living, vibrating human beings being the secret of great and enduring writing. Egri suggested that if you truly know yourself, deeply and intimately, you will be able to create great, complex, and interesting characters.

That's because we have all experienced, to a greater or lesser degree, every human emotion. By tapping into our emotional memories, we can create an infinite variety of characters.

WAYS TO ESTABLISH THE BOND

After conceiving a compelling lead character, you must go a step further and figure out how to create an emotional bond with the reader. You can accomplish this by mastering four dynamics: identification, sympathy, likability, and inner conflict.

Identification

Since the lead character provides access to a plot, it follows that the more the reader can identify with the lead, the greater the intensity of the plot experience. With identification, you create the wondrous feeling that the story, in some way, is happening to *me*.

Identification means, simply, that the lead is like us. We feel that we could, under the right circumstances, find ourselves in the same position in the plot, with similar reactions.

The lead appears to us to be a real human being.

What are the marks of a real human being? Look inside yourself. Most likely, you are: (1) trying to make it in the world; (2) a little fearful at times; and (3) not perfect.

In *The Girl Who Loved Tom Gordon*, Stephen King gives us nine-year-old Trisha McFarland, who is walking in the woods with her mother. The trouble begins when Trisha gets lost, and why does she get lost? Because she petulantly stomps away from her mother to relieve herself. It's such a simple, human response that we easily identify with it. That's how King draws us into his lead character's immediate crisis.

Trisha's not perfect. She has normal human flaws.

Your key question here is: What does your lead do and think that makes her just like most people? Find those qualities, and readers will begin to warm to the lead.

This works even with (perhaps most crucially with) the heroic lead. Take Indiana Jones. In *Raiders of the Lost Ark*, it would have been tempting to leave him as some sort of superman, overcoming all odds without a hitch. But the filmmakers wisely gave him an understandable human flaw: a fear of snakes. This humanizes Jones and makes him more accessible.

Another word for identification is *empathy*.

Sympathy

In contrast to mere empathy, sympathy intensifies the reader's emotional investment in the lead. In my view, the best plots have a lead with whom some sympathy is established. Even if the lead has negative qualities, like Scarlett in *Gone with the Wind*, you can find ways to generate sympathy nonetheless.

There are four simple ways to establish sympathy. Choose wisely. Don't overload them, as it may make the reader feel manipulated.

1. **JEOPARDY.** Put the hero in terrible, imminent trouble and you've got the sympathy factor at work right away. In *Tom Gordon*, Trisha is lost in dangerous woods after she stomps away. That's immediate, physical jeopardy.

Jeopardy can also be *emotional*. Dean Koontz often uses this device. In *Midnight*, FBI agent Sam Booker is close to an emotional abyss. His teenage son hates him, and he is fighting to find reasons to continue living. He is in emotional jeopardy. Part of the depth of the book comes from his finding reasons to carry on.

2. **HARDSHIP.** If the lead has to face some misfortune not of her own making, sympathy abounds. In *The Winner*, David Baldacci gives us a poor, southern woman who grew up without love, education, or good hygiene (even her teeth are bad). So when she takes steps to overcome her state of affairs, we are rooting for her. Forrest Gump, who suffers from physical and mental challenges as a boy, gains our sympathy from the start.

The key to using hardship is not to allow the character to whine about it. Sure, there can be moments when the character lashes out emotionally due to the hardship, but don't let her stay there. We admire those who take steps to overcome.

3. **THE UNDERDOG.** America loves people who face long odds. John Grisham has used the underdog in many of his books. One of his best, *The Rainmaker*, is the classic David-and-Goliath story modernized and moved into the courtroom. We can't help rooting for Rudy Baylor as he battles a huge defense firm. Rocky Balboa became a permanent part of our culture when Sylvester Stallone brought him to the screen in *Rocky*. The movie was a phenomenon not only because it was about a pug fighter's chance to beat the champ but because it was like Stallone's own story as a struggling actor.

4. **VULNERABILITY.** Readers worry about a lead who might be crushed at any time. In *Rose Madder*, Stephen King follows a battered wife who, after years in a hellish marriage, finally gets up the courage to run away from her psychopathic cop-husband. But she is so naive about the ways of the world, and her husband is so good at tracking people down, we worry about her from the moment she steps out the door.

Likability

A likable lead, not surprisingly, is someone who does likable things. For example, likeable leads do favors for people. Or they are witty in conversation.

They are supportive and engaging. They are not selfish. They have an expansive view of life. These are people we like to be around. Think about people *you* like, and then incorporate some of those characteristics into your lead.

A witty character, a character who doesn't take himself too seriously, is likable. So is the character who cares about others without calling attention to himself.

Irwin Fletcher, in the *Fletch* books by Gregory MacDonald, is witty and self-deprecating. So is Elvis Cole, the private investigator creation of Robert Crais.

But note that people who try too hard to be likable often miss the mark. It's a fine line your characters walk, but worth the effort to get it right.

You *can* write about an unlikable lead *if* you compensate in other areas. Giving the Lead power is one good method. Scarlett O'Hara has a certain power over men. She also demonstrates her power to overcome obstacles as the story progresses.

In *The Godfather*, Michael Corleone is a monster, and a powerful one.

Make the unlikable lead fascinating in some way, or readers will be turned off.

Inner Conflict

Characters who are absolutely sure about what they do, who plunge ahead without fear, are not that interesting. We don't go through life that way. In reality, we have doubts just like everyone else.

Bringing your lead's doubts to the surface as your plot unfolds pulls the reader deeper into the story.

In *How to Write a Damn Good Novel II*, James N. Frey writes that inner conflict "can be thought of as a battle between two 'voices' within the character: one of reason, the other of passion—or of two conflicting passions."

Many times it is fear on one side, telling the lead not to act. Inner conflict is resolved when the lead, by listening to the other side—duty, honor, principle, or the like—overcomes doubt and acts accordingly.

Present the Story World

What sort of world does your lead inhabit? Not merely the setting, though that is important. But what is life like for the lead?

In *Mystic River*, Dennis Lehane gives us Jimmy Marcus's story world in the first chapter after the prologue:

> After work that night, Jimmy Marcus had a beer with his brother-in-law, Kevin Savage, at the Warren Tap, the two of them sitting at the window and watching some kids play street hockey. There were six kids, and they were fighting in the dark, their faces gone featureless with it. The Warren Tap was tucked away on a side street in the old stockyard district ...

We get a sense of Jimmy's life and routine here. He's an average guy in a working-class location (near the stockyard). The rest of the section gives us more explanation of Jimmy's situation—how he'd been in prison, but now has a wife and three daughters and owns a store. He's a guy just trying to make it in the world.

Sometimes we begin with the lead practicing his chosen profession. This allows for some explanation, as in Lawrence Block's *Eight Million Ways to Die*:

> She said, "You used to be a policeman."
>
> "A few years back."
>
> "And now you're a private detective."
>
> "Not exactly." The eyes widened. They were very vivid blue, an unusual shade, and I wondered if she were wearing contact lenses. The soft lenses sometimes do curious things to eye color, altering some shades, intensifying others.
>
> "I don't have a license," I explained. "When I decided I didn't want to carry a badge anymore I didn't figure I wanted to carry a license, either." Or fill out forms or keep records or check with the tax collector. "Anything I do is very unofficial."
>
> "But it's what you do? It's how you make your living?"
>
> "That's right."

Notice this isn't just raw exposition. Block shows us the narrator's close observations, and some of his attitude about "official" things.

Set the Tone

Chapter one of Steve Martini's *The Judge* begins like this:

"You have two choices," he tells me. "Your man testifies, or else."

"Or else what? Thumbscrews?" I say.

He gives me a look as if to say, "If you like."

Armando Acosta would have excelled in another age. Scenes of some dimly lit stone cavern with iron shackles, pinioned to the walls come to mind. Visions of flickering torches, the odor of lard thick in the air, as black-hooded men, hairy and barrel-chested, scurry about with implements of pain, employed at his command. The "Cocoanut" is a man with bad timing. He missed his calling with the passing of the Spanish Inquisition.

We are seated in his chambers behind Department 15 ...

A legal setting and a tough tone from the narrator; a lawyer facing a tough, unfair judge. We know this is going to be a certain kind of book with a distinct voice.

Contrast that to the following excerpt from Tom Robbins's *Another Roadside Attraction*:

> The magician's underwear has just been found in a cardboard suitcase floating in a stagnant pond on the outskirts of Miami. However significant that discovery may be—and there is the possibility that it could alter the destiny of each and every one of us—it is not the incident with which to begin this report.

Notice any difference in tone? I think you do. Readers want to settle into a consistent tone. That does not mean a serious novel can't have comic relief, or a comic novel some drama. In fact, that variety is a good thing—it keeps readers engaged.

But the overall impression one gets from a novel should be consistency of tone.

HOOK READERS WITH THE FIRST PAGE

"Don't warm up your engines," Jack M. Bickham counseled in *The 38 Most Common Fiction Writing Mistakes*. "Start your story from the first sentence."

Bickham warns of three beginning motifs that can stall your story on the very first page.

Creating Characters

1. **EXCESSIVE DESCRIPTION.** If description is what dominates the opening, there is no action, no character in motion. While some brief description of place is necessary, it should be woven briefly into the opening action. If a setting is vital to the story, at least give us a person in the setting to get things rolling.
2. **BACKWARDS LOOKS.** Fiction is forward moving. If you front-load with backstory—those events that happened to the characters before the main plot—it feels like stalling.
3. **NO THREAT.** "Good fiction," wrote Bickham, "starts with—and deals with—someone's response to threat." Give us that opening bit of disturbance quickly.

COMPEL THE READER TO MOVE ON TO THE MIDDLE

All of this Act I material described above exists to move the reader on to Act II. Why should they care to read on?

Because you have given them the following in Act I:

- A compelling lead
- Whom they bond with
- And whose world has been disturbed

And when the lead passes through the first doorway of no return into Act II, we must know who or what the opposition is.

Not that a complete identity has to be established. It is perfectly all right that there is a mysterious opponent out there, someone to be revealed later. But that there *is* an opponent is all-important.

Make sure the opponent is as strong as or, preferably, stronger than the lead. And do not scrimp on the sympathy factor! Give the opponent his due, his justifications. Your novel will be the stronger for it.

Handling Exposition

Nothing will slow down plot faster than an information dump. This is where the author merely tells the reader something he thinks the reader needs to know before moving on with the plot.

It's bad enough when this is done in the narrative portion, but dreadful when it is done in dialogue.

For example, you might run across a paragraph like this:

> John was a doctor from the east. He went to medical school at Johns Hopkins where he was a star student. He completed his residency in New York City when he was 30 years old. He lived with relatives on Long Island while he was an intern. John loved New York.

Now, in certain contexts this might be perfectly fine. Sometimes telling is a shortcut, and if it is indeed short, it can work. But take a look at all exposition like the above in your manuscript, and ask yourself if you can be more creative in how you give this information to your readers.

I have a few rules about exposition in the beginnings of books. I have formulated these only because I saw in my own writing the tendency to put in a lot of exposition up front, thinking the reader needed this to understand the story.

Not so. Most of the time I could cut with impunity and not lose the flow of the story; in fact, my novels started to take off from the beginning.

Don't start slowly with useless exposition. Thus, the rules:

- **RULE 1: ACT FIRST, EXPLAIN LATER.** Begin with a character in motion. Readers will follow a character who is doing something and won't demand to know everything about the character up front. You then drop in information as necessary, in little bits as you go along.
- **RULE 2: WHEN YOU EXPLAIN, DO THE ICEBERG.** Don't tell us everything about the character's past history or current situation. Give us the 10 percent above the surface that is necessary to understand what's going on, and leave 90 percent hidden and mysterious below the surface. Later in the story, you can reveal more of that information. Until the right time, however, withhold it.
- **RULE 3: SET INFORMATION INSIDE CONFRONTATION.** Often the best way to let information come out is within a scene of intense conflict. Using the characters' thoughts or words, you can have crucial information ripped out and thrown in front of the reader.

Creating Characters

TWO EXAMPLES OF SUCCESSFUL BEGINNINGS

In the first chapter of *Midnight*, Dean Koontz skillfully weaves in exposition during a tense jog at night:

FIRST SENTENCE: Janice Capshaw liked to run at night." Follows the rule: Open with a character—named—in motion.

NEXT TWO SENTENCES: Author explains something about her running, gives her age and something about her appearance (healthy).

NEXT FIVE SENTENCES: We learn the time and place (Sunday night, Sept. 21, Moonlight Cove). Description of the place. Mood established (dark, no cars, no other people). Background on the place (quiet little town).

NEXT THREE SENTENCES: Mood details in the action (as she runs).

NEXT TWO SENTENCES: Background on Janice's likes about night running.

NEXT FIVE SENTENCES: Deepening details about Janice (why she likes night).

NEXT THREE SENTENCES: Action as she runs. More details and mood.

NEXT SENTENCE: Action as she runs. How she feels.

NEXT SEVEN SENTENCES: Deepening Janice by describing her past with her late husband.

NEXT TWO SENTENCES: First sign of trouble.

NEXT THREE SENTENCES: Her reaction to the sign.

And so on throughout. Read this opening chapter. It is a great example of handling exposition.

For the next example, let's widen our scope and look at how *Final Seconds*, by John Lutz and David August, progresses within the first six chapters:

> **PROLOGUE:** New York public school has bomb scare. Harper, a grizzled veteran, and his young partner, arrive. Tension builds as he tries to undo the bomb. Finally, left holding a bit of explosive, Harper is almost there when ... boom. His hand is mostly blown off.
>
> **CHAPTER ONE:** Two-and-a-half years later, Harper is going to see his partner (who was sort of at fault for the accident). He's working security for techno-thriller author Rod Buckner. Harper is no longer with the NYPD.
>
> **CHAPTER TWO:** Harper can't talk his old partner into coming back to the NYPD. As he's driving away from this very secure complex, a tremendous explosion is heard. The whole house, along with Buckner and all the others, is blown up.
>
> **CHAPTER THREE:** Harper tries to get information on the investigation into his ex-partner's death, but his old captain isn't giving any. Tension builds here.
>
> **CHAPTER FOUR:** We see Harper's home life. Then he gets a message from an old FBI friend to come see him about the case.
>
> **CHAPTER FIVE:** Addleman, a profiler who is now a drunk and eccentric, says he has a theory. There is a serial bomber out there, targeting celebrities!
>
> **CHAPTER SIX:** Now a scene with the bomber, the villain, getting stuff from a contact in a remote area. The contact is surly. When the deal is finally made, the contact takes the money. But it is laced with napalm, and a trick detonator. The guy burns up.

We are now on page 64, the plot is set up, and the cat and mouse begins.

SOME GREAT OPENINGS

Let's have a look at some great openings from best-selling novels and see what the writers are doing. We'll begin, once again, with the master, Dean Koontz, and *Sole Survivor*:

> At two-thirty Saturday morning, in Los Angeles, Joe Carpenter
> woke, clutching a pillow to his chest, calling his lost wife's name
> in the darkness. The anguished and haunted quality of his own
> voice had shaken him from sleep. Dreams fell from him not all
> at once but in trembling veils, as attic dust falls off rafters when
> a house rolls with an earthquake.

Again, notice that Koontz gives us a specific name and a haunting first line. But then he expands upon that line with two others that are almost poetic in their descriptive power and emotional impact. This is one of the greatest opening paragraphs in any thriller you'll ever read.

From *The Stand* by Stephen King:

> "Sally."
>> A mutter.
>> "Wake up now, Sally."
>> A louder mutter: *lemme alone.*
>> He shook her harder.
>> "Wake up. You got to wake up!"
>> Charlie.
>> Charlie's voice. Calling her. For how long?
>> Sally swam up out of sleep.

King uses the dialogue starter, which always gives the impression of instant motion. Somebody is saying something, so we've got action (dialogue is a form of action, a physical act to gain a result or reaction). As the dialogue continues, we know only that Charlie is in some distress, and that Sally, swimming out of sleep, is about to find out what it is.

If you're writing a comical novel, there is another possibility for a grabber opening: using the look and sound of the text itself to create an oddball impression. From *Sacred Monster* by Donald E. Westlake:

> "This won't take long, sir."
>> Ooooooooooooooooooohooooooooooooooooooooooooooooo
>> hooooooooooooooooooooooooohooooooooooooooooooooooo
>> oohoooooooooooooooooooooooooooooooooooooooooooooooo
>> oohoooooooooooooooooooooooooooooooooooooooooooooo, wow.

Relate to Readers with a Lead Character   135

> I hurt all over. My *bones* ache. God's giant fists are squeez-
> ing my internal organs, twisting and grinding. Why do I *do* it, if
> it makes me sick?
> "Ready for a few questions, sir?"

Westlake makes sure we are sufficiently intrigued, too, by making us wonder just what it is the narrator does to make himself so sick.

Now let's have a look at some great openings in literary novels. Can we get any more literary than Herman Melville's *Moby Dick*?

> Call me Ishmael. Some years ago—never mind how long precisely—
> having little or no money in my purse, and nothing particular to in-
> terest me on shore, I thought I would sail about a little and see the
> watery part of the world. It is a way I have of driving off the spleen,
> and regulating the circulation. Whenever I find myself growing
> grim about the mouth; whenever it is a damp, drizzly November in
> my soul; whenever I find myself involuntarily pausing before coffin
> warehouses, and bringing up the rear of every funeral I meet; and
> especially whenever my hypos get such an upper hand of me, that
> it requires a strong moral principle to prevent me from deliberately
> stepping into the street, and methodically knocking people's hats
> off—then, I account it high time to get to sea as soon as I can. This
> is my substitute for pistol and ball.

When writing in the first person, it is the voice that must reach out and grab. Melville's does.

The famous first line, "Call me Ishmael," had perhaps a deeper meaning to nineteenth-century American readers, steeped as they would have been in the Bible. Ishmael was the son of Abraham by Hagar, a servant. Thus he was not the child of God's covenant, as Isaac, son of Sarah, was. Ishmael was sent away by Sarah so he would not share in Isaac's inheritance. He was an outcast. That is what Melville establishes immediately.

Then the narrator goes on, in this haunting passage, to say, basi-cally, that he goes to sea to keep from killing himself. But Melville is poetic—*damp, drizzly November in my soul.*

There's also a touch of humor to keep things from getting too maudlin—Ishmael says he sometimes wants to methodically knock people's hats off.

He's got an attitude. That's one key for literary novelists. If you're doing the book in first person, then give us a voice that intrigues us.

Don't start with descriptions of setting, weather, and the like. This is not an ironclad rule but simply a helpful tip. Readers today are impatient and want to know why they should keep reading.

So if you want to use description to start, make sure it does three things: (1) sets mood; (2) gets a character involved early; (3) gives us a reason to keep reading!

Here is how Janet Fitch's *White Oleander* begins:

> The Santa Anas blew hot from the desert, shriveling the last of the spring grass into whiskers of pale straw. Only the oleanders thrived, their delicate poisonous blooms, their dagger green leaves.

Already we have a mood. The weather does not just exist; it portends. The first sentence gives us desolation. The second gives us something that thrives, but it is dangerous. Read the rest of the book to find out how this applies!

Now Fitch gives us the narrator, getting the character involved early:

> We could not sleep in the hot dry nights, my mother and I. I woke up at midnight to find her bed empty. I climbed to the roof and easily spotted her blond hair like a white flame in the light of the three-quarter moon.
>
> "Oleander time," she said. "Lovers who kill each other now will blame it on the wind."

Now this is a character I want to know more about. Who says things like this? We read on to find out.

In *The Big Rock Candy Mountain*, Wallace Stegner gives us a character who is literally in motion:

> The train was rocking through wide open country before Elsa was
> able to put off the misery of leaving and reach out for the freedom
> and release that were hers now.

Why wasn't Elsa free before? What is she going to do with this new freedom? Where is she headed?

> She tucked her handkerchief away, leaned her shoulder against the
> dirty pane and watched the telegraph wires dip, and dip, and dip
> from pole to pole, watched the trees and scattered farms, endless
> variations of white house, red barn, tufted cornfield, slide smoothly
> backward. Every mile meant that she was freer.
>
> The car was hot; opened windows along the coach let in an acrid
> smell of smoke, and as the wind flawed, the trailing plume swept down
> past her eyes, fogging the trackside. Two men up ahead rose and took
> off their coats and came back toward the smoker. One of them wore
> flaming striped suspenders and stared at her.

A small detail—the man staring. It adds to the sense of vulnerability of
this woman, and that, as we have seen, is a subtle form of jeopardy. Our
sympathy is beginning to build.

W. Somerset Maugham begins *Of Human Bondage* with description,
but then gets us immediately to that change, or disturbance that is so crucial:

> The day broke gray and dull. The clouds hung heavily, and there
> was a rawness in the air that suggested snow. A woman servant
> came into a room in which a child was sleeping and drew the cur-
> tains. She glanced mechanically at the house opposite, a stucco
> house with a portico, and went to the child's bed.
>
> "Wake up, Philip," she said.

Why is Philip being awakened? The mood is somber (gray, dull, heavy
clouds, raw weather). We want to find out what's happening:

> She pulled down the bed-clothes, took him in her arms, and carried
> him downstairs. He was only half awake.
>
> "Your mother wants you," she said.
>
> She opened the door of a room on the floor below and took the
> child over to a bed in which a woman was lying. It was his mother. She

Creating Characters

stretched out her arms, and the child nestled by her side. He did not ask why he had been awakened. The woman kissed his eyes, and with thin, small hands felt the warm body through his white flannel nightgown. She pressed him closer to herself.

"Are you sleepy, darling?" she said.

Her voice was so weak that it seemed to come already from a great distance. The child did not answer, but smiled comfortably. He was very happy in the large, warm bed, with those soft arms about him. He tried to make himself smaller still as he cuddled up against his mother, and he kissed her sleepily. In a moment he closed his eyes and was fast asleep. The doctor came forwards and stood by the bed-side.

"Oh, don't take him away yet," she moaned.

The doctor, without answering, looked at her gravely. Knowing she would not be allowed to keep the child much longer, the woman kissed him again; and she passed her hand down his body till she came to his feet; she held the right foot in her hand and felt the five small toes; and then slowly passed her hand over the left one. She gave a sob.

A mother being separated from her child. Why? Emotional jeopardy is here in force.

So what have we seen?

Any type of novel can hook a reader, set tone, give a sense of motion, connect us with a character, and set the wheels in motion.

Why would you want your plot to begin any other way? The only alternative is that you start with none of this, hoping the reader will stick with you.

But even if you write with a style that makes angels weep, you're not going to keep readers interested for too long on style alone.

Why not make angels and readers both happy?

Grab 'em from the start.

....

JAMES SCOTT BELL is a best-selling and award-winning suspense writer. He has authored four WD Books: *Plot & Structure* (2004), *The Art of War for Writers* (2009), *Conflict & Suspense* (2012), and *Revision & Self-Editing for Publication* (2012).

PART V

ANTAGONISTS

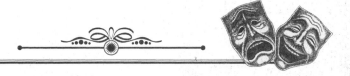

CHAPTER 17

CREATING AN ANTI-HERO

BY JESSICA PAGE MORRELL

If you dare to write about less-than-charming characters, you don't need to redeem them with an ending in which they see the error of their ways, mend their faults, and allow their flinty hearts to be transformed into a choir loft of goodness. You see, Hollywood movies have greatly influenced audience expectations to such a degree that bad people are expected to become good, endings are expected to be tidy and hopeful, and outcomes are expected to be laced with sunshine. Fiction can, and should, mimic life, with all its messes and discomfort and disquiet. Fiction should also prove just how complicated and troubled many people are.

In fiction, sometimes it's difficult to categorize the various character types, especially when the characters' morality cannot be easily defined. This chapter is about a kind of protagonist who sometimes has the morality we've traditionally come to associate with bad guys, which is where the term *anti-hero* comes from. An anti-hero is a protagonist who is as flawed or more flawed than most characters; he is someone who disturbs the reader with his weaknesses yet is sympathetically portrayed, and who magnifies the frailties of humanity.

In days of old, especially in the eighteenth century, protagonists were often heroes and antagonists were usually villains, and they were often depicted in stories as either good or evil, clearly delineated as black and white. My hope is that this chapter will prove that, as in real life, characters come in many shades and types. An anti-hero is a protagonist who typically lacks the traditional traits and qualities of a hero, such as trustworthiness, courage, and honesty. If he were assigned a color, it would be gray.

Often, an anti-hero is unorthodox and might flaunt laws or act in ways contrary to society's standards. In fact, and this is important, an anti-hero often reflects society's confusion and ambivalence about morality, and thus he can be used for social or political comment. While an anti-hero cannot slip into a white hat, he will always:

- have the reader's sympathies, although sometimes his methods will make this difficult.
- have easily identified imperfections.
- be made understandable by the story events, meaning that the reader will come to know his motivations and likely will be privy to his inner demons.
- have a starring role in the story.

An anti-hero is often a badass, a maverick, or a screwup. You might want to picture Paul Newman playing the title character in the film *Cool Hand Luke*, Clint Eastwood as Harry Callahan in *Dirty Harry*, or Bruce Willis playing John McClane in *Die Hard*—slightly scruffy and worn, sometimes moral, but sometimes not. If the character is a woman, perhaps her slip is showing and her lipstick is smeared, she sleeps with men she doesn't know well, and she often cannot fit into traditional women's roles.

An anti-hero can also play the part of an outsider or loner—a "little man." This kind of anti-hero often possesses a fragile self-esteem, has often failed at love, and is sometimes estranged from people from his past. Perhaps the best-known anti-hero of our time is Tony Soprano of the television series *The Sopranos*. Bridget Jones of Helen Fielding's *Bridget Jones's Diary*, Sam Spade of Dashiell Hammett's *The Maltese Falcon*, Philip Marlow in Raymond Chandler's stories, Gulliver of Jonathan Swift's *Gulliver's Travels*, and Randall McMurphy of Ken Kesey's *One Flew Over the Cuckoo's Nest* are also well-known anti-heroes. The reader loves these characters because they are realistic and relatable—just like the people in the reader's life, they're imperfect and roiling with contradictions.

Anti-heroes can be rebels in search of freedom or justice, and they're usually willing to take the law into their own hands. They often occupy a gray area between good guy and bad guy—John D. MacDonald's Travis McGee comes to mind, as does Jack Sparrow in the *Pirates of the Caribbean* films. Robin Hood was an anti-hero, as was Wolf Larsen in Jack London's *The Sea-Wolf*. Of course, there have always been real-life anti-heroes, such as Butch Cassidy and the Sundance Kid, Wild Bill Hickock, Calamity Jane, and Bonnie and Clyde. Sometimes fast living, sometimes an outcast, and never superhuman, this character type provides you with lots of latitude in exploring themes and issues, often amid a true-to-life environment.

Anti-heroes can be obnoxious, pitiful, or charming, but they are always failed heroes or deeply flawed. Often riddled with paradoxical traits and qualities, they resemble real people more than any other type of fictional characters do, and they are increasingly popular these days in fiction, film, and television.

One of the most important qualities to remember is that anti-heroes rarely, if ever, reflect society's higher values—or what we like to think of as our society's values. Their thinking and values are often antithetical to those of the norm. For example, the sort of traits valued by most members of society—such as honesty, strength, integrity, and compassion—will not always be exhibited by an anti-hero in a story. Or he might have a character arc where he grudgingly adopts some of these traits. Traditional depictions of fictional characters meant that main players were good guys with traits that we all want to emulate. Anti-heroes turn that assumption upside down.

And here is the trick to creating anti-heroes: They always possess an underlying pathos. Most characters come with flaws, neuroses, and "issues." But with an anti-hero, these problems are more noticeable and troublesome, and they sometimes get in the way of forming intimate attachments. There is always something that is screwing up the anti-hero's plan, and that something is usually from his past. A story with an anti-hero in a starring role might depict how a person cannot easily escape from the past, particularly the deep losses of the past.

CHARACTERISTICS OF AN ANTI-HERO

It takes a fine hand to draw an anti-hero because this character requires a great deal of nuance to arouse complicated reactions in the reader. As we've just discussed, an anti-hero is a character that the reader roots for, despite his flaws and the bad things he's done or how he justifies these misdeeds. Sometimes the anti-hero is able to toe the line between good and evil, but often he's a danger to himself and others. Sometimes an anti-hero also has remarkable ability to compartmentalize. Perhaps he kills an enemy or a bad guy, then in the next scene shows up at a kid's birthday party, apparently unruffled by his recent grisly task.

Like all main characters, understanding an anti-hero's character arc is crucial in designating his role in your story. After all, you'll need to know if his good behavior is accidental, or if he is redeemed by the story's events. One trick to creating an anti-hero is to fashion his primary traits so that his essential nature and personality are clear to you as you craft each scene he appears in. Then you need to know the *why* of these traits and beliefs—in essence, how he came to be. If your character is lawless, rebellious, or obnoxious, it is likely that your character's past will somehow justify these behaviors.

An anti-hero is not simply a badass who cannot follow the rules. The *reasons* for why he acts as he does, along with his self-concept, are important to the story. Another trick to creating a complicated anti-hero is to shape his less-than-moral traits and acts into a profound statement about humanity. As you create anti-hero characters, consider that they:

- are not role models, although we secretly would like to kick ass like they do.
- can be selfish and essentially bad people who occasionally are good.
- are sometimes unglamorous and unattractive in character as well as in appearance.
- can be motivated by self-interest and self-preservation, but there is usually a line anti-heroes won't cross, which sets them apart from villains.
- often have motives that are complicated and range from revenge to honor.
- forced to choose between right and wrong, will sometimes choose wrong because it's easier.
- can play both sides with good guys and bad guys, profiting from both.
- can sometimes be coerced to help underdogs, children, or weaker characters, and they sometimes do so voluntarily.

Creating Characters

- can embody unattractive traits and behaviors, such as sexist and racist attitudes, and violent reactions when wronged.
- can show little or no remorse for bad behaviors.
- are usually a mess of contradictions.

HEROES VS. ANTI-HEROES: IDENTIFYING THE DIFFERENCES

The role of a hero as the main player who drives the story has been around for centuries. Heroes somehow embody the forces of good and overcome great odds to succeed in the story. In classical stories, a hero was always extraordinary, might have divine ancestry, and was more of a demigod than human. Hercules is this type of hero.

Over time, the term *hero* came to be no longer associated with god-like types, but instead came to mean an extraordinary man or woman who overcame great obstacles, who often sacrificed himself or herself for a cause, who displayed courage when facing the story's problems, and who held moral and exemplary traits. Heroes appeared in myths, epic poems, operas, fairy tales, and, in fact, most story types.

In order for the story to contain suspense, heroes are never perfect; in fact, in the tradition of Aristotle, they possess a fatal flaw that can be their undoing. But because they are heroes, part of their quest is to rise above this flaw so that their grace, perseverance, and greatness of spirit can inspire and uplift readers. Heroes in fiction are also designed to learn from their mistakes; often they rise from the ashes to defeat the bad guys.

In many of the character types discussed in this chapter, there are no absolutes, as in "a villain will always be 100 percent evil" or "a hero will be 100 percent good." If there were absolute truths about every character type, it would make our jobs as writers easier, but we'd also end up with parodies or caricatures of the human condition. Likewise anti-heroes can be difficult to classify because they vary so broadly, and there are few absolute traits shared by every type. You'll know an anti-hero is in story because he's in the starring role though his morals and motives are questionable, and despite his moral traits, or lack thereof, you will still sympathize with him. Here are some general differences that I hope will clarify on which side of morality you'll find an anti-hero and how an anti-hero is the antithesis of a traditional hero:

HERO	ANTI-HERO
A hero is an idealist.	An anti-hero is a realist.
A hero has a conventional moral code.	An anti-hero has a moral code that is quirky and individual.
A hero is somehow extraordinary.	An anti-hero can be ordinary.
A hero is always proactive.	An anti-hero can be passive.
A hero is often decisive.	An anti-hero can be indecisive or pushed into action against his will.
A hero is a modern version of a knight in shining armor.	An anti-hero can be a tarnished knight, and sometimes a criminal.
A hero succeeds at his ultimate goals, unless the story is a tragedy.	An anti-hero might fail in a tragedy, but in other stories he might be redeemed by the story's events, or he might remain largely unchanged, including being immoral.
A hero is motivated by virtues, morals, a higher calling, pure intentions, and love for a specific person or humanity.	An anti-hero can be motivated by a primitive, lower nature, including greed or lust, through much of the story, but he can sometimes be redeemed and answer a higher calling near the end.
A hero is motivated to overcome flaws and fears, and to reach a higher level. This higher level might be about self-improvement, a deeper spiritual connection, or trying to save humankind from extinction. His motivation and usually altruistic nature lends courage and creativity to his cause. Often a hero makes sacrifices in the story for the better of others.	An anti-hero, while possibly motivated by love or compassion at times, is most often propelled by self-interest.

A hero (usually when he is the star of the story in genre fiction, such as Westerns) concludes the story on an upward arc, meaning he's overcome something from within or has learned a valuable lesson in the story.	An anti-hero can appear in mainstream or genre fiction, and the conclusion will not always find him changed, especially if he's a character in a series.
A hero always faces monstrous opposition, which essentially makes him heroic in the first place. As he's standing up to the bad guys and the troubles the world hurls at him, he will take tremendous risks and sometimes battle an authority. His stance is always based on principles.	An anti-hero also battles authority and sometimes go up against tremendous odds, but not always because of principles. His motives can be selfish, criminal, or rebellious.
A hero is a good guy, the type of character the reader was taught to cheer for since childhood.	An anti-hero can be a bad guy in manner and speech. He can cuss, drink to excess, talk down to others, and back up his threats with fists or a gun, yet the reader somehow sympathizes with or genuinely likes him and cheer him on.
A hero can be complex, but he is generally unambivalent; an anti-hero is a complicated character who reflects the ambivalence of many real people.	An anti-hero's actions and ways of thinking demand that the reader think about issues and ask difficult questions.

ROLES FOR ANTI-HEROES

The roles for anti-heroes in contemporary fiction seem endless, as society is coming to terms with the notion that morality is not always absolute. Here are some roles that you might consider for your anti-hero.

Everyman

Picture this category of anti-hero as the opposite of Superman. Not only does an everyman anti-hero not possess supernatural talents or abilities, he also might have a lackluster appearance and come with a beer gut, a bad back, and a bald spot. When you create an everyman type for a story, you'll be featuring a story character that the reader can easily identify with, because the real world is populated with these types. Often a person of humble origins, the everyman is never elite, exceptional, or even charismatic. The everyman is ordinary—the grocer, the baker, the candlestick maker. Writers use everyman characters so that the reader can imagine himself amid the story events. Because this type of character isn't extraordinarily brave or talented, he'll react realistically to story events and often won't rush in to save the day or solve the story problem. In fact, often he is dragged kicking and screaming into a fight and likewise often only changes under duress.

John Updike's Rabbit Angstrom in *Rabbit, Run* is a famous example of this category of anti-hero, as are the unnamed lead character in Philip Roth's *Everyman*, Richard Ford's everyman character Frank Bascombe, who's featured in three novels, *The Sportswriter, Independence Day*, and *The Lay of the Land*, and Saul Bellow's Tommy Wilhelm in *Seize the Day*.

The everyman character is usually in some way bumbling, inept, or in over his head. Sometimes the character is seriously adrift; sometimes he is thrust into a position of danger where his lack of bravery or talents will make his situation tenuous and dangerous. An everyman will always possess at least several unsympathetic, or even despicable, traits. Sometimes this character is an optimist, sometimes he is a cynic, but he is always a realistic depiction of humanity.

Vigilante or Tarnished Knight

A vigilante is a person with his own moral code who takes the law into his own hands, as in the days of the Old West. In many ways, this type of anti-hero is closest to heroes in literature because of his *aims* in the story. Dirty Harry Callahan, played by Clint Eastwood in the film series, exemplifies this type. While a vigilante still might be part of the system, he is often an ex-cop or ex-military man, and he has often left his previous position because of a mistake or because he simply cannot play by the rules. Often self-employed, he may work as a private investigator, security professional, or bodyguard. A vigilante often takes on the dangers of the role with excess relish or dispassion.

In George Pelecanos's *The Night Gardener*, Dan "Doc" Holiday exemplifies this type. He left the police force because of his drinking and shady dealings, but he now doesn't have much to live for. After sleeping off a drinking binge, he stumbles onto a body in a community garden and is pulled back into unsolved cases from early in his career. The story uses a cast of good and bad cops, and it shows that the police often operate in a moral limbo; right and wrong are not always simple, and playing it straight isn't always the way to solve a case.

Charming Criminal

The suave Cary Grant as John Robie in the film *To Catch a Thief* is a good example of this type. Readers and film audiences know crime is bad, but they just cannot help but like, or at least sympathize, with this likeable rogue. He's not made for the nine-to-five routine, so he skirts the law, usually by stealing or scamming. Professional gamblers might fall under this type also. With a charming criminal at the helm, these stories usually feature nonstop action and witty dialogue, with the reader or film viewer enjoying being in the know as the plans are laid for the heist or scam.

While charming criminals tend to rip off companies or banks, Red, the convicted murderer in Stephen King's "Rita Hayworth and the Shawshank Redemption," is an exception. Although Red murdered his wife, he's aware of the depravity of this crime. In fact, he claims he's the only guilty man serving in Shawshank, and at the story's end, he is paroled to a new life. Sometimes an author places this more likeable type amid less savory characters, as Elmore Leonard does with his character Ernest Stickley Jr. in *Stick* and *Swag*. When the charming criminal is the lesser evil in a story, his humanity is emphasized. Often a story will center on a complicated scam or heist, as in the film *Ocean's Eleven*, where Brad Pitt and George Clooney play characters who are part of an ensemble cast of likeable thieves.

Dark Hero

Dark heroes, also called Byronic heroes, are angst-ridden, and are often misunderstood loners. Picture James Dean as Jim Stark in the film *Rebel Without a Cause* and Clint Eastwood as William Munny in *Unforgiven* to understand this type. Also picture this dark hero character dressed in black. This tradition of a dark hero has been around since John Milton wrote *Paradise Lost*, but it was firmly in place with characters in Gothic novels of the eighteenth century and is, in fact, the precursor to the anti-hero as a character type. Typically this character is a young and attractive male with attitude and a lousy reputation, although the Ellen Ripley character, played by Sigourney Weaver, in the film *Aliens* also falls under this category.

Bad Boy

Bad boys are anti-authority and cannot handle conventional morality; they instead possess a personal moral code that is sometimes disturbing to others. While they have many bad habits, they are often portrayed sympathetically, even if the reader cannot identify with them. Bad boys might be guns-for-hire or assassins. They are most often found in comics, Westerns, action films, thrillers, vampire novels, science fiction, and Gothics. Sometimes their quest can ennoble them. Bad boys typically bring a lot of fire, defiance, and eroticism to a story, along with a sense of danger. Lestat de Lioncourt of Anne Rice's *Interview With the Vampire* and *The Vampire Lestat* is an extreme example of this character type. A more typical example of a bad boy is Paul Newman as the title character in *Cool Hand Luke* and as "Fast" Eddie Felson in *The Hustler*.

Reluctant Hero

A reluctant hero is a tarnished or ordinary man with several faults or a troubled past, and he is pulled reluctantly into the story or into heroic acts. During the story, he rises to the occasion, sometimes even vanquishing a mighty foe, sometimes avenging a wrong. But he questions whether he's cut out for the hero business. His doubts, misgivings, and mistakes add a satisfying layer of tension to a story. Han Solo, the smart-aleck smuggler of the Star Wars series, is an example of the type. Like many anti-heroes, the reluctant hero is a loner, selfish and self-serving, and he reluctantly puts aside his own interests for the good of humankind. Sometimes this character has also experienced a fall from grace and may have been disgraced or dishonorably discharged from the military or the police force, or, in the case of Solo, part of the Imperial Starfleet.

Ezekiel "Easy" Rawlins, Walter Mosley's series character in Easy Rawlins, is another example of the reluctant hero. In the series, which takes place over several decades beginning in the 1940s, Rawlins is an unwilling detective in the Watts section of Los Angeles. He's usually pulled into the puzzle at the heart of a story by a friend, often because it seems that black people won't achieve justice without his help. Rawlins walks a crooked line between the established order and his own code of honor, and his street smarts and underground contacts are often what help him solve the case. Like many anti-heroes, Rawlins suffers a troubled past and his character's core is pain and rage—emotions that make his actions endlessly fascinating.

Loser

This type of anti-hero has traits similar to the everyman, but the loser usually begins the story at a low ebb in his life. For example, Quoyle of E. Annie Proulx's *The Shipping News* is a quintessential loser. Unattractive, lumpy, and sometimes dim-witted, it seems like he can barely muddle his way through daily life. After his ill-fated marriage, the reader is especially worried that someone so clueless is not going to be able to survive, much less raise two daughters on his own. A loser is known for a terrible ineptness, bad luck, especially troubling flaws, and qualities that make him seem especially ill-suited for the task at hand. This sort of ineptness keeps the story teetering at the edge of disaster. Willie Loman of Arthur Miller's *Death of a Salesman* is another good example of a loser. Loman's identity is so tied to his worth as a salesperson and his pursuit of the American Dream that when he fails to produce, he fails to feel any worth.

Outcast

This category of anti-heroes includes characters who often accept or even glory in their roles as social outcasts. They often defy conventions of society, behavior, or morality, but the reasons for why they are outside society are many. They are not interested in the trappings of middle-class life, so most outcasts won't be homeowners with a wife, two children, a Golden Retriever, and an SUV. Their roles in the story will always shine a light on beliefs or systems that most of us take for granted or give little thought to. In Joseph Heller's *Catch-22*, Captain John Yossarian is a classic example of an outcast. The book has many themes, including the idiocy of a military bureaucracy, the senselessness of war, and the impossibility of living by the rules of a greater society. Mark Twain's Huck Finn is an outcast because of his social status, but when he takes off with Jim, a runaway slave, it solidifies his position as outcast.

Screwball

Screwball characters are usually depicted in the midst of a fairly complex situation, such as a mystery with romance, lots of sexual tension, and a series of complications factored into the story. Usually the character is strong-willed, unpredictable, and sometimes zany, such as Joan Wilder in the film *Romancing the Stone* and Stephanie Plum in Janet Evanovich's suspense series. These characters are used to create hilarity and surprising plot twists. Stories with screwball characters are fast-paced, veer toward absurdity, and feature lots of laughs amid the characters' antics. Carl Hiaasen is especially known for creating screwball characters in his novels, as are Elmore Leonard and Pete Hautman.

Disgraced Hero

A disgraced anti-hero might have once been a true hero, but he was somehow undone by his own demons; so he cannot assume that role now, although at times his actions can be heroic. Like a vigilante, a disgraced hero is more closely aligned with heroes than other anti-types, such as outcasts. Robert B. Parker's Jesse Stone is a good example of this highly flawed type of character. After drinking himself out of a job in Los Angeles, Stone takes a job as small-town sheriff in Massachusetts. The underlying question in each story is: Can Stone overcome his personal demons so that he can handle his job? Disgraced heroes are kin to dark heroes, and they are often leading the helm of mysteries and thrillers. They are always scarred by something in their pasts, such as a mistake that cost another person his or her life, the death of a loved one, a childhood trauma, or a military stint. This type of character is often a loner and will always be haunted by the past and struggle with self-destructive behaviors.

Oddball

An oddball character can be a nerdy geek who wears a pocket protector, or an autistic savant, among many other types of people. The point is, they don't fit in, and because of their oddities, other people often ridicule or avoid them. Their presence in a story creates extreme sympathy along with tension because oddballs can range in nature from explosive to outlandish. Sometimes only a few characters in the story will see beyond the oddball's strangeness. Such is the case of the Dean Koontz series character who is boldly named Odd Thomas.

Odd is a short-order cook by trade, but his particular psychic skills bring him into the company of the dead and newly murdered citizens of his town, along with other wandering dead, such as Elvis. Besides being able to commune with the dead, Odd is also able to see other depraved spirit creatures, called bodachs, so that he knows when violence or carnage is forthcoming. Odd seems to signify that the world is not safe and the dead are restless.

In *The History of Love*, Nicole Krauss's characters are mostly oddballs, including Leo Gursky, the lonely octogenarian who mourns the loss of his true love, as well as his estrangement with his only son—a famous writer—and his own great manuscript. Krauss seems to use all her cast to make the reader think about aloneness and estrangement. The novel focuses mainly on the slowly converging stories of Leo Gursky and Alma Singer. Leo is an eighty-year-old retired locksmith in New York, a survivor of a Nazi massacre in the Polish village where he grew up sixty years before the novel opens. Alma is a fourteen-year-old girl whose father has recently died, whose mother shields herself from loneliness by working nonstop as a literary translator, and whose nine-year-old brother, Bird (over whom she vigilantly watches), thinks he might be the Messiah. Leo and Alma—and all the many other characters in this slender, densely woven novel—are connected with other characters across time and space by *The History of Love*'s impact on their lives. The key to using oddballs in a story is that they're sympathetically and intricately drawn; you must find fresh quirks and eccentricities that make them endearing to the reader, although perhaps not so to their fellow cast members.

Rebel

Although many anti-heroes have a rebellious nature, sometimes an anti-hero exists almost solely as a rebel with a cause. This character type will fight or resist the status quo, and their reasons for rebelling often fuel the plot and place them in direct opposition with other characters. Rebels can be tragic, or they can succeed at their cause; they can be loners, or they can be part of a group. A rebel steps outside the norm to create a new artistic form or new culture, such as the beatniks and hippies of the 1960s and 1970s. Like outcasts, rebels serve the plot to shine a light on some aspect of society that they believe needs to be changed. Often, they question authority and demand that society is not dehumanizing or corrupt. Randall McMurphy in Ken Kesey's *One Flew Over the Cuckoo's Nest* is a good example of a tragic rebel antihero because he loses to the evil Nurse Ratched, and the lobotomy that makes him a placid patient also robs him of his humanity.

Creating Anti-Heroes Based on Opposing Traits

Most people possess a paradoxical nature or a jumble of traits that don't quite seem to jibe. When a character has opposing traits, the reader will have a deeper and more profound relationship with him because people in real life are complex and textured, and fictional characters who possess these same dichotomies are relatable. Also, because characters who are strictly one-dimensional are predictable and dull, the reader wants characters to possess contradictory or oppositional traits. After all, in real life, we can change moment to moment or day to day. We experience varying moods, sometimes we ride a high cycle of success, sometimes we plummet to the depths of despair during periods of loss or disappointment. Sometimes people become cynical after a series of failures, sometimes people are corrupted by success. And some people are simply a roiling blend of traits that seem to be a mishmash of characters.

Mario Puzo's blood saga *The Godfather* is one of the best-selling novels of all time, and it is the basis for three films. In the tale, the godfather, Don Vito Corleone, struggles among the underworld bosses for power while the storyline depicts how family values and criminal traits are transferred from one generation to the next.

Many of the characters are sympathetically drawn and built from a complex set of traits. Puzo humanizes the members of the crime family by showing them in intimate moments, such as gathering for Sunday dinner and dancing at a wedding, and somewhere between the cannoli and the spaghetti and the guns, the reader tends to think of them as people first and criminals second. So, oddly, the reader finds himself siding with the family, although common sense dictates that they are ruthless criminals.

The central character, Don Corleone, is an icon of American fiction and an anti-hero, as described in the book:

> But great men are not born great, they grow great, and so it was with Vito Corleone. ... It did not happen in a day, it did not happen in a year, but by the end of the Prohibition period and the start of the Great Depression, Vito Corleone had become the Godfather, the Don, Don Corleone.

One of the reasons Corleone is so memorable is because he's so paradoxical, and thus fascinating. He's a sentimental father seen weeping over his son's corpse, an astute businessman, and a ruthless scourge, whose olive oil business is a front for a far-reaching crime syndicate. He is pro-family and anti-social. He is compassionate, yet he will slit your throat if you cross him. He appears benevolent, but he is a despot who stops at nothing, including bribing politicians and officials, to hold on to power. He is a prince of justice helping out other Italians who have been victimized, but he is also a blackmailer, murderer, thief, and tyrant.

Corleone is also a realist:

> ... [Corleone] had long ago learned that society imposes insults that must be borne, comforted by the knowledge that in this world there comes a time when the most humble of men, if he keeps his eyes open, can take his revenge on the most powerful. ...

And because he's a realist, he's also paranoid; "Keep your friends close, but keep your enemies closer" is one of his mottoes.

Corleone is a man of few words, but he can be amazingly eloquent, as when he says, "I made him an offer he couldn't refuse." He demands ultimate loyalty and friendship, and when he's crossed, he dispenses fierce justice. Shrewd and always in charge, his son Michael says of him, "It's all personal, every bit of business ... He takes everything personal. Like God."

Keeping Corleone in mind, let's consider how some of the uglier traits in an anti-hero can also be tempered with a positive side, thus creating a character who is endlessly complicated.

NEGATIVE TRAIT	POSITIVE TRAIT
Controlling	Efficient, great managerial abilities
Hot-tempered	Passionate
Manipulating	Able to see the big picture
Overbearing	Charismatic
Scheming	Capable, competent
Selfish	Focused
Greedy	Generous to family, works hard to provide their comforts
Ruthless	Ambitious, tender with children and elderly mother
Dishonest in business dealings	Honest with wife, children
Intolerant, insensitive	Perceptive
Brusque	Forceful, decisive

You have many choices when it comes to creating the central traits for your anti-hero, and sometimes these traits will be similar to those ordinarily bestowed on heroes or likeable protagonists. Your anti-hero can be courageous, truthful, analytical, charismatic, independent, quick thinking, and resourceful. On the other hand, he could be ruthless, cynical, aloof, selfish, and controlling. These traits need to be demonstrated in scenes and via the character's thoughts, especially when he's making tough choices. You always want to demonstrate the fallout of a character's negative traits. If he has a hair-trigger temper, then his spouse and children might suffer. If he's impetuous and mouthy, he creates enemies. If he relies too much on logic and analysis, maybe he misses out on love and laughter.

And here is another trick to creating an interesting anti-hero (or villain): Make his central traits also his downfall or curse. Thus his strengths and core traits also get him into trouble. Corleone—because he was assured, powerful, and at the top of his game—feels safe in his world. His enemies think otherwise, and, in a bid for power, they attempt to assassinate him. This assassination attempt changes everything in the story, including who becomes the next Don.

Creating Characters

If your character is a loner, make certain that this quality dooms him to a showdown or tight spot where he's outclassed, outgunned, and sorely in need of allies. If he's truthful, make certain that this leads to hurt feelings and misunderstandings. If he's highly self-sufficient, make certain that this trait, too, comes with a cost.

An anti-hero can be a guy living an ordinary or undistinguished life. He can also be a character who is at the bottom of his downward character arc or one who is on his way to greatness. He can be as vain as a peacock, or he can possess a fragile sense of self-worth. While anti-heroes are necessarily complex, beware of making them too angst ridden or too wacky to be understood or sympathetic. Unlike a villain, an anti-hero can have a character arc in which he is redeemed or transformed by the end of the story; in fact, he can become heroic. The most important thing to remember when crafting an anti-hero as your main character is that he is the antithesis of the ultracompetent hero.

JESSICA PAGE MORRELL is the author of *Writing Out the Storm* (Collectors Press, 1998); *Between the Lines: Master the Subtle Elements of Fiction Writing* (Writer's Digest Books, 2006); *Voices from the Street* (Gray Sunshine, 2007); *The Writer's I Ching: Wisdom for the Creative Life* (Running Press, 2007); *Bullies, Bastards & Bitches: How to Write the Bad Guys in Fiction* (Writer's Digest Books, 2008); and *Thanks, but This Isn't For Us: A (Sort of) Compassionate Guide to Why Your Writing Is Being Rejected* (Tarcher, 2009). Her work also appears in anthologies and *The Writer* and *Writer's Digest* magazines. Morrell founded and coordinates three writing conferences: Summer in Words, Making it in Changing Times, and Claim Your Story.

CHAPTER 18

THE THREE-DIMENSIONAL VILLAIN

BY DONALD MAASS

Villains are some of the worst characters I meet in manuscripts, and not in a good way. What I mean is that they frequently are cardboard. Most are presented as purely evil: *Mwoo-ha-ha villains*, as we call them around the office.

Cardboard villains never work. Far from frightening us, they generally have us rolling our eyes. It's not that I don't enjoy a good baddie, understand; it's just that too many writers get lazy when it comes to these antagonists. Unchallenged by doubt, free of obstacles, never set back, blessed with infinite time and resources, able to work their nefarious schemes on a part-time basis (or, at least, that's how it seems since they crop up only occasionally), these villains strike us as unrealistic and therefore silly.

Even worse can be stories in which there is no villain as such. Literary fiction, women's fiction, romances, and coming-of-age tales are just a few types of story that do not necessarily call for a classic wrongdoer. In such manuscripts, those who oppose the protagonist are often poorly developed and inactive. Lacking strong resistance, one wonders why the protagonist is having a hard time. It is possible to build conflict out of internal obstacles, of course, but over the long haul it's wearisome and hard to maintain readers' interest that way.

People are the most fascinating source of obstacles: that means antagonists, those who work against your protagonist. They can be active opponents or even friendly allies who cast doubt upon your protagonist's actions or undermine his resolve.

Do you go through your days without experiencing friction from others? I doubt it. Do you have ongoing problem people in your daily routine, possibly even active enemies? If you do, then you know that those who oppose you are not easily deterred, and they may even have the best of intentions. Have you ever noticed how your critics are eager to help you? They willingly share what they see as wrong with you and have valuable suggestions for your improvement. Our enemies do not hide.

Keith Ablow's series of thrillers featuring FBI forensic psychologist Frank Clevenger has been noted for its original and chilling villains. The fifth in the series, *The Architect* (2005), revolves around a killer who leaves his victims with one part of their anatomy (their spine, say) exquisitely and meticulously dissected, as if laid open for a medical school class. It's a different piece of anatomy each time, too. All the victims come from money, so Clevenger's task is to make connections and find who is responsible.

Ablow, meanwhile, clues us in. The sick pervert who dissects people is an architect; not only that, a brilliant architect named West Crosse. Crosse is smart. Crosse is successful. Crosse is handsome. Bored yet? We would be except for the creepy and unusual touches that Ablow adds. For instance, when Crosse was twenty years old, he deliberately ruined his perfect face by cutting a jagged facial scar on himself. Professionally, he is blunt to the point of alienating potential clients. Toward the novel's beginning, Crosse brings preliminary plans for a new home in Montana to a rich Miami couple who are choosing an architect. Crosse is openly contemptuous of their ultramodern digs:

> Crosse sat down. The chair felt stiff and cold. He placed his rolled drawing on the table, laid a hand on the glass. Then he looked Ken Rawlings directly in the eyes. "You're living—or trying to live—in someone else's house. Because it feels safe. But it isn't."
>
> "I'm not following you," Rawlings said.
>
> "This is Walter Gropius's house," Crosse said. He glanced at Heather Rawlings. "It has nothing to do with you, nothing to do with your wife." He felt his own passion beginning to stir, the

> passion to liberate people from the tombs of fear that kept them
> from expressing the truest parts of themselves, kept them from
> feeling completely, exquisitely alive. ...

This from a guy who dissects different body parts on living victims? It is exactly that contradiction that makes Crosse so fascinating: He gives life through design; he takes life by design. What is up with this sicko? Of course we read ahead to find out. More to the point, Ablow has created a villain who helps his victims. If he finds them lacking in some respect, he fixes them. Just being helpful, you see? That's far from your usual *Mwoo-ha-ha* villain, and it works.

National Book Award nominee Charles Baxter devised in *The Soul Thief* (2008) a villain who doesn't kill but rather steals lives. Baxter's protagonist is Nathaniel Mason, a graduate student in Buffalo, New York, in the 1970s. Nathaniel is infatuated with an artistic beauty, Theresa, who unfortunately is the lover of a romantic poseur named Jerome Coolberg.

Coolberg plays head games with Nathaniel, stealing his shirts and notebooks, claiming that episodes of Nathaniel's life happened to him instead. Events occur that are both tragic and that set Nathaniel's life on a disappointingly conventional track. Years later Nathaniel begins to feel that Coolberg had manipulated his fate in even more sinister ways. He tracks down his nemesis, now a famous interviewer on national radio in California, only to find that Coolberg expects him. They walk on to a pier, where Coolberg explains himself:

> "... Are you looking down? Nathaniel? Good. Do you suffer from
> vertigo? I do. But you see what's down there? I don't mean the
> ocean. I don't mean the salt water. Nothing but idiotic marine
> life in there. Nothing but the whales and the Portuguese and
> the penguins. No, I mean the mainland. Everywhere down
> there, someone, believe me, is clothing himself in the robes of
> another. Someone is adopting someone else's personality, to his
> own advantage. Right? Absolutely right. Of this one truth I am
> absolutely certain. Somebody's working out a copycat strategy
> even now. Identity theft? Please. We're all copycats. Aren't we?

Of course we are. How do you learn to do any little task? You copy. You model. So I didn't do anything all that unusual, *if* I did it. But suppose I did, let's suppose I managed a little con. So what? So I could be you for a while? And was that so bad? Aside from the collateral damage? ..."

That Nathaniel's life was messed up by Coolberg is bad; that Coolberg can rationalize what he did is even worse. (Worse still is Nathaniel's passive acquiescence, which is made sickeningly clear in the novel's last line.) To put it another way, there's no villain so scary as one who is right.

Not all antagonists are creepy or bad. Some are as human as a novel's protagonist. An example can be found in John Burnham Schwartz's *Reservation Road* (1998), a novel about the aftermath of a hit-and-run. The victim is a ten-year-old boy standing by a roadside near a gas station in a northern Connecticut town. His father, Ethan, sees him killed.

The driver of the car is Dwight, whose point of view is one of the three through which Schwartz tells his story. Dwight is at fault but is intended to be sympathetic. For the author, that is a challenge. How can a hit-and-run driver be sympathetic?

In the opening pages, Schwartz deftly sketches in Dwight's circumstances. He is driving his son Sam home from a Red Sox game. The game went to extra innings, so they are late. That's a problem because Dwight's ex, Sam's mother, is a bitch on wheels. Worse, Dwight screwed up a few years earlier after she told him she was leaving him for another man. Dwight struck both her and Sam; he landed on probation, lost his law practice, and was left with tenuous visitation rights to his son.

Thus Dwight finds himself driving too fast down a nighttime road, one headlight out, distracted and worried. He hits Ethan's son, killing him. This is a crucial moment for Schwartz. Why doesn't Dwight stop? Schwartz has Dwight's son Sam dozing in the car, his face pressed against the passenger door handle. There is the impact. Schwartz executes the moment this way:

> The impact made the car shudder. My foot came off the gas.
> And we were coasting, still there, but moving, fleeing. Unless

I braked now: *Do it*. My foot started for the brake. But then Sam started to wail in pain and I froze. I looked over and he was holding his face in both hands and screaming in pain. I went cold. "Sam!" I shouted, his name coming from deep down in my gut and sounding louder and more desperate to my ears than any sound I'd ever made. He didn't respond. "Sam!"

In the rearview mirror I saw the dark-haired man sprinting up the road after us. His fury and his fear were in his half-shadowed face, the frenzied pumping of his arms. He was coming to punish me, and for a moment I wanted him to. My foot was inching toward the brake. But suddenly I felt Sam warm against my side, curling up and holding on and bawling like a baby. I put my foot on the gas.

Dwight makes a tragic mistake, but as *Reservation Road* progresses, it is Ethan who does something wrong, allowing himself to become consumed with a desire for revenge. His reasons are carefully developed—so carefully than when he discovers Dwight's name and goes to his house with a gun, it is unclear what will happen. Motives, in other words, abound on both sides. The two antagonists are perfectly understandable. We feel equally for them both.

That is the power of a three-dimensional antagonist: the power to sway our hearts in directions we would not expect them to be swayed. To get us to see, even accept, the antagonist's point of view. You may not want your story to be neutral. You may embrace right and wrong and write an outcome that makes your values obvious. That is your choice.

....

DONALD MAASS heads the Donald Maass Literary agency in New York City, which represents more than 150 novelists and sells more than 150 novels every year to publishers in America and overseas. He is a past president of the Association of Authors' Representatives, Inc., and is the author of several books, including *Writing the Breakout Novel* (Writer's Digest Books, 2002), *The Fire in Fiction* (Writer's Digest Books, 2009), and *Writing 21st Century Fiction* (Writer's Digest Books, 2012).

CHAPTER 19

AMP UP YOUR ANTAGONISTS

BY LAURA DISILVERIO

Dear Author: We antagonists, villains, bad guys, femme fatales—call us what you will—don't get no respect. We're overlooked, underdeveloped and squeezed into a space that would cramp your average gerbil. When we get short shrift, your books aren't nearly as good as they could be. They lack tension and depth. They're forgettable. Not that I'm one for pointing fingers, but I've got to tell you, it's your fault. Who was given pages and pages of backstory in your last novel? That's right—the protagonist. Whose motives and character arc were fully fleshed out? Right again—the so-called "good" guy's. Who did you "interview" and construct a character bible for? Yeah, him again. Well, I don't mind getting second billing, but I have to point out that if you gave readers a chance to truly know and understand me, your books would be a lot more memorable and engaging. We might even get a movie deal, like my idol, Hannibal Lecter.

Sincerely, Eva N. Carnate

I don't know how the above e-mail got into my in-box, but it caught my attention immediately. Did Eva have a point? It didn't take me long to review my work-in-progress, analyze some novels I'd read recently, and realize that she did. Many authors are guilty of discriminating against their antagonists. Yet antagonists are just as important to good stories as the protagonists are. If your antagonist is not fully realized, lacks depth, or is a caricature of evil, your story will suffer.

Luckily transforming your antagonist from a one-dimensional paper doll into a force to be reckoned with—and remembered—is completely possible if you implement a few simple but powerful methods for creating antagonists and expanding their roles. You can build a worthy adversary during the outlining process or beef one up when you revise your already completed draft. It's never too late.

The antagonist is, quite simply, the person who acts to keep your protagonist from achieving his goals. Note the key words *person* and *acts*. I'm using *person* here as a catchall for a sentient being or creation of any kind that is capable of emotion and has the intellectual ability to plot against your protagonist. Thus a personified car (as in Stephen King's *Christine*) could be an effective antagonist, but an abstraction such as "society" or "Big Pharma" cannot. (More on this later.)

The antagonist must *act* to prevent your heroine from achieving her goals, whether that action is whispering reminders that she's totally useless, plunging a knife into her back, or anything in between. The type of action your antagonist takes will depend on his nature and the kind of story you're writing. But your story must have an antagonist. (In some stories—*Dr. Jekyll and Mr. Hyde* comes to mind—the protagonist is actually his own antagonist.) Without an active antagonist, your hero could take a leisurely Sunday stroll toward his goal. Lacking the obstacles a worthy antagonist would provide, he would also lack the opportunity for growth or the necessity to change, and his character arc would flatline (as would your book sales).

With the following tips in mind, reread your manuscript with an eye toward making your antagonist as compelling as your protagonist. Some effort on your part could even put your villain in the heady company of Professor Moriarty, the White Witch, Simon Legree, and Nurse Ratched.

REMEMBER THAT ANTAGONISTS ARE PEOPLE, TOO

I stop reading novels in which the antagonist is obviously nothing more than a device to move the plot in a certain direction. If I can't empathize with the antagonist, believe in her motives or understand why she's dishing out evil, I put the book aside. Flesh out your antagonist. Give us an origin story (how she became the way she is) or show that she regrets something and might change if given a chance.

If working with a nonhuman antagonist, personify him at least a little bit. Think of Frankenstein's loneliness, HAL's (the computer in *2001: A Space Odyssey*) jealousy, or Shere Khan's hatred of the "man cub" (*The Jungle Book*). Show the antagonist doing something nice. Even villains love their mothers or cockapoos, volunteer at soup kitchens, or help snow-stuck motorists push their cars out of intersections. Do this early on. Give him believable, even laudable, motives.

Inspector Javert from Victor Hugo's *Les Misérables* is a strong antagonist because his obsession with finding Valjean stems from his belief that stealing is wrong. How many readers would disagree with that? Javert's insistence that theft is always, without exception, wrong, however, turns his crusade into persecution. His inability to believe that good and evil can coexist in a single man leads him to suicide. His death is one of the story's tragedies because he has been so thoroughly developed as a character and because we have, from the beginning, understood his motives and his flaws.

ESCHEW THE TOTALLY EVIL ANTAGONIST

Pure evil is dull, unbelievable, and predictable. Readers cannot relate to it. Sometimes evil characters devolve into cartoons and become jokes, thus killing suspense or tension. Other times they're boring: *Yeah, yeah, the serial killer who tortured small animals as a child and is now stalking women that remind him of his mother … yawn.* One way to prevent a truly dark character from becoming a caricature is to make her a viewpoint character—because *no character is the embodiment of evil in her own mind.* No one is the villain in his own story. George R.R. Martin did this effectively in his A Song of Ice and Fire series. In its first book, *A Game of Thrones*, Jaime and Cersei Lannister, the incestuous brother and sister, seem to be evil personified, the characters readers love to hate. In subsequent books, however, they become viewpoint characters, making it difficult not to empathize with them.

If your book's structure makes it impossible to show the antagonist's viewpoint, place one of the viewpoint characters in that position and have him try to understand his perspective. Perhaps your heroine is struggling to find day care for her infant while your villain is looking at nursing homes for his aging father. Or they could both lose something dear to them or confront job-related problems. It could even be something small: Your protagonist could get stuck in a traffic jam, while your antagonist's flight is delayed by the weather. The point is to show similarity, humanity, and an overlap of feelings and experience between the protagonist and the antagonist. This will enlarge the reader's perception of the antagonist, even if subconsciously.

YOUR ANTAGONIST SHOULD NOT BE ABSTRACT

Abstractions make for distant, unrelatable antagonists. If you think "organized religion" or "corporate greed" is your hero's antagonist, your story might be more effective as an essay. Put a human face on the abstraction. A hypocritical pastor might make a good antagonist in the first instance, or a ruthless Wall Street corporate raider in the second (Gordon Gekko, anyone?). Those people can represent the abstraction and take action against the protagonist.

In Anton Myrer's *Once an Eagle*, it would be easy to think of "war" as Sam Damon's antagonist. Myrer thrusts Damon into every war from the early twentieth century to "Khotiane" (Vietnam) and paints a grim picture of the suffering it causes him. Yet "war" does not act against Damon; it is war's human face, Courtney Massengale, who maneuvers to defeat Damon and ensures he loses out on the promotion that might have allowed him to persuade policy makers not to get the United States involved in Khotiane. Without this human antagonist, Damon's life (and *Once an Eagle*) would have less meaning; he would be fighting against uncontrollable, impersonal geopolitical forces with no hope of changing the outcome. His almost lifelong tussle with Massengale, however, is one every individual can identify with: the battle to live each day as a human being devoted to a higher cause than self-interest. If your work-in-progress features an abstraction as the antagonist, rework it to give the abstraction a Massengalian face.

MAKE YOUR PROTAGONIST AND ANTAGONIST EQUALS

There's no tension in a story where the protagonist is a Mensa member and Delta Force commando and his foe is a wimpy dolt. Do you enjoy watching a football game when the score is 72–0, or a horse race when one thoroughbred wins by twenty lengths? No, such uneven matchups are boring. The same is true in novels. So, to heighten tension throughout the story, your antagonist needs to be your hero's equal, or superior to your hero, at least in some arenas. Consider giving the antagonist complementary traits (he's calm and detail-oriented if your heroine is impulsive; she's a great team-builder or motivator if the hero is a loner).

In graphic novels, archenemies frequently embody the exact opposite qualities of the superheroes and are more than a match for them. Whereas Superman's strength is, well, strength, Lex Luthor's advantage is intellect.

KEEP YOUR ENEMIES CLOSE

If your protagonist's dream is to return to college at forty and her husband tells her she's too old, he's the antagonist, even though they love each other. This "beloved antagonist" scenario happens frequently in women's fiction and mainstream literature. A husband might act, sometimes unconsciously, to keep the heroine from reinventing herself. Or an adult child might be convinced that the aging protagonist would be happier in a nursing home. Think of any character who uttered the phrase, "It's for your own good." When writing this kind of antagonist, capitalize on the conflict inherent in the relationship and on the drama that arises when someone with our best interests at heart—someone we care about—stands between us and a goal. Our protagonists don't want to destroy beloved antagonists or see them jailed or rendered impotent.

They want to change their minds and maneuver around them. It can be challenging to keep the tension high in such a story, because you may not want to inflict pain on either the protagonist or the antagonist. Bite the bullet—make life hard for both of them.

CONSIDER GIVING YOUR ANTAGONIST PROXIES

Forcing the protagonist to defeat proxies in order to reach the final battle with the primary antagonist is an excellent way of raising the stakes. One of the best examples in recent literature is the Harry Potter series. In the first book, the ultimate antagonist, Lord Voldemort, receives scant mention; Rowling gradually reveals his importance as the series progresses. Harry and his allies must confront an array of proxies throughout the series, including a basilisk, Death Eaters, dementors and a host of others before coming face-to-face with Voldemort for the climactic battle. Voldemort is, of course, working against Harry from behind the scenes even before the first book opens, but he must use the proxies to carry out his schemes until he regains a body and his strength.

In most fiction, bringing the antagonist and protagonist face–to–face on more than one occasion will heighten the tension. When this is not possible for plot reasons, proxies can work, as can behind-the-scenes machinations such as anonymous threats and indirect attacks against the protagonist's reputation, family, or self. Rowling enables mental contact between Harry and Voldemort before their physical confrontation; that type of "mind meld" won't work for all stories, but it reminds us to be creative in the ways we structure protagonist–antagonist interactions.

By internalizing these six tips, you can amp up your antagonist and make him better than he was before. Stronger. Wilier. Worthy of making your protagonist's life a bubbling cauldron of conflict … and worthy of giving readers a story experience they won't soon forget. If we start giving antagonists the respect they deserve, maybe we won't get any more snarky e-mails from our villains, and maybe our book sales will zip toward the stratosphere. (Note to Eva N. Carnate: Don't get any ideas. You're still not getting your own series.)

....

LAURA DISILVERIO is the author of twelve mystery novels (and counting) and a retired Air Force intelligence officer. President of Sisters in Crime and frequent faculty member for Mystery Writers of America University, she plots murder and parents teens in Colorado, trying to keep the two tasks separate.

CHAPTER 20

SYMPATHY FOR THE DEVIL

BY JESSICA PAGE MORRELL

It cannot be said too often: Antagonists—and villains, in particular—are complicated, three-dimensional, and robustly knowable people. After all, it is the process of *learning* about fascinating characters in terrible difficulties that draws readers in. Readers especially want to learn about what makes a badass tick.

Let's delve into why sympathy is often mentioned with fictional characters, what it really means, and how it applies to badasses, particularly to villains. Since this chapter is about creating sympathy, I want you to think of sympathy as a much broader concept than the typical definition. In this context, sympathy doesn't necessarily stem from likeability, but rather from readers recognizing characters' basic human qualities, aspirations, and sensibilities. Just to note, empathy for characters means that the reader feels like he's identified with or is experiencing a character's goals, emotions, or way of thinking. Empathy, whereby the reader and character are emotionally entwined, is most often associated with protagonists and sometimes with antagonists, but rarely with villains.

So we're going to explore how to reveal the souls and psyches of villains and other complicated types so that they're unmistakable. Many of the techniques outlined in this chapter can also work with antagonists and anti-heroes, including dark heroes and bad boys. So, although the term *villain* will often appear in the discussion here, consider how these techniques might be applied to other unconventional main characters who require a special degree of intricacy.

There are a number of lessons I want you to take away from this chapter; most of them evolve from having a very intimate knowledge of your characters. Every writer has his own way "in" to the story. Some plan, some dream. Some writers piece a story together like a puzzle as bits of inspiration slip into consciousness. For most writers, plot and conflict are so entwined with characters that one cannot be known without the other.

However, if you're the sort of writer who likes to plan and outline, you might want to begin writing a novel by getting to know your characters within the framework of your plot. Characters without a plot idea are lifeless sketches since each character must fit the particular needs of the story. So it rarely works to merely create characters without imagining the world they'll inhabit and the problems they'll encounter. Once you have even a hazy knowledge of your plot, you can begin to create a cast.

Start by making major choices for your main characters since it will be easier to plot if you first decide on the dominant traits and morality of your main players. As you outline your protagonist's traits and major actions in the story, you'll also make crucial distinctions about him, such as if he's likeable or unlikeable, heroic or ordinary. As your protagonist takes shape, your antagonist—especially if your story calls for a villain—will likely be forming alongside him.

If you're featuring a villain in your story, your essential choice is whether he will be sympathetic (as in someone the reader comes to know and discerns his humanity) or unsympathetic (as in someone whose humanity eludes the reader). The other crucial distinction in creating a villain is deciding whether he's villainous at heart or if *circumstances* have turned him into a villain. Once these bigger considerations are out of the way, the more intimate details about his backstory and front story can be shaped.

While it sounds antithetical to describe a bad guy as sympathetic, when you create any type of badass, you need to look deep into his troubled soul and explore his motivations, desires, and past for the roots of his deformed psyche. He might long for power, acceptance, or fame; perhaps these are desires similar to the protagonist's. While in some stories a stock villain—a person who simply is evil, the type that the reader loves to hate—might be needed, most stories benefit froom a villain who has primal, understandable human drives.

While a villain may be sympathetically drawn because you've given him multiple dimensions and included his backstory, his *goals* won't necessarily be ones that the reader identifies with because those goals are going to be harmful, immoral, illegal, or even evil. (Remember that with anti-heroes or other badasses, their goals are also sometimes difficult for readers to identify with.) If a villain's sympathetically drawn, it doesn't mean that when he thunders after a victim with a chain saw, the reader is thinking, *Oh, I bet he doesn't* really *mean to hurt him.* A guy with a chain saw, unless he's chopping up firewood, will always be dangerous, and the reader needs to believe in his dangerousness. What sympathy provides is understanding.

Creating a sympathetic villain also doesn't mean creating a character who's weak or ineffective, although there is often something rather pitiful about a villain. This pity is typically stirred because the villain doesn't have full access to his humanity, or because he has somehow shut himself off from others or reality.

Sympathy means you'll want to *humanize* a villain so that the reader might come away with a haunting understanding of his twisted soul. A reader doesn't need to like your character, but when he can understand a character, the story has deeper power. Conversely this also works well with creating protagonists and heroes. If the reader believes in a protagonist's (especially a hero's) *flaws*, he'll believe in the story. If the reader believes in the antagonist's or villain's *humanity*, he'll believe in the story.

Also, sometimes the reader might believe that there is a tiny spark of decency buried within a villain that makes him worth redeeming. In some stories, this spark gets snuffed out when the villain whacks his next victim, sometimes this spark simmers throughout the story, and sometimes it never exists.

FIRST COMES KNOWLEDGE

In many amateur writers' manuscripts, the story suffers from not so much a lack of imagination, but a lack of nuance, emotional range, and detailed knowledge of the human psyche. The results are story people who are merely caricatures.

While you can draw from your own life experiences, writing fiction in which a villain appears—especially a villain who is psychologically damaged, such as a sociopath—is firmly grounded in research into human psychology, mental illness, and how the brain and emotions evolve through different stages of development.

In writing your villain, you'll want to talk with experts and read articles on abnormal psychology and the latest psychological research. You'll also want to know the basic characteristics of specific criminal types; you'll want to know if they are capable of empathy or if their lack of empathy sets them apart from the rest of humanity. If your story type warrants it, you'll also need an understanding of the criminal justice system. And, for your information, watching *CSI* and television shows of that ilk doesn't qualify as research.

In real life, most of us prefer to lump people into categories. There's our nice neighbor and our cranky neighbor. Our reliable friends and our flighty ones. The awesome ex-boyfriend and the psycho ex-boyfriend. The wonderful boss and the awful boss. Sometimes these judgments and classifications have validity. If your friend is late nine times out of ten, you'd be silly to expect her to show up on time the next time you meet. If your neighbor throws wild parties every weekend with people vomiting on the lawn and music blaring until three in the morning, it wouldn't make sense to classify this neighbor as thoughtful. So classifying people is simply expedient. But as a fiction writer, you need to be careful about classifications and generalizations.

Because we sometimes paint people with these broad strokes, we might wander through life ignoring all the shadings people possess, discounting their more complicated traits and nuanced reasons for acting as they do. Humans long to bring order to the world—to categorize, judge, and sort people based on a few incidents or missteps. This habit often takes hold during our childhood and adolescence. A teacher gave you a *D* on a report you slaved over, so he now gets lumped into the "bad" teacher file. A neighbor yells at you for walking on his lawn, so he gets filed under "crank." A friend stands you up, so she is categorized under "flake." Meanwhile you forget that the teacher is often a fascinating lecturer, that the neighbor sometimes gave you rides to school in bad weather, and that your friend listened to you for hours when you lamented ad nauseum about breaking up with your sophomore-year sweetheart. It's likely that although you're an adult now, you might still hang on to these tendencies of classification and simplification. As you create your characters, you must go deeper and defy the urge to typecast. Otherwise your characters will likely be thinly drawn, and thus be unsympathetic.

It's also important to realize that good people break our hearts, break their promises, disappoint us, and betray us. Good people can be insensitive or selfish; even the best of us are not always tolerant, patient, and kind. This business of being good while walking through life is enormously difficult. Each day, people and events get on our nerves and strain our patience. A story can be especially dramatic when a decent person missteps, but even more so when a bad person does.

Knowledge of human nature and psychology is essential to fiction writers because we live in a sophisticated age. Your readers might regularly tune in to Dr. Phil or Oprah, read various self-help and inspirational books, and listen to psychologists on talk radio. They've heard theories about why serial killers go on killing sprees, why meth is so addictive, and why intimacy is so difficult for many people. In fact, we're bombarded with information in our society, and much of it strives for an understanding of why people do what they do.

So, while in real life you might quickly classify or lump people into various types, if you're writing a villain in your story, with a few exceptions, he cannot be simplistic. If your villain is a *type* rather than a fully-fleshed person, he will be trite and anemic, a marionette twitching when you pull his strings. You need a source code for his actions, and you need to know how you want your reader to react. Do his actions stem from human weakness, mental illness, misguided principles, or rationalization? Is your villain broken, cynical, or amoral? Is he a poseur? Is he conflicted? Is there pathos at his center?

As a fiction writer, you're aware that you're writing for a sophisticated audience that expects depth, knowledge, and intimacy when reading fiction. Readers don't always need to identify with your characters, but they do want consistency and to meet story people they've never met before. Respect this, and deliver stories brimming with an assorted cast that has complicated reasons for doing what they do.

Think of the villains in Alfred Hitchcock's films as you ponder the lessons in this chapter. It was Hitchcock who said that the better the villain is, the better the movie is. Some of his villains were urbane, some were con men, thieves, and traitors. Sometimes a villain was a married man who'd grown tired of his wife and turned murderous. But most of them had some depth and some humanity, and often they left us wondering about how they came to be. Hitchcock's films also teach writers that the more screen time or pages you lavish on the villain or any character, the more complexity is necessary since readers and filmgoers want to follow rounded characters.

When a villain is in the story, the reader generally will be filled with dread and horror. But you want to engage both the reader's intellect and his emotions. Shakespeare's plays feature complicated characters, most of whom are not simply good or evil. A more contemporary example of a compelling villain is Mitch Leary, played by John Malkovich, in the film *In the Line of Fire*. It's an assassin-on-the-loose thriller, but in this case, Leary is an ex-CIA operative who has suffered a breakdown. He also feels betrayed by this organization and wants payback. Malkovich embodies the complicated and wily Leary, and he is both believable and menacing in the role.

INTIMACY: SLEEPING WITH THE ENEMY

In real life, people become known to us when we spend lots of time with them, listen to their childhood stories, and witness how they handle themselves in a variety of situations. As most married people will attest, true knowledge of a person comes after you've lived together and shared a bed.

I'm talking about both literal and broader interpretations of sleeping with people, so bear with me. For instance, maybe in your childhood, you shared a bedroom with a sibling, and his snores, breathing, rustling, and habits became the rhythms of your night and created a deep understanding of the person. Perhaps you attended summer camp and felt like you knew your bunk mates intimately by the end of your two weeks together. This type of intimate knowledge can come from sharing a marriage bed or living with a lover or roommate. Spending nights in such close proximity lets you know a person in ways you'll never know co-workers or neighbors. We are all vulnerable and exposed in our sleep, and sharing this particular space makes for a fascinating breadth of knowledge.

In creating your badass characters, especially your villains, imagine this level of intimacy. If you can imagine this sort of depth, your villain will be humanized; he may even seem ordinary. An ordinary person with a capacity to harm others is much scarier than an invincible, ten-foot robot that is typecast complete with a maniacal laugh.

Let's think about this: When you sleep with someone, you know what he or she is like the first thing in the morning—bleary eyed and foggy or instantly alert; what he or she wears or doesn't wear while sleeping; and if he or she suffers from nightmares or insomnia. In this level of intimacy, you know if a person hogs the blankets, sleeps in a fetal position, or prefers the windows open year-round. Now, start asking yourself how you can bring this level of knowledge into your story and characters.

You might be wondering how the style of pajamas a character wears makes a difference in your story. The point isn't whether a character wears pajamas or sleeps nude. It likely doesn't matter much if he's a tea drinker or starts the day with a double espresso. The point is to imagine your character with the same depth that you can imagine your husband, wife, roommate, sister, or brother in a variety of situations.

As with the people you have shared intimate space with, you should be able to make a long list of your characters' preferences, mannerisms, and habits. Know the sort of mess they leave in the bathroom after a shower; in more intimate relationships, know the smell and quality of their skin, the texture of their hair, what parts of their bodies are like—the nape of the neck, the inner elbow, the crooked toes, the hidden mole. Once you know these small and penetrating details, you will have the level of knowledge that helps you understand how and why their minds work. You should also know what sort of routines they follow and what habits and interests make them tick. And most of all, know their drenching sorrows or wounds, exactly how they feel when they're scared, and what they do when they're afraid.

Keeping this level of intimacy in mind, imagine your badass in a variety of circumstances. Imagine him when he's trying to appear charming and normal at a cocktail party or at tea with his godmother. Imagine him when he cannot find a parking space, when he's forced to wait in a long line, when a salesclerk is inept or impertinent with him, or when he must perform a task he's sure is beneath him. Imagine him thwarted at big and small goals, imagine him longing to brag about his exploits but needing to keep quiet, and, most of all, imagine him when his best-laid and most intricate plans go awry.

After all, even villains are going to be depicted under stress and possibly not always at the heights of their power. Perhaps your character will need to rely on underlings who are incompetent, will juggle a family or job along with criminal activities, or will act against his best judgment. Always keep in mind that the events of the story often also exhaust the villain and push him to the limits of endurance, tolerance, and patience. There is nothing that steals credibility in a story like characters who never tire or sleep or eat or pause to nurse a wound.

SHAPING THE BACKSTORY

If you've ever visited a natural history museum where the skeleton of a dinosaur or another huge mammal was reconstructed, you might have imagined the extreme care and delicacy that was involved in assembling the beast. Keep this delicate task in mind as you put the pieces of your villain, bone by bone, into place. You'll be fabricating a range of skills and talents, along with insecurities, flawed thinking, and misplaced motives. It will require the daintiest tools in your repertoire, your most finely honed awareness of human nature.

When it comes to villains, there are deep considerations on how to make him not only a compelling threat, but also a compelling person. In shaping your villain, here are some questions you need to consider:

- What is his "regular" or "normal" world before the story begins?
- What does he do on a normal day?
- Did he come from an intact family or a divorced family? Would he consider his childhood happy, difficult, or best forgotten?
- Did he have a large extended family? If so, how important were these influences?
- Was his family financially stable? If not, how does this affect him now?
- Is he a loner? If not, who are his peers?
- Is he capable of intimacy?
- What was his biggest disappointment? What did he do about it?
- Has he suffered from physical, emotional, or sexual abuse? If so, how are you going to demonstrate the repercussions of this in his present actions?
- Is there a history of addiction, such as alcoholism, in his family? If so, how has he been affected?
- Is he considered the black sheep of the family? If not, what role is he assigned?
- Is there a history of mental illness in his family? If so, what are his coping methods and personality traits as a result?
- Does he have a personal or family secret that is rarely mentioned?
- Was there a tragedy in his family, such as the death of a child, that is rarely mentioned?
- Is there a particular trauma from the past that is going to influence his front story?
- If the trauma were severe, does he suffer from Post Traumatic Stress Disorder? If so, how does it manifest in his actions and daily life?
- Does he have a history of committing juvenile crimes, such as violence against animals?
- Has he ever been incarcerated?

Creating Characters

- Has he ever had obsessive fantasies or been a stalker?
- What items does he have in his wallet, safe-deposit box, or hiding place that he doesn't want people to know about?

These questions aren't necessarily appropriate to every member of your cast, but some of them might help shape your villain's situation.

A Villain's Origins

If people come from a fragile or troubled family, research proves that they're often at risk to go on to create the same problems or patterns as adults. As children in a dysfunctional home, they often learn these cardinal rules: don't trust; don't talk; don't feel. This means that if a parent is a raging alcoholic, has a propensity for violence, or is involved in criminal activities, the kids will often cover it up and something within them will shut down.

Now, some kids will act out (family therapists have labeled these kids *scapegoats*), and some will act heroic to keep the family system afloat. The scapegoat kid typically reflects the extreme stress felt in the family and is often seen as the problem in the family, but it's usually a parent's drinking or abuse that is the real problem. Often the first strategy for the children is to move away as soon as possible and somehow distance themselves from their families of origin.

If your villain or other character comes from a dysfunctional family, you'll want to research the various roles played by family members and reflect on how all that has happened in childhood will play out. Has the character lost access to his emotions? Does he trust anyone? Has he re-created a dysfunctional situation, or has he risen above his background?

It cannot be said often enough that the protagonist's backstory, or events that happened before the story begins, haunts the front story with the pain and insistence of a migraine. However, it must also be noted that the villain's backstory has an equal, or mostly likely a greater, influence over all the story's events.

It is rare that bad people just happen, though family members and professionals attest that some children seem simply to be born bad or with a propensity for violence or dishonesty. More commonly, genetic factors are pointed out—for example, a child of a sociopathic parent is more likely to be a sociopath than the rest of the population—or children who have learning disorders or Attention Deficit Disorder, for example, can eventually take on destructive behaviors if they are not treated and monitored properly.

There is also a possibility that a villain had a fairly normal childhood, but then something happened to turn him to the dark side. Perhaps he became involved with drugs or addictions, which, in turn, led him to crime or an outsider's lifestyle. Or perhaps a tragedy struck later and has shaped your villain, such as his beloved wife or child was killed by a drunk driver and he becomes an avenger. Perhaps a woman is brutally raped, a child is exploited by a pedophile, a teen joins a gang, or a computer geek stumbles onto an online get-rich-quick scheme. Or, at an impressionable age, a villain might meet an influential person, such as a hardened criminal, who turned him away from normalcy. If a villain starts out with a fairly normal upbringing but then turns toward crime or evil, it's essential that you know the turning point and the motivation that transformed him into such a tormenting presence.

And before you start worrying that all this knowledge of backstory and the like will bog down your story, remember that, as the writer, you'll always know more about your characters than what ends up on the page. Depending on the storyline, you must decide how much information your reader needs to know so that your characters' actions have a proper context. Thus, as the creator of your characters, you'll know everything about them, even when the information is not explicit in the story.

Legacy of Trauma

In the overall prison population, many of the convicts were exposed to some kind of trauma or abuse in childhood. The same is true for fictional villains, so it is your job to research exactly how traumas affect and motivate people as they go through life.

Sometimes a villain's backstory won't necessarily be traumatic, but it will still color his adult perceptions. But most characters in fiction are

Creating Characters

somehow scarred by loss, and this is especially true for villains. I like to think of this as the "runt of the litter" approach. If you've ever seen a litter of puppies or kittens and noticed how the runt is left behind and cannot feed as often as the others, your sympathy for the smaller littermate is activated. But sometimes the runt grows up with a fierce sense of entitlement. The degree of trauma in the villain's backstory will directly relate to the degree of villainy in the front story. The more powerful your villain is, the more important it is that you give him a compelling reason for his adult viewpoints and actions.

SYMPATHY STRATEGIES

Let's talk about some of the ways you can make your villains sympathetic—keeping in mind, of course, that sympathetic is not synonymous with likeable. As with creating a character arc for all types of story people, one way to make a villain sympathetic is to show that he's capable of change. This doesn't mean he'll change his evil ways by the story's end; it's more likely that you will show he was once not so twisted, or maybe you will reveal the loss or trauma that changed him. Some aspect of change is always a bedrock of sympathetic fictional characters, even villains.

Here is a list of sympathy strategies more specific to villains, but keep in mind that all the strategies center around the knowledge that the reader sympathizes with characters going through trials and feeling emotions that he understands:

- Make certain that there is nothing illogical about the villain's actions. Otherwise it will seem as if you are pulling the strings behind the scene.
- Avoid coincidences that bring the villain together with the protagonist to make things happen in the story.
- Beware of giving the villain a backstory that is so horrific or downtrodden that it's supposed to excuse creepy or illegal behavior. While a villain's backstory can start him on the road to crime, it must be realistically drawn and also involve him making bad choices.

- Since sympathy for all characters happens when the reader watches them struggle, especially with conflict or an uphill battle, don't allow the villain to breeze through the story without stirring a hair or breaking a sweat. His struggle to defeat the hero, for example, might cause wonder or begrudging admiration in the reader.
- If you're writing a villain who is up against an ordinary person, make sure the villain has some ordinariness as well. When invincible types are in the story, it kills sympathy.
- Remember that, as with good guys, the reader's sympathy is ignited for villains when he witnesses the villain experience vulnerability, anguish, and embarrassment.
- For most stories, make certain that the villain is too evil to live (even if that means a life sentence in prison).
- Give the villain an opportunity to make a choice, even if that choice is the wrong one.
- Show a crack in the villain's armor, such as willfulness, arrogance, or excessive pride.
- Depict the villain interacting with other characters, perhaps even showing his deep feelings for a loved one, or kindness or empathy toward a vulnerable character.
- Stop thinking about your villain as a character, and instead think of him as a person.

These are basic strategies, but you can come up with your own plans to create a realistic and believable villain. For inspiration, read other authors' works, and make a note when an author implants a revelation about a character's humanity that you weren't expecting.

Remember, you have fiction's basic toolbox—exposition, dialogue, action, gestures, mannerisms, setting—at your disposal to create believability and sympathy. When you find stories in which you particularly believe in the characters, dissect the author's methods. Based on your reading, you might want to use a narrator to stand apart from the story and comment on the story milieu, or on the motives or backstories of characters. If the reader comes to trust the

Creating Characters

narrator, he comes to understand the characters, including the villain under discussion.

If you want to create depth in a villain, you can also use indirect means. Perhaps a secondary character can offer opinions about the villain, or the villain can be revealed through newspaper accounts, a trial transcript, a psychologist's therapy sessions, or police investigation notes.

Or perhaps you'll want to place the reader squarely in the villain's thoughts so he can experience this inner world. In real life, we often long to know exactly what a partner, spouse, or child is thinking. In fiction, we have the opportunity to slip into a character's mind. And this experience can be especially delicious when the character is a villain because the reader understands the rarity of this experience. If the villain is friendless, tortured, egomaniacal, or unable to control murderous impulses, the reader will experience these sensations and feel the chilling reality of this troubled soul. Or, conversely, you might want to shape a villain who is self-deprecating or ruthlessly honest about his own motives, or make his bravado rather admirable.

EMPATHY

When a villain is onstage in a story, you want to elicit a whole range of complicated emotions in the reader. The reader should be fascinated by the villain, worried about his capabilities, and in some way feel that he has met this nightmarish creature. But a story works best when the reader also understands a villain and can see beneath the actions that brand him.

When this understanding is also laced with empathy for how a villain came to be, it can be especially emotional for the reader. Sometimes you might want to cause the reader's sympathies to yo-yo—for a moment, he feels sympathy or empathy with the villain, then when the scoundrel pulls off a caper or harms a vulnerable character, these feelings will shut down, only to be activated again when another piece of the villain's backstory shows a deprived childhood.

Author Thomas Harris is perhaps best known for his complex villain Hannibal ("The Cannibal") Lecter, but in his novel *Red Dragon*, he thrusts the reader deep into characters' hearts, vulnerabilities, and souls so that the reader's emotional involvement is complicated and erratic.

The villain in question in *Red Dragon* is Francis Dolarhyde, and he seems to have a benign occupation—processing film in a lab. The lab handles photos snapped at family vacations and birthday parties—records of everyday life that he's never part of. You see, he was born with a cleft lip and palate and rejected by his mother. He was raised by his grandmother, not out of the goodness of her heart, but out of a grudge between mother and daughter. His grandmother, a cold-hearted monster, wanted to keep him close as a pawn in a high-stakes game only she could win.

The story begins when Will Graham, who had been nearly killed by Hannibal Lecter during his capture, is coerced out of early retirement by the FBI's Jack Crawford to help solve two murders. Happily married and a stepfather, Graham reluctantly agrees to work on the case. Much of the opening chapters detail how Graham begins his investigation and starts uncovering small clues. He has never been the same since his dustup with Lecter, and his fragility in the story creates an extra dose of tension.

Serial killers often have a safe place to have their private chamber of horrors, as is the case with Dolarhyde, who lives in a house where the nearest neighbor is a half-mile away:

> Dolarhyde always made an inspection tour of the house as soon as he got home; there had been an abortive burglary attempt some years before. He flicked on the lights in each room and looked around. A visitor would not think he lived alone. His grandparents' clothes still hung in the closets, his grandmother's brushes were on her dresser with combings of hair in them. Her teeth were in a glass on the bedside table. The water had long since evaporated. His grandmother had been dead for ten years.

From this description, the reader follows him through an evening alone, including when he watches a home movie of his murder victims. The film is spliced with shots of him sexually aroused, raping his victim, then a final shot of an entire family arranged in a tableau with Dolarhyde capering naked and blood smeared among them.

I don't know about you, but a person as depraved and whacked-out as Dolarhyde doesn't exactly draw tears of sympathy. Especially after another scene where he's alone with a ledger of souvenirs from his victims and newspaper clippings of his crimes, after his feelings of allegiance toward Hannibal Lecter are revealed, and after he kidnaps tabloid reporter Freddy Lounds, forces him to recant something he wrote about him, bites off his lips, sets him on fire, and rolls him into the front door of the newspaper office.

By the time Lounds is screaming in agony, the reader has witnessed Dolarhyde's bottomless rage, often a feature of killers. But then to complicate matters, Harris also reveals that Dolarhyde is driven by a desperate loneliness, and that people who are physically deformed will always be outsiders and will always be scorned. The reader has witnessed how, because he's had reconstructive surgery, he has a speech impediment, and fellow employees make fun of him.

Harris tosses another hand grenade into the story when Dolarhyde falls in love with Reba McClane, one of his co-workers. Reba is blind, spunky, likeable, and interesting. Now he has a reason to control his violent urges, but can he?

In reading *Red Dragon*, the reader is worried about Graham and his fragile recovery, especially after Lecter attempts to send Dolarhyde Grahams's address and his family is forced to flee their home. But when Reba becomes intimate with Dolarhyde and enters his house, the place where his grandmother treated him so shabbily, the reader's skin is prickling with worry and anticipation. Then, apparently in a move to save Reba, Dolarhyde shoots himself and sets the house on fire, which brings the reader back to empathy with Dolarhyde. Or does it?

Recovering from her ordeal, Reba is tormented and doubting herself. Graham tells her:

"... There was plenty wrong with Dolarhyde, but there's nothing wrong with you. You said he was kind and thoughtful to you. I believe it. That's what you brought out in him. At the end, he couldn't kill you and he couldn't watch you die. People who study this kind of thing say he was trying to stop. Why? Because you helped him. That probably saved some lives. You didn't draw a freak. You drew a man with a freak on his back. ..."

Harris, a master grenade launcher, tosses in a final round because Dolarhyde isn't dead after all—the body found in the house was one of his victims.

Just as we're utterly horrified by Dolarhyde, especially when we learn that he considers his massacres his life's work, Harris starts weaving in his backstory and lobbing missiles until we're so caught up in the drama, that, while we're not rooting for Dolarhyde, we're experiencing conflicting feelings about what is left of his tarnished humanness. We understand that people suffering from such severe psychosis cannot see reality in the way that we can. We can imagine Dolarhyde as a much different person if his mother hadn't rejected him, if his grandmother hadn't been so cruel, if his reconstructive surgery had been more successful, if somewhere during his lonely childhood someone would have loved him or at least intervened when he first started showing signs of deviant behavior.

In a similar fashion, if you can create a villain that makes the reader understand him with this depth, you'll have succeeded in humanizing him and creating intricate emotions in your reader.

The forces that shape villains in fiction and in real life can rarely be undone. Thus, when you're creating sympathy for a villain, you're doing so because of his situation and backstory. Not only do readers want to walk along in your protagonist's clothes, they want a close-up meeting with the villain, a meeting so physical and fully wrought that the character's smell, posture, and menacing or seemingly benign presence will take over their senses. Readers want a glimpse or, better yet, a tour of the inner workings of someone drastically different from them.

....

JESSICA PAGE MORRELL is the author of *Writing Out the Storm* (Collectors Press, 1998); *Between the Lines: Master the Subtle Elements of Fiction Writing* (Writer's Digest Books, 2006); *Voices from the Street* (Gray Sunshine, 2007); *The Writer's I Ching: Wisdom for the Creative Life* (Running Press, 2007); *Bullies, Bastards & Bitches: How to Write the Bad Guys in Fiction* (Writer's Digest Books, 2008); and *Thanks, but This Isn't For Us: A (Sort of) Compassionate Guide to Why Your Writing Is Being Rejected* (Tarcher, 2009). Her work also appears in anthologies and *The Writer* and *Writer's Digest* magazines. Morrell founded and coordinates three writing conferences: Summer in Words, Making it in Changing Times, and Claim Your Story.

PART VI

SUPPORTING CHARACTERS

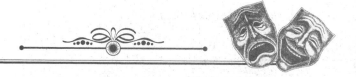

CHAPTER 21

DEVELOPING YOUR SUPPORTING CAST

BY JOSEPH BATES

Supporting characters better our understanding of the main character and the circumstances she finds herself in, whether long-term (I need to solve this homicide case) or the short-term (I need a ham sandwich). And if your supporting characters aren't working toward an understanding of the main character or situation in some way, you might ask yourself what they're really doing there, hogging time and space in your book. Your novel isn't an open house for complete strangers to walk through as they wish. Everything you spend time on must be for a reason, including those minor characters who appear to be simply passing through.

That said, your supporting cast can't seem like they're only hanging around to provide information or further the plot. Rather your secondary characters, even the ones who appear in the book for only a couple of paragraphs and then are gone forever, must appear in those paragraphs as independent people with unique personalities, motivations, and desires of their own ... and you often have to accomplish this in just a few choice words or lines.

For example, let's start with a simple enough premise and conflict—a man and woman on an uncomfortable dinner date—and consider what that situation calls for in terms of supporting characters. They're at a restaurant and are unhappy with their relationship, for whatever reason, though the tension in the scene comes from their being unwilling or unable to express their unhappiness. So a secondary character working with and against this problem might be a waitress who, unlike our two quietly suffering characters, comes over and tries to say everything. Who is simply trying to be cheery—and trying to make a sale—and whose fake outgoingness helps highlight our main characters' quiet desperation. The waitress might not pick up on the fact the two are having a fight of sorts and might start suggesting every dinner- or drink-for-two on the menu, clueless to the tension between them.

We'd find ways to deliver her character clearly from the way she speaks, acts, dresses—loud, overbearing, pieces of flair on her suspenders, lipstick on the tooth—and we'd see that she has a clear, simple motivation all her own: taking an order and trying to push tonight's special. But her actions in following through with the motivation give us a way of seeing the main characters and their predicament in fuller, if depressing, terms. (Note, too, that we'd have even more minor characters in the scene—young couples in love, old couples in silence, an obnoxious kid's birthday party—and that all of them, even though rendered quickly, would be serving the same function of showing our suffering couple more clearly.)

This is the case for every minor character you make part of your cast, whether the character comes in once to fulfill a specific function and then leaves or becomes a rregular, someone who plays an important role in building the story as part of a subplot.

ROUNDING FLAT CHARACTERS

If you find yourself having trouble seeing your characters, whether major or minor, as full people in their own right, here are a few questions you might ask to help nudge them in the right direction.

What's the character's internal motivation; what does he or she really want?

This might particularly be a question to ask of a flat protagonist, the result of a main character who seems motivated by nothing but plot-level or external circumstances. Remember that your hero is also a person like you or me ... and consider what *we'd* feel in a similar situation. (And don't forget that even minor characters have motivations, and lives, of their own.)

How might you locate a character's internal motivation and conflict if these seem to be absent?

If your character's motivation seems purely external, perhaps as part of his obligation or job—for example, if you're writing a detective novel, and the character has simply taken on a new case—try to consider what it is about the character, personally, that informs his or her professional work, how it influences his ability to do the job, or speaks to the reason he entered this profession in the first place. Also consider how this particular job is different from yesterday's job, or tomorrow's, or last year's. Presumably part of what makes this job or case different is that it is personally different, there's something personal at stake. How might that be the case?

What peculiar traits—of appearance, personality, behavior, mannerisms, speech—might you highlight about the character to make him seem fuller?

I don't mean that giving a monocle and a handlebar moustache to a character automatically makes him full. Instead consider what unusual or distinctive features might exist for your character naturally ... and might help us see him or her. Are you playing both with and against type? No character is 100 percent good or evil, kindhearted or callous, capable or clueless, so consider not only how to set up our expectation of character but also how to subvert that expectation, how to complicate our view of a character. Hannibal Lecter would be a lot of fun to share a glass of wine with, discussing art and music and philosophy and the finer things. So long as he didn't kill and eat you.

How is the heart of the character, the motivation, evident in a work you admire?

Consider this with any novel or work that means something to you, no matter the genre. Try looking back at the main character you find compelling and play armchair psychologist a bit, looking at how the external and internal motivation and conflict play with, or play off of, each other.

OVERACTIVE OR INACTIVE SUPPORTING CHARACTERS

If in the second act you find your novel veering off course either because a minor character has come in and tried to run the place or because your minor characters seem to be doing nothing but sitting on your couch, eating your food, not really contributing, you should put them to the test: Determine why they're there, if they can be brought in line somehow, or, if not, how you might excise them from the novel.

Minor characters who become personal "darlings" for the author can be very hard to kill, and often a writer will find some way to justify keeping around an inactive but favorite minor character based on very thin reasoning, such as saying that the character adds comic relief (yes, but comic relief to your depressing postapocalyptic Gothic revenge story?) or that the character adds a romantic element (yes, but does your chain-saw murderer bipolar anti-hero really need a love interest?) or, or … .

If an inactive supporting character does indeed seem to fulfill some function like this—but is otherwise inert—you might see if another and better-established supporting character could fulfill that role just as easily. Or you might consider streamlining several supporting characters into just one who does the trick.

Ultimately who stays and goes is not up to you as the author but up to your story. When in doubt, try to listen to what the story is telling you to do and follow that advice; it's almost always going to be right.

....

JOSEPH BATES is the author of *The Nighttime Novelist* (Writer's Digest Books, 2010) and *Tomorrowland: Stories* (Curbside Splendor, 2013). His short fiction has appeared in such journals as *The Rumpus, New Ohio Review, Identity Theory, South Carolina Review,* and *InDigest Magazine.* Visit him online at www.josephbates.net.

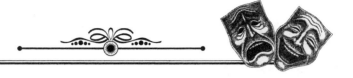

CHAPTER 22

THE CHARACTER HIERARCHY

BY ORSON SCOTT CARD

Not all characters are created equal.

You must know—and let your readers know—which characters are most important to the story, so they'll know which are worth following and caring about, and which will quickly disappear.

It's hard to measure the exact importance of a character—importance doesn't come in quarts or by the inch. But there are three general levels of importance, and the distinctions can be useful.

1. **WALK-ONS AND PLACEHOLDERS.** You won't develop these characters at all; they're just people in the background, meant to lend realism or to perform a simple function and then disappear, forgotten.

2. **MINOR CHARACTERS.** These characters may make a difference in the plot, but we aren't supposed to get emotionally involved with them, either negatively or positively. We don't expect them to keep showing up in the story. Their desires and actions might cause a twist in the story but play no role in shaping its ongoing flow. In fact, a rule of thumb is that a minor character does one or two things in the story and then disappears.

3. **MAJOR CHARACTERS.** This group includes the people we care about; we love them or hate them, fear them or hope they succeed. They show up again and again in the story. The story is, to one degree or another, about them, and we expect to find out what happens to them by the end. Their desires and actions drive the story forward and carry it through all its twists and turns.

193

Remember, though, that there is no wall dividing one level from the others. In your story, Pete and Nora may be the main characters, but their friends Morry and Dolores and Pete's boss Edgar and Nora's brother Shawn are also fairly major, and we expect to know more about them; and then there's Pete's secretary and the doorman, who both do some pretty important things in the story, though we aren't aware of deep personal dilemmas in their lives; and we certainly will remember the weird taxi driver and the Indian cop and . . .

So where is the dividing line between major and minor? There isn't one. But we know that Pete and Nora are the most important; Morry, Dolores, Edgar, and Shawn are somewhat important; Pete's secretary and the doorman are somewhat important but still pretty minor; and the weird taxi driver and the Indian cop are definitely minor but certainly not mere walk-ons. The different levels shade into each other. And as you master the techniques appropriate to each level, you'll be able to create each character at exactly the level of importance the story requires.

WALK-ONS AND PLACEHOLDERS

Unless your story takes place in a hermitage or a desert island, your main characters are surrounded by many people who are utterly unimportant in the story. They are background; they are part of the milieu. Here are a few samples that show what I mean.

> Nora accidentally gave the cabby a twenty for a five-dollar ride and then was too shy to ask for change. Within a minute a skycap had the rest of her money.
>
> Pete checked at the desk for his messages. There weren't any, but the bellman did have a package for him.
>
> People started honking their horns before Nora even knew there was a traffic jam.
>
> Apparently some suspicious neighbor had called the cops. The uniform who arrested him wasn't interested in Pete's explanations, and he soon found himself at the precinct headquarters.

Creating Characters

Notice how many people we've "met" in these few sentences. A cabby, a skycap, a hotel desk clerk, a bellman, horn honkers in a traffic jam, a suspicious neighbor, a uniformed police officer. Every single one of these people is designed to fulfill a brief role in the story and then vanish completely out of sight.

Part of the Scenery

How do you make people vanish? Any stage director knows the trick. You have a crowd of people onstage, most of them walk-ons. They have to be there because otherwise the setting wouldn't be realistic—but you don't want them to distract the audience's attention. In effect, you want them to be like scenery. They really aren't characters at all—they're movable pieces of milieu.

So you dress them in drab or similar clothing, and make your main characters' costumes contrast sharply with the crowd. If possible, you make the walk-ons hold absolutely still; if they have to move, you make them move as smoothly and gently as possible. You do not allow them to make noise except when you want general crowd noises. You make them keep their attention riveted either on their own quiet task or on the main action of the scene. You turn them so they're facing generally upstage. You never let any one walk-on stay onstage for very long, or the audience starts expecting him to do something.

The surest way for a walk-on to get himself fired from a play is to become "creative"—to start fidgeting or doing some clever bit of stage business that distracts attention from the main action of the scene. Unless, of course, this is one of those rare occasions when the walk-on's new business is brilliantly funny—in which case, you might even pay him more and elevate the part.

You have the same options in fiction. If a character who isn't supposed to matter starts getting out of hand, distracting from the main thread of the story, you either cut her out entirely or you figure out why you as a writer were so interested in her that you've spent more time on her than you meant to and revise the story to make her matter more.

Most of the time, though, you want your walk-ons to disappear. You want them to fade back and be part of the scenery, part of the milieu. How do you do it in fiction?

Stereotypes

Sometimes stereotyping is exactly the tool of characterization you need.

A stereotype is a character who is a typical member of a group. He does exactly what the readers expect him to do. Therefore they take no notice of him—he disappears into the background.

As ordinary human beings, we may not *like* a particular stereotype if we happen to be the member of a group we think is viewed unfairly. But as writers, writing to our own community, we can't help but be aware of and use our community stereotypes in order to make placeholding characters behave exactly according to expectations.

If we think that a particular stereotype is unfair to the group it supposedly explains, then we're free to deliberately violate the stereotype. But the moment we do that, we have made the character strange, which will make him interesting and attract the readers' attention. He will no longer simply disappear—he isn't a walk-on anymore. He has stepped forward out of the milieu and joined the story.

MINOR CHARACTERS

There's nothing wrong with a background character violating stereotype and attracting attention—as long as you realize that he isn't part of the background anymore. The readers will notice him, and they'll expect his strangeness to amount to something.

The audience still isn't supposed to care much about him; he isn't expected to play a continuing role in the story. He might be momentarily involved in the action, but then he'll disappear. Still, his individuality will set a mood, add humor, make the milieu more interesting or complete. The way to make such characters instantly memorable without leading the audience to expect them to do more is to make them eccentric, exaggerated, or obsessive.

Creating Characters

Eccentricity

Remember the movie *Beverly Hills Cop*? There were hundreds of place-holders in that film—thugs who shot at cops, cops who got shot at, people milling around in the hotel lobby, people at the hotel desk. They all acted exactly as you would expect them to act. They vanished. Unless you personally knew an actor who played one of the walk-ons, you don't remember any of them.

But I'll bet that as you walked out of the theater, you remembered Bronson Pinchot. Not by name, of course, not then. He was the desk attendant in the art gallery. You know, the one with the effeminate manner and the weird foreign accent. He had absolutely nothing to do with the story—if he had been a mere placeholder, you would never have noticed anything was missing. So why do you remember him?

It wasn't that he had a foreign accent. In southern California, a Spanish accent would merely have stereotyped him; he would have disappeared into the background.

It wasn't his effeminacy. The audience would merely see him as a stereotypical homosexual. Again, he would disappear.

But the effeminacy and the accent were combined—the "foreigner" stereotype and the "effete homosexual" stereotype are rarely used together, and so the audience was surprised. What's more important, though, is that the accent was an eccentric one, completely unexpected. Pinchot based his accent on the speech of an Israeli he once knew; the accent was so rare that almost no one in the audience recognized it. It was a genuinely novel way to speak. He was not just a foreigner, he was a strange and effeminate foreigner. Furthermore Pinchot's reactions to Eddie Murphy—the hint of annoyance, superiority, snottiness in his tone—made him even more eccentric. Eccentric enough to stick in our minds.

How memorable was he? From that bit part, he went directly into the TV series *Perfect Strangers*. Which goes to show that you can still parlay a bit part into a career.

And yet in *Beverly Hills Cop*, though we remembered him, we never expected his character to be important in the story. He existed only for a few laughs and to make Eddie Murphy's Detroit-cop character feel even more alien in L.A. Pinchot managed to steal the scene—to get his promotion from walk-on—without distorting the story. He was funny, but he made no great difference in the way the story went. He simply amused us for a moment.

Since he was a minor character, he did exactly what he needed to do. Likewise in your stories you need to realize that your minor characters should *not* be deeply and carefully characterized. Like flashbulbs, they need to shine once, brightly, and then get tossed away.

Exaggeration

Another way to make a minor character flash: You take a normal human trait and make it just a little—or sometimes a lot—more extreme, like the character Sweet-Face in *Butch Cassidy and the Sundance Kid*. Butch and the Kid are in a whorehouse; the Pinkerton detectives ride up on the street below. There we see a pudgy-faced character who looks like the soul of innocence and believability. Butch tells Sundance a brief story about him— that with Sweet-Face covering for them, they're safe because everybody believes him. His innocent look is an exaggeration, but sure enough, when Sweet-Face points out of town, as if to say "they went thataway," the Pinkertons take off in that direction.

A few moments later, the Pinkertons ride back, confront Sweet-Face again; Sweet-Face panics and points straight toward the room where Butch and the Kid are watching. His panic and betrayal are as exaggerateed as his innocence was before. He sticks in the memory, and yet we never expected him to be important again in the plot.

Obsessiveness

Let's go back to the example I gave before, of Nora's cabby, the one she paid a twenty for a five-dollar ride. The stereotypical reaction—"Hey, thanks, lady"—is so ordinary we can omit it entirely. But what if the cabdriver is obsessive?

"What is it, you trying to impress me? Trying to show me you're big time? Well, don't suck ego out of me, lady! I only take what I earn!"

Nora had no time for this. She hurried away from the cab. To her surprise, he jumped out and followed her, shouting at her with as much outrage as she'd expect if she hadn't paid him at all. "You can't do this to me in America!" he shouted. "I'm a Protestant, you never heard of the Protestant work ethic?"

Finally she stopped. He caught up with her, still scolding. "You can't do your rich-lady act with me, you hear me?"

"Shut up," she said. "Give me back the twenty." He did, and she gave him a five. "There," she said. "Satisfied?"

His mouth hung open; he looked at the five in utter disbelief. "What is this!" he said. "No tip?"

Now that's a guy who won't let go. If you saw that scene in a movie or even read it in a novel, chances are you'd remember the cabdriver. Yet you wouldn't expect him to be important in the plot. If he showed up again it would be for more comic relief, not for anything important. For instance, when the story is all but over and Nora is coming home with Pete for a well-earned rest, it could be funny if they get in a cab and it turns out to be the same driver. The audience would remember him well enough for that. But they would be outraged if the cabdriver turned out to be an assassin or a long-lost cousin.

This would *not* be true, however, if this were the first scene in the story. At the beginning of the story, all the characters are equal—we don't know any of them at all. So if in fact you wanted to tell the story of how Nora got involved with this obsessive-compulsive cabdriver—or how the cabdriver managed to get Nora's attention so he could start dating her—this would be a pretty good beginning.

The other side of that coin is that if the cabdriver is in fact supposed to be minor, you could *not* begin the story with this scene. If these were the first five paragraphs of the story, we would naturally expect that the story was going to be *about* Nora and the cabby, and when Nora goes on through the story without ever seeing or even thinking of the cabdriver again, at some point many readers are going to ask, "What was that business with the cabdriver all about?"

This is because much of what makes the difference between major and minor characters is the amount of time you spend on them. And the amount of time is not absolute—it is relative to the total length of the story. In a 1,500-word story, this 150-word section would be 10 percent of the total—and that's a lot. In an 80,000-word novel, this 150-word section would be almost vanishingly brief. So the cabby would seem more important in a short story than in a novel.

However, if this scene comes at the *beginning* of a story and the reader doesn't know yet what the story is about, then the cabby is present in the entire 150 words of the story's first scene. At that point he seems to the reader to be almost as important as Nora—he is diminished only by the fact that he is not named and Nora is the point-of-view character. The reader has every reason to expect that the cabby will amount to something.

This is why it's a good idea to introduce at least a few major characters first, so that the first characters the reader meets—the characters who occupy 100 percent of the opening—really will turn out to matter to the story.

MAJOR CHARACTERS

By now it should be obvious that the major characters are the ones who really matter, the ones the story is, to one degree or another, *about*. Their choices turn the story, their needs drive the story forward.

These are also the characters who most need to be characterized. Because they really matter to the story, you can devote as much time to them as strong characterization might require.

There are other cues you use to let the audience know which characters are major, besides the raw amount of time devoted to characterization.

Choices

If a character is relatively powerful—powerful enough to make choices that change other characters' lives—the audience will remember her better and expect her to amount to something more in the story. If the other characters all regard a character as dangerous or powerful, the readers will, too.

Focus

This leads to one of the most effective theatrical techniques for making the audience notice a character—have everyone on stage *look* at him, *listen* to him, or *talk about him* behind his back. If you do enough of this, you never have to bring the character onstage. We never see the title character in *Waiting for Godot*, for instance, and yet he is arguably the most important character in the play, and his failure to arrive is the most important "event."

You can use the same technique in fiction to focus the readers' attention on a character whether he's present or not. In The Lord of the Rings, the character of Sauron appears in person only once; beyond that, he personally intervenes in the story only a handful of times. Yet he is the engine driving almost every plot thread, the focus of everyone's attention far more often than any other character. The result is that readers "remember" Sauron as one of the most important characters in The Lord of the Rings—even though he almost never appears in the story at all.

Frequency of Appearance

If a character keeps coming back, even if she's not all that exciting or powerful, we begin to expect her to do something important—or else why would the writer keep bringing her up? This is why, when movie stars are evaluating a script, they'll keep track of how many scenes their character will be in. If they aren't in enough scenes, they won't loom large enough in the audience's mind—and therefore the film won't be a "star vehicle."

Sometimes a character who should remain minor will keep coming back just because of her job—a bartender at the club where two major characters regularly meet, for instance. Then you need to reduce her importance—have her say very little or have substitute bartenders show up on her night off, something to let the reader know that it doesn't matter much whether the bartender is there or not.

Action

A character doesn't have to appear all that often, as long as every time he *does* appear, what he says and does has an important effect on the plot. On the other hand, a character who is often present but does almost nothing can quickly fade in the readers' memory. In the play *Romeo and Juliet*, Romeo spends a lot of time with his two friends, Benvolio and Mercutio. In fact, as I remember it Benvolio is present in more scenes than Mercutio, including the first scene in which we see Romeo himself. Yet Benvolio is completely forgettable, while Mercutio is one of the most memorable characters in the play. Why? Because Benvolio never does anything but listen to people and make a few bland comments, while Mercutio is flamboyant and provocative and funny and outrageous, and when he is onstage he either incites or is deeply involved in every action.

Rule of thumb: Passive characters will never seem as important as active characters.

Sympathy

The more endearing or charming a character is, the more the audience comes to like her as a human being, the more important that character will be to the audience, and the more they'll expect to see what becomes of her.

Point of View

One of the most potent devices for making a character important to your readers is to use the character's point of view. Rule of thumb: When a character in the story is used as the narrator or viewpoint character, his importance is greatly increased.

There are also some variables that are out of your control. A character might be extremely important to some readers because they think they resemble him, or because the character resembles someone they love or hate. Or a character you think of as important may seem unimportant to some readers because they have seen too many characters like him—to them, the character has become a cliche. In fact, if your story is very popular, it is likely to be imitated—and the fact that the market is flooded with imitations of your best character will soon make your character feel like an imitation, too, even though he's the original!

But since these things are generally out of your control, you can't very well use them to help you establish your hierarchy of characters. The techniques you *can* control are:

- Ordinariness vs. strangeness
- The amount of time devoted to the character
- The character's potential for making meaningful choices
- Other characters' focus on him
- The character's frequency of appearance
- The character's degree of involvement in the action
- Readers' sympathy for the character
- Narration from the character's point of view

As you use these techniques to varying degrees with the many characters in your story, an unconscious ranking of the characters will emerge in the readers' minds, starting with the least important background characters, moving up through the minor characters, to the major characters, and finally to two or three main characters or a single protagonist—the people or person the story is mostly about.

Chances are you won't be fully aware of the hierarchy of characters in your own story—it's almost impossible for a storyteller to have all these techniques completely under conscious control. But if you find that readers seem not to notice a character you think is important, or if a character starts "taking over" the story when you don't want him to, you can use these techniques to adjust the character's relative importance. And when these techniques *are* under your control, you can play your characters the way a harpist plays each string on the harp: a few at a time, for exactly the right balance and harmony.

ORSON SCOTT CARD is the author of the novels *Ender's Game* (Tor Books, 1985), *Ender's Shadow* (Tor Books, 1999), and *Speaker for the Dead* (Tor Books, 1986), which are widely read by adults and younger readers, and are increasingly used in schools. His most recent series, the young adult Pathfinder series and the fantasy Mithermages series, are taking readers in new directions. Besides these and other science fiction novels, Card writes contemporary fiction, biblical novels, the American frontier fantasy series The Tales of Alvin Maker, poetry, and many plays and scripts.

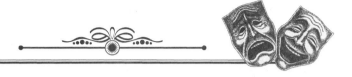

CHAPTER 23

CRAFTING EFFECTIVE SUPPORTING CHARACTERS

BY HALLIE EPHRON

Sir Arthur Conan Doyle gave Sherlock Holmes a full panoply of supporting characters. There was Dr. Watson, the quintessential "sidekick," to act as a sounding board; Scottish landlady Mrs. Hudson, to cook and clean and fuss over Holmes; Scotland Yard Inspector LeStrade, to provide a foil for Holmes' intuitive brilliance, as well as access to official investigations; the Baker Street Irregulars, to ferret out information; and Mycroft Holmes, Sherlock's politically powerful older brother, to provide financial and strategic support. Like Doyle's, your cast of supporting characters should reflect what your protagonist needs.

BALANCING CHARACTER TRAITS

An amateur sleuth needs a friend or relative with access to inside information—a police officer, a private investigator or a crime reporter will fit the bill. A character who's arrogant and full of himself needs a character to keep him from taking himself too seriously, maybe an acerbic co-worker or a mother. You might want to show a hard-boiled police detective's softer side by giving him kids or a pregnant wife.

The most important supporting character in many genres, though, is the sidekick. Virtually every mystery protagonist has one. Rex Stout's obese, lazy, brilliant Nero Wolfe has Archie Goodwin—a slim, wisecracking ladies' man. Carol O'Connell's icy, statuesque, blonde Detective Kathy Mallory has garrulous, overweight, aging, alcoholic

Detective Riker. Robert B. Parker's literate, poetry-quoting Spenser has black, street-smart, tough-talking Hawk. Harlan Coben's former basketball-star-turned-sports-agent, Myron Bolitar, has a rich, blond, preppy friend, Windsor Horne Lockwood, III.

See a pattern? It's the old opposites attract. Protagonists and their sidekicks are a study in contrasts. Sidekicks are the yin to the protagonists' yang. The contrast puts the protagonists' characteristics into relief. For instance, the thickheaded Watson makes Holmes look smarter.

The place to start in creating a sidekick is with the profile you developed of your protagonist, so think about what kind of opposites will work.

TORMENTING YOUR HERO

Every protagonist needs an adversary, too. This is not the villain, but a good-guy character who drives your sleuth nuts, pushes his buttons, torments him, puts obstacles in his path, and is generally a pain in the patoot. It might be an overprotective relative or a know-it-all co-worker. It might be a police officer or detective who "ain't got no respect" for the protagonist. It might be a boss who's a micromanager or a flirt.

For Sherlock Holmes, it's Inspector LeStrade and his disdain for Holmes' investigative techniques. In the same vein, Kathy Reichs' forensic anthropologist Temperance Brennan has a tormentor in the person of Montreal police sergeant Luc Claudel. Their sparring is an ongoing element in her books. In *Monday Mourning*, Brennan finds out Claudel is going to be working with her on the case. She describes him:

> Though a good cop, Luc Claudel has the patience of a firecracker, the sensitivity of Vlad the Impaler, and a persistent skepticism as to the value of forensic anthropology.

Then she adds:

> Snappy dresser, though.

Conflict is the spice that makes characters come alive, and an adversary can cause the protagonist all kinds of interesting problems and complicate your story by throwing up roadblocks to the investigation.

Creating Characters

An adversary may simply be thickheaded—for example, a superior officer who remains stubbornly unconvinced and takes the protagonist off the case. Or an adversary may be deliberately obstructive. For example, a bureaucrat's elected boss might quash an investigation that threatens political cronies, or a senior reporter may fail to pass along information because he doesn't want a junior reporter to get the scoop.

In developing an adversary, remember it should be a character who's positioned to thwart, annoy, and generally get in your protagonist's way. With an adversary in the story, your main character gets lots of opportunity to argue, struggle, and in general show his mettle and ingenuity.

Fleshing Out the Supporting Cast

A supporting character can be anyone in your sleuth's life: a relative, a friend, a neighbor, a co-worker, a professional colleague; the local librarian, waitress, town mayor; even a pet pooch. A supporting character may get ensnared in the plot and land in moral peril, or even take a turn as a suspect. In a series, supporting characters return from book to book and can have ongoing stories of their own.

Supporting characters come with baggage, so pick yours carefully. If you give your protagonist young kids, you'll have to deal with arranging for child care. A significant other? Be prepared to handle the inevitable attraction to that sexy suspect. A pet Saint Bernard? Beware, he'll have to be walked. Twice a day.

Supporting characters give your character a life, but each one should also play a special role in the story. Supporting characters might start out as stereotypes: a devoted wife, a nagging mother-in-law, a bumbling assistant, a macho cop or a slimy lawyer. It's OK to typecast supporting characters during the planning phase. When you get into the writing, if you want them to play bigger roles, you'll want to push past the stereotype and flesh them out, turning them into complex characters who do things that surprise you—and, in turn, the reader.

As a general rule, remember: You don't want supporting characters to hog the spotlight, but bland and uninteresting characters shouldn't be clogging up your story, either.

NAMING SUPPORTING CHARACTERS

Give each supporting character a name to match the persona, and be careful to pick names that help the reader remember who's who.

Nicknames are easy to remember, especially when they provide a snapshot reminder of the character's personality (Spike, Godiva, or Flash) or appearance (Red, Curly, or Smokey). Throwing in some ethnicity makes a character's name easy to remember, too (Zito, Sasha, or Kwan). Avoid the dull and boring (Bob Miller) as well as the weirdly exotic (Dacron).

It's not easy for readers to keep all your characters straight, so help them out. Don't give a character two first names like William Thomas, Stanley Raymond, or Susan Frances. Vary the number of syllables in character names—it's harder to confuse a Jane with a Stephanie than it is to confuse a Bob with a Hank. Pick names that don't sound alike or start with the same letter. If your protagonist's sister is Leanna, don't name her best friend Lillian or Dana.

Create a list of names that you consider "keepers," and add to it whenever you find a new one you like.

INTRODUCING MINOR CHARACTERS

Minor characters should make an impression when they come on the scene, just not a big splash. Here's an example from *Devices and Desires* by P.D. James. With a flash of description, action, and dialogue, Manny Cummings makes his debut:

> The door was already closing when he heard running footsteps and a cheerful shout, and Manny Cummings leapt in, just avoiding the bite of the closing steel. As always he seemed to whirl in a vortex of almost oppressive energy, too powerful to be contained by the lift's four walls. He was brandishing a brown envelope. "Glad I caught you, Adam. It is Norfolk you're escaping to, isn't it? If the Norfolk CID do lay their hands on the Whistler, take a look at him for me, will you, check he isn't our chap in Battersea."

Is Manny tall or short? Fat or thin? Balding or sporting a crew cut? Who knows and who cares. It's what he does that counts: He leaps into the elevator, arriving like a whirlwind, delivers three lines of dialogue with a hint of an Irish brogue, and gives the protagonist an all-important brown envelope that pushes the plot along.

A minor role is no place for a complex character. Don't imbue one with a lot of mystery that your reader will expect you to explain. A name, a few quirky details, and a bit of action or dialogue are more effective than a long, drawn-out description.

ADDING AUTHENTICITY

Remember that the world of your novel will also be full of walk-on characters who provide texture and realism. Each one may also have some small role in facilitating the plot, but for the most part, walk-on characters are there to make scenes feel authentic. Your protagonist takes a stroll, the street needs pedestrians; she goes to the bank to withdraw money, the bank needs bank tellers and security guards; and so on with hotel clerks, waitresses, salesmen and all the rest.

When crafting your more important minor characters, don't get carried away and forget that walk-ons should get no more than a sentence or two of introduction. They don't need names, and a touch of description is plenty. Choose details that can be a kind of shorthand commentary on the neighborhood or context. Maybe the playground skateboarder is dressed in baggies and a Rasta hat. Or perhaps a PTA mother has a four-carat rock on her finger.

Used in this way, walk-ons remain as much elements of setting as they are characters—and that setting will be a fitting backdrop to help both your protagonist and your more important supporting characters stand out.

HALLIE EPHRON is the best-selling, award-winning author of nine novels and *Writing and Selling Your Mystery Novel: How to Knock 'Em Dead with Style* (Writer's Digest Books, 2005).

PART VII

CONFLICT

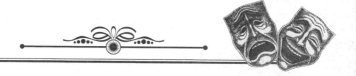

CHAPTER 24

A CHARACTER'S EMOTIONAL THREAD

BY JORDAN E. ROSENFELD

While all people undergo some change in life, characters in fiction have a dramatic imperative to change in order to give meaning to the narrative they star in. These transformations, however, can't happen all at once, or too easily. The reader tends to be suspicious when a character starts out mean and becomes kind too quickly, for example. So how can you change your characters in ways that lend credibility to each scene and feel authentic in the course of your narrative? Gradually.

Though each narrative has its own variation on shape and structure, it is helpful to think of breaking your novel or story into three parts (or you can use the theatrical term *acts* if you like). Doing so allows you to step back and really watch as your characters grow and change over the course of your narrative, all the while creating a satisfying arc for the reader. Let's focus on the beginning act of your narrative.

EARLY SCENES

The first third of your narrative is all about establishing the nuts and bolts of characters and their basic conflicts and plot problems, and setting in motion all the seeds for conflict and challenges to come. In these opening scenes, the reader is meeting your characters just as if they were new guests over for dinner. Their words, actions, and reactions to other people will all serve as introductions, and these first impressions will be remembered and will set the stage for their behavior deeper into the book. We'll now look at the ways you can establish information and set up your characters for change in the first third of your narrative.

Establishing Character-Related Plot Threads

While you establish that your protagonist is a smack-talking hooligan with seductive eyes and a mop of brown curls, or a lonely librarian who reads mystery novels and winds up investigating an actual crime, to use this first section of your narrative, you also need to establish:

- **INVOLVEMENT:** What is your protagonist's relationship to the events of the significant situation? Is the event his fault, centered around him in some way; did he accidentally stumble into it; or is he integral to it?
- **THE STAKES:** What he stands to lose or gain as a result of the above-mentioned events will create necessary tension and drama.
- **DESIRES:** What he desires, from material goods to deep and abiding love, will inform the stakes and his intentions.
- **FEARS:** What he fears, from bodily harm to not obtaining his desire, will also inform the stakes.
- **MOTIVATION:** What reasons does he have to act upon the events of the significant situation? What is he driven by?
- **CHALLENGES:** How does the significant situation challenge his life, views, status, other people, his status quo, needs, etc.?

We'll walk through these points using excerpts of early scenes from the first part of the novel *House of Sand and Fog* by Andre Dubus III.

Involvement

Co-protagonist Kathy Nicolo (married name Lazaro) is a cleaning woman whose self-absorbed husband divorced her eight months ago. Since then, her life has been a wreck: Financially, she just scrapes by, and her stability as a recovered alcoholic and addict is severely tested. The only material thing of significance to her is the house she inherited from her father, where she lives.

How is she involved in the significant situation? In the first scene she wakes up to find a locksmith and a cop at her door with a notice of eviction for back taxes—an erroneous notice at that. It doesn't matter; until she can prove in court that she has done nothing wrong, they have the right to evict her, and they do. Kathy loses her house and must go live in a motel while she sorts things out. In the time it takes her to get a lawyer, her house goes up for auction and is purchased by co-protagonist Colonel Behrani, a once wealthy man from Iran who is now a struggling immigrant with iron pride.

For simplicity's sake, I'm going to focus on Kathy's storyline, though Dubus does a thorough job of developing both characters fully and weaving their stories together seamlessly.

It's pretty clear what Kathy's relationship to the significant situation is: She's been evicted from her house. Though Kathy claims it's a mistake, the reader doesn't have enough evidence yet to know if this is true. She seems volatile, and the reader isn't sure if she's trustworthy; she *could* be the kind of woman who might fail to pay taxes:

> "That's all right 'cause I'm not leaving." My throat felt dry and stiff.
> The locksmith looked up from his work on my back door.
> Deputy Burdon rested one hand on the countertop, and he had an understanding expression on his face, but I hated him anyway. "I'm afraid you have no choice, Mrs. Lazaro. All your things will be auctioned off with the property. Do you want that?"
> "*Look, I inherited* this house from my father, it's paid for. You can't evict me!" My eyes filled up and the men began to blur. "I never *owed* a fucking business tax. You have no right to do this."

The Stakes

The stakes are pretty clear: Without her house, she's got nowhere to go but to a motel, and on her small income, even that expense is a big one—Kathy could wind up in dire straits pretty quick. This evokes some sympathy for the woman, even though the reader doesn't really know who she is yet. Your stakes must be equally clear to the reader; don't make the reader guess. Remember to:

- Show what the protagonist has to gain
- Show what the protagonist stands to lose

Let the reader see in the scenes from the first part exactly what is at stake for your protagonist. Does he stand to be kicked out of his tribe if he speaks his mind; lose his worldly possessions if he loses his job; lose his child visitation rights if he can't pay child support? These questions and their answers must be enacted in scenes in the first part of your narrative.

Desires

Next, through passages of interior monologue, the reader gets a peek into Kathy's desires, which center mostly on her relationships. She remembers the few rare good times before her husband Nick left her; she reflects on the days with her first husband, Donnie, when she was barely an adult and became addicted to cocaine. The reader feels her palpable loneliness—she's so lonely that even the bad memories are a comfort to her. Because of her desire for love, when Lester Burdon, the deputy who first came to evict her, shows up to check on her, even though he helped facilitate her current unhappy state, her desire makes it plausible that she takes to him:

> "I thought I'd check on you, see how you're holding up."
>
> He sounded like he meant it, and he seemed even softer than the day before when he'd led those men in kicking me out of my house. When we got to his car, a Toyota station wagon parked at the edge of the lot near the chain-link fence, I kind of hoped he'd keep talking; Connie Walsh was the first person I'd had a real conversation with in over eight months, and that was more of an interrogation than a talk. I wanted one, even with a sheriff's deputy in the fog.

Kathy's pressing desire to be loved will get her into a lot of trouble later on in the narrative. Her other, more immediate desire, which will drive her actions in much of the rest of the narrative, is more straightforward: to get her house back.

Desires will come in many shapes in your narrative and can be expressed or shown:

Creating Characters

- In dialogue between characters
- In the form of thoughts (interior monologue), as in the previous example
- In subtle actions—your protagonists may simply take (or try to take) what they desire

What matters is that the reader has a feeling for what these desires are, straight away. Desires and motivations fuel a character's intentions in every scene; they help give purpose to the character's actions, so you'll want to make them as clear as possible.

Fears

Kathy's fears are a bit less direct, but they are there in the subtext of the scenes. The reader knows that she is a recovering addict of both drugs and alcohol, with a penchant for men who like to be in control of her. This tells the reader that Kathy is not a person with high self-esteem, nor is she someone who feels particularly in control of her own life. The reader sees that she is someone who prefers dependence on others over independence and that the act of being out of her house throws her whole life into chaos. Kathy is afraid to be alone and afraid to be an adult in the world, to take responsibility for herself. These fears will get her into trouble in the middle of this novel.

Your protagonist should have some kind of fear, whether it is a rational one like the fear of fire, or an irrational one, like a fear of butterflies or of the color yellow, because those innocuous things trigger memories of terrible experiences. No character should be too brave—even heroes have weaknesses. Establish what your character is afraid of early on, because in the middle of the narrative you're going to exploit those fears.

You can establish fear:

- Through speech (for instance, he can admit to a friend that he is "terrified of spiders")
- Through behavior (your protagonist, upon seeing a passenger jet overhead, hits the dirt like he is about to be bombed)

- Through a flashback scene in which the reader sees that the protagonist was traumatized by a specific event

Fear is as much a part of your protagonist's motivations as desire, and it is through fear and desire that you exert change on your characters.

Motivation

Kathy's surface motivation is pretty clear: She's motivated to get her house back because it's all she has, and she sees it as the cornerstone of her ability to live a stable life. This motivation leads her to get legal aid and fight to get her house back. But Kathy is also motivated by older, deeper issues regarding her family and her relationship to her parents. These motivations are the ones that cause her to get involved with Lester Burdon, a married man and a cop; these motivations also cause her to become volatile and enraged at Colonel Behrani, who has her house; and they begin to set the stage for the drama that unfolds in the second part of the narrative.

Your protagonist's motivations will be clear to the reader so long as you:

- Make it clear what the protagonist's desires are
- Make it clear what the protagonist's fears are
- Offer opportunities to thwart the desires and trigger the fears

Motivations—which stem directly from your protagonist's fears and desires—are the foundation of scene intentions. Once you know how your protagonist is motivated, and by what forces, then you can direct him to act in every scene in a way appropriate to the circumstances of your plot.

Challenges

Kathy's challenges are myriad. She lacks money and resources; she has a weakness for using alcohol to drown her feelings; she is attracted to men who are bad for her; and she is literally challenged by Colonel Behrani's takeover of her home.

Creating Characters

Challenges are the situations in which you thwart your protagonist's desires and trigger his fears, and they are good and necessary. The more of them you can comfortably create—that is, the more you can create that pertain to your plot and make sense to the character—the better, because they generate a sense of urgency and concern in your reader. In the first part of your narrative, your job is to set up which intentions are going to be opposed and thus lead the way to the middle part, where these intentions will meet with greater opposition and create more conflict.

Assessing Your Character

The scenes in the first part are all about potential conflict. You want to ask yourself, have I destabilized my protagonist, given him problems and conflicts that begin to worry both him and the reader? Has my protagonist been directly involved in a significant situation that has brought initial conflict and challenges? Make sure that by the end of the first part, your protagonist is showing signs that he feels tested, forced into action, and driven toward change. Nothing should yet be too conclusive, too fixed in stone, because if it is, the reader has little motivation to keep reading.

....

JORDAN E. ROSENFELD (www.jordanrosenfeld.net) is author of the suspense novels *Night Oracle* and *Forged in Grace*, and the writing guides *Make a Scene* (Writer's Digest Books, 2008) and *Write Free*, with Rebecca Lawton (Kulupi Press, 2008). Her two forthcoming books from Writer's Digest Books are *A Writer's Guide to Persistence* and *Deep Scenes*, with Martha Alderson.

CHAPTER 25

PUSH YOUR CHARACTER TO THE LIMITS

BY DAVID CORBETT

Most of us at some point in our reading lives have come upon a scene where one of the characters does something so odd it doesn't just defy expectation, it stops us cold.

We're not pleasantly intrigued, we're baffled—or annoyed. The dreamlike illusion we've enjoyed up to that point has been ruptured not in some Brechtian breach of the fourth wall, but through plain bad writing. We scratch our heads, thinking: *The character just wouldn't do that.*

As writers, we don't ever want our readers to feel that kind of disconnect—but that doesn't mean our characters should be neatly and easily defined, either. Pushing our characters to their limits, in fact, is what makes for compelling fiction.

So how, then, can we determine the limits of what's believable in how a character behaves?

CHARACTER IN CONTEXT

In life, when someone we know acts "out of character," the subtext is almost always: *Something must be wrong.* The strange behavior, we assume, must be the result of some strain of which we're unaware.

Sometimes we learn the person has a health problem. Sometimes we learn he was under the influence. The intoxicant may be drink or drugs, the pressure of fear or the rush of love (or some other kind of rapture), but the result is the compromise of the person's inhibitions.

In the most unsettling cases, we come to realize we don't know the person as well as we thought. The behavior we found puzzling resulted from an aspect of personality we simply didn't know, recognize, or understand. (This kind of revelation isn't limited to others. You may even have shocked yourself on occasion, behaving in a way that made you think: *Where the heck did that come from?*) One great advantage reality has over fiction is that it doesn't have to make sense. It just happens. In the case of real people, there's no stopping the movement of time to say: *I don't buy that.*

The great challenge of fiction is creating characters who feel logically, emotionally, and psychologically consistent—who make sense—but retain the enigmatic power to surprise.

It should come as no shock that the trick is to learn from real life.

Just like their real-world avatars, characters who defy our expectations are almost always either:

- Under a strain
- Feeling free of some customary inhibition
- Revealing something about themselves that had previously been hidden

Put otherwise, the key factor in the seemingly strange behavior is normally one of the following:

- Conflict
- Permission
- Deceit/Disclosure

Conflict: I Wouldn't Do This If I Didn't Have To

When the principal motivator for the unexpected act is conflict, the character enters the scene with a strong desire and a plan for achieving it, only to run smack into an equal—or overpowering—counterforce. As the character learns his plan is insufficient, ill-conceived, even ridiculous, he tosses aside this element or that—or pitches the whole thing overboard—and is forced to adapt and improvise.

The limits of what the character can do in the service of improvisation are defined first by the parameters of her mental and emotional makeup. But those parameters acquire elasticity depending on the depth of the character's desire, the ferocity of the opposition, and the stakes.

For example, in the film *Three Days of the Condor*, Joseph Turner (Robert Redford) is a mild-mannered analyst. But when he returns from lunch one day to discover his co-workers murdered, he kidnaps Kathy Hale (Faye Dunaway) as he tries to find a safe place to regroup. Turner's not "the kind of guy" who under any other circumstances would abduct a woman. But his behavior is believable because his adversaries are ruthless. He's not acting as he *might*; he's acting as he *must*. And the real key to the credibility of his otherwise out-of-character behavior is that he himself acknowledges the abnormality of what he's doing.

Likewise, in Tennessee Williams' *A Streetcar Named Desire*, Blanche DuBois is desperate to find not just a resting place but a home with her sister, Stella. It becomes obvious, however, that Stella's heart and home now belong to her husband. Blanche struggles harder and harder to get Stella to come out and say it—"my home is your home"— using flattery, nostalgia, guilt, sisterly simpatico, humor, but her efforts continue to fail. Finally, there's nothing to do but something wildly out of character; Blanche tells her sister the unvarnished truth: "You're all I've got in the world." But, being Blanche, she can't help but add a little manipulative dig: "And you're not glad to see me."

These scenes work because the characters don't improvise wildly; they start with the familiar, using tactics they know well. The level of strangeness rises in sync with their desperation as the conflicts build and those tried-and-true methods fail.

The scenes also succeed because on some level the characters express or recognize the unusualness of what they're doing. Turner apologizes. Blanche quickly reverts to form.

Permission: As Long As You Say It's Okay

Drink doesn't just steady the nerves. It grants the drinker tacit permission to let her inhibitions down, act as she pleases, and say what she feels. And the "uncharacteristic" behavior is usually something that, when the person is sober, is kept under wraps.

Returning to *Streetcar*: For Blanche, drink isn't just an intoxicant, it's an indulgent friend who assures her it's all right. She can return to her fantasy world of romance and mystery and forget the scandalous realities that have rendered her homeless, penniless, and the subject of scorn.

Looked at more broadly, the role of permission reveals how much we frame our conduct around our circumstances. Propriety, duty, conformity, habit—they limit what we believe we're allowed to do or say. But then we go on holiday—wherever, however—and the rules of gravity no longer apply.

In the film *Rachel, Rachel*, Rachel Cameron (Joanne Woodward) is a middle-aged spinster in a small Connecticut town. She lives wrapped in a straightjacket of righteous conformity—until a man shows up and she falls in love. She takes her holiday right there at home, finally letting herself feel the pleasure she's been denying herself for decades.

Here the issue isn't adaptation in the face of *present* conflict. It's exploration or discovery of a suppressed, unsettling, or even dangerous side of the personality that's been there all along, just unexpressed. But that raises the question of *why* it's been unexpressed, and the answer often leads us to *past* conflict.

You won't know how far you can push a character's liberated feelings without exploring her backstory: Why has this side of her personality been denied? When was the last time she demonstrated it? What happened? Who in the character's past enforced that prohibition? In answering such questions, envision a crucial scene: a self-absorbed parent ignoring a long-anticipated performance; a judgmental teacher launching into a tirade over an innocent mistake; a so-called friend mocking the latest love interest. Let that one vivid scene stand for a history of abuse, neglect, or being shut down.

And when the suppressed behavior at last finds expression, keep that internal naysayer in mind. As when faced with present conflict, the character might not suddenly leap from the familiar to the unrecognizable in one reckless bound, but instead experiment, her boldness growing with her confidence. Then again, the behavior she's kept under wraps may escape with explosive force, as though to destroy the image of that person who, for years, has been saying over and over with insidious force: *no*.

Deceit/Disclosure: That Wasn't Really Me

Here the inexplicable conduct hasn't been repressed—it's been deliberately hidden. Of the three types of surprise behavior we've covered, this one lends itself best to a sudden, big reveal. It's also the easiest and most straightforward to portray.

In *The Scarlet Pimpernel*, Marguerite St. Just is baffled by what's become of the brave, charming man she married. Sir Percy Blakeney has become a parody of himself, playing the part of the slow-witted dandy. Ultimately Marguerite discovers the foppery is a disguise, intended to conceal Sir Percy's role as the leader of a band of noblemen dedicated to saving the lives of aristocrats facing death under the Reign of Terror.

In Daphne du Maurier's *Rebecca*, the gentile Maxim de Winter erupts in inexplicable bursts of caustic temper that take on such a menacing aspect that he seems increasingly likely to crack apart. In the story's crucial revelation, he at last confesses why this is—his wife Rebecca's death wasn't an accident after all.

Once we know the puzzling behavior results from something that has been concealed, we accept it readily, unless for some other reason it feels unbelievable. The paraplegic may very well get up and dance, but if he does, it better be magic or deception at play. Anything else is just bad writing.

If I Did This More Often I'd Be Better At It

Regardless of what's prompting your character to reach her limits, strange behavior shouldn't come easily. Characters who demonstrate instant skill or comfort with something they've never tried before reside largely in the realm of shlock. The less familiar the behavior, the clumsier and more uncomfortable it should be. Trying anything out of the ordinary means complication, difficulty, intensified focus. Portray that in your scenes, and you'll increase tension, enhance suspense, and intensify reader empathy.

THE ROLE OF CONTRADICTIONS

What much of the behavior we're discussing exemplifies is the capacity of human beings to be contradictory.

Simply stated, a contradiction is something about a person that piques our interest because it betrays what we expect, given what else we know or observe about him.

Once you train your eye to look for contradictions, they crop up virtually everywhere, expressing a paradox of human nature: that people do one thing *and* exactly the opposite; they're this but they're also that.

In Jungian psychology, this largely unexplored, contradictory aspect of the personality is referred to as the Shadow. Psychic wholeness requires integrating into the conscious personality the nebulous traits embodied in the Shadow, and a great many stories are premised on exactly that kind of self-realization.

That said, some of the contradictions that prove useful in characterization are not psychological at all, but physical: the bully's squeaky voice, the ballerina's chubby knees. But the most interesting contradictions always reflect something internal, even dispositional: A man is both garrulous and shy, outgoing but suspicious, brutal but childlike. Omar Little from the TV show *The Wire* isn't just a shotgun-toting vigilante; he's also an openly gay man who treats his lovers with startling affection and tenderness. The effect: We never know which half of the personality will assert itself in any given situation. That's suspense—the best kind.

Some contradictions are behavioral: We feel divided—optimistic and yet wary, accepting and yet guarded. Other contradictions reflect the need to act properly in a variety of contrasting social situations: the dinner table, the office, the stadium, the chapel, the bedroom. We feel differing degrees of freedom to "be ourselves" in each of these environments, depending on who else is present.

Beyond purposes of verisimilitude, contradictions serve two key dramatic purposes:

1. They defy expectation and thus pique our interest.
2. They provide a straightforward method for depicting complexity and depth. Specifically they provide a means to portray:
   - Subtext (the tension between the expressed and the unexpressed, the visible and the concealed)
   - The situational subtleties of social life ("I must be many things to many people")
   - The conflict between conscious and unconscious behavior
   - Suspense (we want to know what the contradiction means, why it's there)

But again, there are limits to what is credible. Contradictions that seem implausible may enhance a comedic portrayal—the mob boss with the Yorkie, the cop who's terrified of cats, the chain-smoking nun—but they can undermine a dramatic one, if handled carelessly. Ask whether the contradiction draws you, the writer, toward the character, or permits you an emotional distance. If the latter, you're "looking at" the character rather than emotionally engaging with her, and the characteristic you're considering is likely not working. If you can justify the contradiction, root it in backstory, and unearth scenes from your imagination that reveal how this character developed these seemingly irreconcilable inclinations, it will become less conceptual, more intuitive and organic.

EMOTION, INTUITION, AND TRUST

The temptation when writing scenes in which characters do the unexpected is to stop and explain what just happened. Many writers think, not without some merit, that to leave things incomplete, ambiguous, or untidy is just sloppiness. Though there's much to admire in this sort of rigor, in the realm of characterization it's sadly misplaced.

Where rigor is necessary is in how vividly, creatively, and comprehensively we conceive our characters. We don't get to know someone new through a recitation of biological data; we get to know her through interacting with her—especially during emotional or demanding times. So, too, we get to know a character by engaging with her in meaningful scenes that reveal the most significant aspects of her life: her wants and contradictions and secrets and wounds, her attachment to friends and family and her fear of her enemies, her schooling and sense of home, her loves and hatreds, her shame and pride and guilt and sense of joy. As important as a character's choices and motivations are in any scene—what she does and why—they don't exist in a vacuum.

This way of understanding the character—relying on emotionally significant scenes, not information—allows us to engage with the character on the level of intuition, not intellect. This permits us to envision our characters clearly and to feel as though we're in dialogue with them, observing them as we observe a dream—not controlling them like marionettes. And it's precisely "plot puppets" that most routinely exhibit traits that feel "out of character."

Readers shouldn't be vexed by a character's behavior, but they should never feel entirely comfortable, either, or they'll be several steps ahead of the story at every turn.

Explaining your character kills her. Whatever she does, the reader or audience needs to feel her actions arise not from some single, explainable source but from the whole of her personality. And the deeper you understand that whole, the more likely you'll be able to portray convincingly the unexpected in her behavior.

So where is that fine line between being puzzled by behavior and finding it contrived? The answer lies in letting the behavior emerge *from the character*, not the writer. We need to create enough of a vivid intuition of a character that the possibility for real, unpredictable, unpremeditated action *on the character's part* seems credible. And this requires envisioning the character in emotionally demanding scenes, filled with conflict, pathos, and risk. In the end, it's not so much a question of how far the character will go, but how thoroughly you're willing to connect with her.

....

DAVID CORBETT (www.davidcorbett.com) is the award-winning author of the instructional title *The Art of Character* (Penguin Books, 2013), and his fifth novel, *Save by an Evil Chance*, is scheduled for an April 2015 release. Corbett's short fiction has appeared twice in *Best American Mystery Stories*; his nonfiction work has appeared in *The New York Times*, *Narrative*, and other publications. He's taught at the UCLA Extension's Writer's Program, LitReactor, Book Passage, and at conferences across North America.

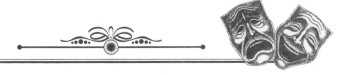

CHAPTER 26

CHARACTER OBJECTIVE AND CONFLICT

BY MARY KOLE

A reader, whether he knows it or not, is picking up a book with the following request in mind: *Make me care.* That's my mantra every time I approach the slush and shelves, too. The best way to accomplish this is to introduce not only a great character but a character with objectives and motivations. Then imbue the character's life with enough conflict, both internal and external, to really get the story engine humming.

We root for people in life when we know their desires and goals. Will they persevere (like we want to with our own goals)? Will they fail (like we're afraid to)? We start to care once we see a person in trouble. This empathy is an important bond to create between reader and character, and you should do it as early as possible.

OBJECTIVE, MOTIVATION, AND ACTION

Objective, motivation, and action are all sides of the same pyramid. One is the desire, the other is the foundation below it, and the third serves the other two.

OBJECTIVE: A character's main goal in life, whether it's a thing (the One Ring), a person (Juliet), or a value that springs from her personality or code of right and wrong (justice for all). A character can have many objectives, but you should always know the overarching goal she's striving toward. Characters can have objectives from moment to moment, scene to scene, and over the course of the novel.

MOTIVATION: I won't care much if you simply tell me what a person wants. Deep-seated personal drivers don't spring out of nowhere. As a reader (and an agent), I'm always asking: Why? Why does she want this? Why did he get this way? Motivation is usually explored in backstory, but whether it ends up explicitly on the page or not, the reader must get below-the-surface insight into a character's objectives.

ACTION: Once your character is motivated by a goal, he acts toward it. I was a theater major, so I hope you'll allow me a digression. In acting theory, your motivation is expressed in the actions you take. For example, Blanche and Stanley are fighting in *A Streetcar Named Desire* by Tennessee Williams. The audience sees one scene, but Stanley first begs, then demands, then grovels to try and get through to Blanche. His objective is the same (get her to stay), but like a rat in a maze, he tries different avenues to achieve his goal. Keep this in mind for later.

Because life is never simple, objectives and motivations must be complex. It's not enough to galvanize a character to action with one simple goal, nor is it sufficient to explain a strong objective with one easy motivation. (For example, "He was hit by a falling tree as a kid so he became a lumberjack in a twisted revenge ploy.")

We must *always* know what your characters want (each and every one of them) when we see them in a scene together. Outline a character's objectives and motivations, and then reinforce them constantly for the reader with actions. I should be able to open the book to any page in your manuscript and intuit exactly what the characters' objectives are on that page, in that scene, in that chapter.

Once a character stops striving, we stop caring, and action loses meaning. Every choice a character makes and everything she does should have bearing on her goal. But it doesn't always have to be linear. Sometimes a character has to make a sacrifice that gets him further away from his objective. Sometimes she's frustrated and does something completely counterproductive. Those instances are always interesting from a character standpoint, but they always have one thing in common: The goal is never out of sight, even if it's taunting your protagonist from the rearview mirror.

Think also about your protagonist's self-doubt after a big decision; his surprise when he doesn't get or, better yet, achieves his objective. What is he thinking in the moment something happens to bring him closer or further from his goal? Let him stumble on his path toward objectives and make mistakes. What does he learn? How does he deal with the ramifications? We get to know a character via his actions and reactions.

It's also important to remember the shadowy, hidden side of objectives. The truth is, we don't always want what's good for us. What dark dreams does your character have?

Finally, most humans are not open books. If we were, both therapists and self-help gurus would be out of a job. We don't always know exactly what we want, why we want it, or how to express it. Here we come to the unconscious objective. For some people, it's to love and be loved by others. For others, it's to be accepted by their peers at any cost.

Characters struggling with unconscious objectives shouldn't be able to articulate them. But those deep desires are something that you, the writer, must absolutely think about. Readers should know what a character's driving conscious goal is, and also have a sense of the unconscious machinery or more basic human need operating underneath it all. And remember, make this but one complex part of your character and never state it outright. It is a rare person who walks around saying, "I just need love," and so your characters shouldn't either.

A CHARACTER IN CONFLICT

Another piece of the characterization puzzle is conflict. There are two kinds of conflict: internal and external. Internal is what's going on in the character's mental life (self-confidence issues, fitting in, depression, etc.), external is the character's friction with relationships and the larger universe of your novel (me versus people, me versus the world).

INTERNAL CONFLICT: The issues that a character has swirling in his head about his identity and his life in general at any one moment.

This is often in reaction to events happening in the outside world. Other times, internal conflict exists in the character's head alone. Good sources of internal conflict can be: loneliness, self-consciousness, lingering heartbreak, fear of failure, etc.

EXTERNAL CONFLICT: There are two levels of external conflict, the interpersonal and the societal. Interpersonal conflict can be a fight with a loved one, problems within a family, losing a job, an argument at work, etc. Societal conflict happens on a grand scale. In a dystopian society, for example, the protagonist is in conflict with the government or ruling class. Flu epidemics, famine, an authoritative regime, prevalent racism, an economic downturn, etc., are all examples of societal conflict.

Both internal and external conflict need to be present, fresh, relatable, and compelling enough to keep a reader's attention. And our access to conflict, especially in terms of how much it affects a character, is through interiority.

You can spend weeks thinking up many layers of delicious conflict for your characters. Just know that a balance between internal and external conflict should be apparent from the first page. We don't want to read about a character who has achieved perfect Zen peace of mind. Fiction runs on friction and trouble.

BALANCING INTERNAL AND EXTERNAL CONFLICT

In fiction, I'm always harping on writers to add more conflict, more stakes, more tension. But there must *always* be a reason behind the angst.

Conflict without the proper motivation is melodrama. And nobody wants to read about a whiner. Make sure that every bit of conflict you write stems from somewhere—that it isn't just conflict for conflict's sake.

And keep in mind that internal conflict isn't enough. As we already know, if you had an entire manuscript of a teen sitting in his room, thinking about all the things that suck in his life, it would be dead in the water. (Lots of writers have tried this and I hope I can save you the trouble.)

You need to imbue your work with external conflict, too. That means friction with other people and with the world at large. You should include this latter layer even if you're not writing a dystopian novel or one that takes place in an otherwise fractured world. Probably no one in the world is truly happy with every facet of society. You don't have to dwell here, but societal conflict is always a good layer to add to your story.

REVEALING OBJECTIVE:

What does your character want and why? What would he give up for what they want? What would he die for? What impossible thing does he crave? What is his most secret longing? What is his version of a perfect world? On the flip side, what is something he wants that he probably shouldn't? Articulate these. Next to each one, write one example of how this objective manifests itself in action. For example, "She wants a sense of home more than anything else . . . so she crawls into bed with her foster parents every night."

REVEALING MOTIVATION: Think of as many reasons or details as you can for each objective and why your character wants what she wants.

CONFRONTING CHANGES: How does your character come to terms with himself after an emotional transition, difficult decision, or mistake? How might his reactions be surprising or unexpected? What are some of the events you're planning in your manuscript that will throw him for a loop of internal conflict?

CONFRONTING FAILURE: What is holding your character back? What is the scene where she tries to confront it? How can she fail? How does she eventually either blow past this obstacle or make peace with it? These are emotions you can harness when building conflict.

ME VERSUS THE WORLD: What is broken or otherwise wrong with society (in your character's estimation)? Why is this a problem for him? How can you bring your character into contact with the source of his tension? Write out how he reacts to society's ills in this moment; try to imagine what you can reveal about his true self here.

CREATING CHARACTERIZING DETAILS AND MULTIDIMENSIONAL CHARACTERS

Some novel details are more important than others, especially when it comes to characters. Certain pieces of information, known as characterizing details, not only give readers facts, they do double duty to teach them about character.

CHARACTERIZING DETAIL: A multilayered piece of information or action that teaches us something deep-seated about a character. For example, that your protagonist has red hair is *not* a characterizing detail. It is part of the set dressing and rather arbitrary. However, if your character drops a cookie, waits longer than five seconds, picks it up and eats it anyway, that not only adds situational humor to your story, it also shows us things about your character that speak to her other traits: Her love of cookies, her tolerance for ick factor, etc. Great characterizing details work on multiple levels.

Writers are often confused about what counts as a characterizing detail, but I wouldn't spend my attention on labels. As long as you understand the concept and use it, you don't have to go through your manuscript and categorize every description and action (unless this helps you nail the idea, of course).

Here's why characterizing details are important: They show us things about the character that contribute to our understanding of him. In the example of a character who eats food from the floor, we may not use that information right away, but we will remember it. If that writer has done his job, this knowledge will come into play at some point down the line.

Characterizing details are always deliberate, mostly delivered through action, and are the ultimate in fictional economy: They accomplish more than one thing with just one sentence or thought.

The best characterizing details are also specific. Compare "She didn't mind germs," to "She waited a whole seven-point-five seconds before picking up the cookie and stuffing it in her mouth."

Often they are also relatable. I love those moments in fiction when it feels like an author has reached inside my mind and put one of my private thoughts or actions on the page. I've often waited a questionable amount of time before picking up dropped food and eating it. But I'm embarrassed about it and try to get it over quickly. If I were to read, "She waited to make sure nobody was looking, checked once more over her shoulder, then dove for the cookie," I'd get chills of recognition up my spine.

So strive to really make your characterizing details revelatory of deeper character traits (working one level below the surface), specific, and true to life. The reader will pick up on these nuggets of information without fail.

STANDOUT CHARACTERS

I'm often surprised by how little it takes to make a character stand out or to render a larger-than-life personality. The writers who spend pages and pages outlining every detail of a character's room or locker or closet, on describing every freckle and pierced ear, are missing the point.

It's not about how much information you give us, it's about the quality of your information, and how much work it's doing on your behalf.

For example, you don't need to pile a quirky or over-the-top character with every idiosyncrasy in the book like they're some demented ice cream sundae. You can do more with so much less. Instead of dressing a drama geek in striped tights *and* Dr. Martens boots *and* a steampunk hat *and* a harajuku jacket from Japan, give us one memorable and specific detail that hints at a world of eccentricity: He carries a 1960s paisley print valise to school instead of a backpack. Now we know that we're dealing with an "old soul" type of oddball, and you didn't just exhaust yourself.

As with imagery, I'd rather have one dynamite characterizing detail than three perfectly okay descriptions. Include only what's going to catch in your reader's memory. (Hint: It's probably one of the first things you thought of when creating this character, and the detail that keeps sticking in mind.) Trim the fat and really ask yourself whether what you're describing speaks to the deeper core of your fictional person or it's just window dressing.

If you're stuck on nailing specific details, get outside of your imagination. Interview real people who've shared a situation with your characters. You shouldn't make up every single thing in your book, and sometimes you *can't* know everything. Should you feel stuck, interview people who know something about the situation you're writing about.

Track down some people who you can interview and get out of your own head. It's often energizing to learn some specific details that you never could've invented on your own. After all, specificity will help your reader suspend disbelief and buy more deeply into your story and characters.

RELATABILITY AND AWARENESS

Let me circle back to the idea of relatability for a moment. We want characters to grab us because we recognize ourselves in them.

Make sure that you don't polish them up so much that they become lifeless. Characters are all about flaws and quirks. Even if your character strains to be perfect at all times, there's a whole dark underbelly to that pursuit that should taint the shiny outer image.

In terms of relatability, you have to make a big decision: How self-aware is your protagonist? Some people are conscious of everything they do and how it affects the outside world. Others have a looser grasp of action and consequence. Some have a firm grip on their feelings and know what's going on inside their heads at all times. Others surprise themselves with their emotions.

If you haven't already, play with this idea when rendering your characters. Doing so will give them a sense of the realistic, and turn them into people that readers can relate to.

CORE IDENTITY

Characterizing details are bits of information that touches something deeper in your characters than just eye color or espresso-drink preference. Here we'll delve into what you need to know about your characters and their core identities in order to forge a three-dimensional protagonist.

Not all of these things will make it into your final draft, and you shouldn't spell them outright for your readers, but you must know the following about your characters' rich inner lives:

Core Strength

When things get tough, what is it inside your protagonist that gives him the courage or resolve to keep going?

Core Virtue

What does she hold highest in herself and in other people? Does she value loyalty? Love? Honesty? What positive emotion, when practiced, makes your character feel noble or dignified?

Core Role

(An offshoot of the core virtue.) If your character is loyal above all, does he prize his role as friend and confidant? (Question taken to the next level: What happens when he can't play that role for whatever reason?)

Core Flaw

What is the flip side or dark side of your character's strength? Of her favorite virtue? The part of her voice that, when taken to the extreme, isn't admirable anymore?

Core Emotions

What does he love? Need? Fear? Hate? What arouses his strongest primal feelings?

Core Boundaries

In her moral framework, what is right and what is wrong? What are the absolute boundaries that your character will not cross? (Question taken to the next level: What happens if she is forced to the very edge of these boundaries, or maybe even over the edge?)

Core Outlook and Fixed Beliefs

To generalize, Depression-era babies sometimes believe that life is a slog for survival and that basic needs are never guaranteed. People raised in the dot-com generation might believe that they can create their dream career as an entrepreneur without working for a corporation like their parents did. A man with a string of bad relationships might not believe in love anymore. High school sweethearts will tell tales of love at first sight. I could go on and on. What is the world "like" to your character? Is it basically good or basically bad? Is there a higher power involved, whether God, fate, or karma, or are we all running around without supervision? In short, what's the view through your protagonist's unique lens? What are his fixed beliefs about how life works? (Question taken to the next level: What happens if he receives evidence that his beliefs about the world are actually false?)

COMPLEX AT THE CORE

There are shades and reverse sides to everything. That's why I try to ask "next level" questions whenever I think about core character identity. Those will help you brainstorm ideas for plot complications.

The best plot points are those that cause tension between your main character and her identity, that force her into a tough choice, that turn her beliefs on their heads. The best secondary characters and relationships also do this. For example, a character's core principle could be a pro-life stance on abortion . . . until he sees his best friend forced to make a very tough decision about a surprise pregnancy.

Difficult plot points and antagonists that attack your protagonist's core identity also give your characters the room to reexamine their firm values. Humans are never 100 percent consistent. Moral dilemmas and difficult choices are key to deepening a reader's understanding of your fictional people because they may not always act like we expect them to.

For every core principle, imagine what would make your protagonist act out of character. What kind of pressure would make him turn away from his identity? These character twists will then feed into the reader's understanding of the character she *thought* she knew, and make the whole persona that much more complex and fascinating.

If you can create a strong character with a healthy sense of core self, then thrust him through a plot that attacks those pillars of identity and surprise the reader with some of his choices, you will have an amazingly layered protagonist on your hands.

ACTIVE CHARACTERS ALWAYS WORK

One of the biggest issues I see in beginning writers' manuscripts is a character who does not have a firm bedrock to define her. She doesn't know who she is or what she wants (ick!). I have never met a human being, teen or otherwise, who was a complete blank canvas with no driving passions, desires, or beliefs.

Passive characters are those who float through a plot without the forward momentum of strong objectives and motivations, and without the foundation of strong characterization. They're like a lifeless crash-test dummy going through a series of stunts . . . and about as relatable. Thrillers, horror, some paranormal, and some fantasy novels are especially vulnerable to this, because the writer spends more time writing action sequences than giving us a strong hero to root for.

If I don't have a complex character on the page, I won't care about your cool dragon battles. And if your character is completely reactive—just letting the plot wash over him without making any difficult choices or confronting anything about himself—I won't know him nearly as much as I would an active character.

Keep that in mind as you attack the exercises below.

DEFINING CORE IDENTITY: Go back to the questions in the core identity section and spend some time defining those for your character. Don't skimp on this. You will learn things about your protagonist that you never knew, especially when you take some of those questions to the next level.

HEROIC QUALITIES: In what unexpected way can your character be a hero? How? When? Standing up to whom? To help whom? Where does the heroic element fit into her identity?

TOUGH DECISIONS: What is your character's toughest decision in this story? Imagine this for all your characters. How does the character come to it? What are the emotional repercussions? What is a twist you can work here? How does this decision end up defining your character? How does it not? How can you set up a series of decisions that escalate in difficulty as you approach the climax?

THE OUTLYING LAYER: What is one layer to your character's core identity that runs counter to all his other values and beliefs? What are three plot moments in your manuscript when this layer can come to light and guide your character's decisions or actions, for better or for worse?

CHARACTERIZING REACTIONS: What are three moments in your story where a character is confronted with something that touches or, better yet, shakes a part of her core identity? How does she react? Go back to that place and rewrite her responses with these ideas in mind.

PAST, PRESENT, AND FUTURE: You can learn a lot about your characters and discover a lot of potential characterizing details by freewriting from their POV in a stream-of-consciousness style that mimics how our minds really operate. We never exist solely in the present; we are always thinking past, present, and future. It's very difficult indeed to be in the moment. What is a few minutes in the head of your protagonist like? What is he fixated on? What is he worried about? What from the past tugs him constantly backward? If you're struggling with this concept or want an example of it achieved brilliantly, read *The Mockingbirds* by Daisy Whitney.

QUIRKS AND PRIVATE MOMENTS: What is a quirk your character has? It's okay to have more than one. Aim to be relatable in that "the author is looking over your shoulder and knows your secrets" sense. Tap your own private moments, embarrassments, and things not even your best friends know about you. Speaking of which, what does your character do when nobody else is looking? What makes her privately happy and content? If she had a day totally alone in the house, how would she spend it?

....

MARY KOLE has worked as an editorial intern for Chronicle Books and a literary agent for the Andrea Brown Literary Agency and Movable Type Management. She blogs about children's book writing and publishing at www.Kidlit.com and offers freelance editorial services at www.MaryKole.com. Her book on writing young adult and middle-grade fiction is *Writing Irresistible Kidlit* (Writer's Digest Books, 2012).

CHAPTER 27

COPING WITH CONFLICT

BY RACHEL BALLON

Conflict is the strength of any exciting character and story. Without it, characters don't have drive, desire, or desperation. Without conflict, there's no story, just words. Conflict is one of the most important building blocks for exciting characters. Through conflict, your characters shed their layers bit by bit until we discover the different aspects of their hidden selves. The characters' internal conflicts create the dramatic action for your story.

This chapter will include various types of conflicts and the overt and covert reactions to conflict. You'll learn how to throw characters into the middle of conflict to give them momentum, tension, and suspense, and to force them to take off their masks.

EMOTIONS AND CONFLICT

Emotional conflict is what all great characters carry inside and what all exciting writing must contain. Every story you write deals with characters in emotional conflict. It doesn't matter if you're writing a thriller, an action adventure, a period piece, or a romance novel, all the characters must be involved with emotional conflicts. That doesn't mean your plot can't have battles, riots, mayhem, terrorist attacks, wars, tornadoes, earthquakes, plane crashes, hurricanes, fires, floods, or famine. Yes, you can put all of these external conflicts in your story, but it's imperative for you to create characters with inner conflicts like fears, resentments, or frustrations.

Since all fiction writing needs to have emotional conflict, how do you develop it? First, you must give your main character a goal and then put obstacles in the path of his goal. These obstacles are necessary to create both internal and external conflict for the character. The greater the obstacles and complications, and the more hurdles your main character has to overcome, the more powerful and absorbing your conflict and story become.

Even if your character doesn't reach his goal, he still has to struggle toward it. Otherwise there is no conflict, and without conflict, there is no drama. Fear is one of the most overriding emotions that fictional characters can face. Fear is a basic emotion and the cause of both inner and outer conflicts. So if you want to create emotional conflict for your characters, fear is a good candidate to deal with.

In John D. MacDonald's *The Executioners* (also known as the movie *Cape Fear*), a prosecutor, Sam Bowden, and his family are suddenly invaded by a terrifying ex-con, Max Cady, who blames Bowden for sending him to jail.

The entire family becomes permeated by fear when Cady makes subtle threats, kills the family dog, and stalks each one of them.

Fear of the unknown is the basic emotion throughout the story. MacDonald's novel shows how fear suddenly makes a grown man unravel, as Sam becomes obsessed with the safety of his wife and children against a cunning, evil killer who is out for vengeance. Bowden's fear is responsible for his emotional downward spiral into how far he'll go to stop Cady—even if it means he has to kill him.

What do your characters want desperately enough to motivate them into taking action and to move the story to its climax? To achieve the ultimate conflict for your characters ask, "What would my characters fight for, and what would they die for?"

Inherent in the answers to these questions is the necessity of creating powerful, emotional conflicts. There are many different types of conflict, and you can make use of one or more of them to establish suspense, emotion, and excitement in your characters.

ACTION VS. EMOTIONAL CONFLICT

Writing is all about conflict. But I'm not talking just about violence, armies, or wars. You must also fill your stories with your character's inner conflict to build tension and suspense. Good storytelling involves human emotions that will get your readers and viewers emotionally involved.

The success of action films or suspense novels not only has to do with suspense, twists, turns, surprise, and shock—all necessary elements in these stories—but also with emotional conflict. In novels such as *The English Patient* or *Gone with the Wind*, it is the emotional conflict between the male and female characters and not the conflicts of war that move and involve the audience. Director James Cameron gave us the lovers, Rose and Jack, in his film *Titanic* because he was wise enough to know that dealing with his lovers would allow the audience to intimately experience their plight because of their love, rather than feel emotional about a sinking ship. Action novels and films that fail are those that only have action conflict but haven't connected to the audience in any deep way.

You can put characters who are in conflict in armies, wars, disasters, and even involved in the ultimate conflict—death. However, unless you focus on the emotional conflicts of your main and major characters, these other conflicts will have little emotional impact.

Think of how you've reacted in the past to novels or films that were filled with relentless, nonstop conflict. As you witnessed massive beatings, wars, and chaos, you weren't involved, and you became insensitive to these massive conflicts. It wasn't because you're a cold, unfeeling person; it was that you weren't emotionally attached to any of the characters. In a story where you're emotionally connected to specific characters, you're more moved by their arguments than you are watching men fight and die.

TYPES OF CONFLICT

Three basic sources of conflict are found within most great novels, as well as throughout history. The pitting of man against himself, man against nature, and man against man. Each of these opens the door for both internal and external obstacles that your characters must face—for better or for worse. Whether he succeeds or fails, your protagonist will inevitably have undergone a mental, possibly even physical change that affects his reasoning, his actions, and his long-term motivations. Let's explore each of these sources of conflict a bit more.

Man Against Himself

Man against himself is one of the most important conflicts in fiction, as well as in life. Think of all the times you've had emotional conflicts because of internal warring emotions. How many New Year's resolutions did you make and eventually break? That's an example of emotional conflict within. You want to achieve something and your inner conflicts fight against the very thing you want to accomplish.

If you want to write a story about man against himself, you need to recall the times you vowed not to do something and ended up doing it, even if it was bad for you. This emotional conflict is evident in all addictive behavior. Addicts know that alcohol, food, drugs, sex, gambling, or other addictions are destructive to them.

Let's say that Adam, a young music producer, who is a cocaine addict, swears to himself and to others that he'll never use again. His addiction has lead to his arrest for possession of drugs. He's made bail, and soon the craving seeps in and eventually hits him full force. He can't think of anything else except to give in to his unstoppable urge.

The craving for instant gratification overpowers his desire to stop the addiction, and he caves in to that relentless urge without considering the consequences of his behavior. He throws caution to the wind and his future down the drain because of his addiction. Adam loses his job, his girlfriend leaves him, and he's arrested again. This time, he ends up with a one-year sentence for mandatory rehab.

Adam's emotional conflict is powerful and unstoppable. You can see that by creating characters who have inner emotional conflicts, you'll create characters whose struggle will engender empathy in your readers and viewers. The greater the urge, the greater the internal turmoil and the greater the conflicts.

In the novel *Requiem for a Dream*, by Hubert Selby Jr., both the mother, Sara, and her son, Harry, spiral downward into a cloudy, confusing drug-induced world. Sara tries to lose weight and becomes hooked on prescription diet pills. Her son uses cocaine and heroin. Their drugs fill them with the possibility of realizing their dreams, but instead they're both living a nightmare.

There are also emotional conflicts that aren't as life threatening as drug addiction. For example, in Helen Fielding's *Bridget Jones's Diary*, Bridget is a neurotic heroine who chronicles her inner battles with self-acceptance, her weight, her drinking, her smoking, and her poor taste in men. In this excerpt from Bridget Jones's Diary, you can see that her major source of conflict is herself:

> On way home in end-of-Christmas denial I bought a packet of cut-price chocolate tree decorations and a 3.69 [pounds sterling] bottle of sparkling wine from Norway, Pakistan or similar. I guzzled them by the light of the Christmas tree, together with a couple of mince pies, the last of the Christmas cake and some Stilton, while watching Eastenders, imagining it was a Christmas special.
>
> Now, though, I feel ashamed and repulsive. I can actually feel the fat splurging out from my body. Never mind. Sometimes you have to sink to a nadir of toxic fat envelopment in order to emerge, phoenix-like, from the chemical wasteland as a purged and beautiful Michelle Pfeiffer figure.

Man Against Nature

You can see the conflict of man against nature in action-packed adventure movies and novels such as *Alien*, *Jurassic Park*, and *Planet of the Apes*. The main character's goal is always thwarted by some act of nature that almost prevents him from reaching his goal. These struggles usually involve life and death issues. Will your characters survive the erupting volcano, the dinosaur, or the killer bees?

A classic example of the man against nature conflict can be found in Ernest Hemingway's *The Old Man and the Sea*. The old man, Santiago, is a fisherman whose physical strength as well as strength of

Creating Characters

character is tested as he battles an eighteen-foot marlin alone. It's an exciting tug-of-war conflict between Santiago and the marlin for survival.

Man Against Man

The most popular type of conflict involves man against man. In this conflict, the main character has a goal and another character stands in the way of him reaching his goal. You can find this conflict in mystery, spy, detective, and war stories. But the most dramatic type of man against man conflict is the small personal story involving families, lovers, friends, and relationships. Examples include *Ordinary People*, *American Beauty*, and *The Great Santini*. These stories involve man against man in an emotional and psychological way, rather than in a good against evil way. These personal conflicts include family members struggling with themselves and with one another. They are powerful because they are universal, and your readers and viewers can and will identify with them.

When you create characters who experience man against man conflicts, you have to build the conflicts within the character in a greater way than you would if you were creating characters who are in a mystery or a plot-oriented story.

In all good writing, the main character and other characters should always have internal conflicts, along with the other types. The most powerful writing involves both internal and external conflicts. You want your characters to feel torn by their emotional conflicts and hopefully resolve them by the end, while also resolving the plot.

Personal stories have more impact on your audience than the greatest movie car crash could ever have. Tobias Wolff wrote *This Boy's Life*, an autobiography about his relationship with his mean stepfather and the emotional and psychological conflicts the relationship created. Wolff shows readers the emotional conflicts of a young boy, who eventually transformed and overcame his emotional adversity as well as his living adversary.

SOURCES OF CONFLICT

Opposing emotional drives create conflict and frustration within humans and within characters. These frustrations result from obstacles in your character's path that keep him from reaching his goal. Inner conflicts come from deep frustration within your character. Just as you have to deal with your own personal conflicts, so do your fictional characters deal with their personal conflicts.

Frustrations occur when a person is prevented from reaching a positive goal or avoiding a negative goal. Frustration is a very basic response to feeling thwarted, blocked, or trapped in negative relationships or situations in which you see no clear way out. Even small babies will become aggressive and throw tantrums when their needs aren't met and they become frustrated.

The two basic types of frustration are environmental and personal. Environmental frustration has to do with such circumstances as lack of money, parental restrictions, lack of housing, lack of food, societal restrictions, physical restrictions, and terrorism. Personal frustration includes inadequate intelligence, disease, physical handicaps, lack of physical strength, mental illness, emotional conflicts, and psychological disturbances. When you create characters, give them either environmental or personal frustrations in order to intensify the level of conflict in your story.

REACTIONS TO CONFLICT

The two direct responses to frustration are either fight or flight. Every day you may employ aspects of the fight or flight reaction to frustration and stress in your life. Your characters also use these reactions to fear.

Fighting usually involves some type of destructive physical act that escalates and leads to further conflict. Gunfights, duels, brawls, or fistfights represent direct reactions to frustrations and conflicts. There are also more indirect ways of fighting, which include verbal abuse such as blaming, arguing, criticism, sarcasm, name-calling, and barbed threats.

Flight is also a direct reaction to frustration and includes actions such as running away, hiding, quitting, leaving home, and ending relationships. The more common methods of using flight against frustrations are indirect actions of tuning out through daydreams, fantasies, disinterest, apathy, detachment, and even suicide. James Thurber wrote a wonderful story called "The Secret Life of Walter Mitty," which demonstrates how a man flees from the humdrum of his daily life through his fantasies.

Another way of reacting to frustration is self-sabotage, which is an indirect response to the flight instinct. When frustrated or conflicted, an individual might turn his frustrations inward against himself and drive recklessly or take excessive drugs to escape his emotional pain.

Since all novels, shorts stories, or scripts are about characters in conflict, let's look at the some of the patterns of conflict you can use for your characters.

PATTERNS OF CONFLICT

The patterns of conflict listed below demonstrate the problems that come from having to make decisions that create conflict and frustration in the individuals.

DOUBLE-APPROACH CONFLICTS cause the individual to choose between two goals. They both could be positive goals like getting married or moving to another city for a career promotion. Most stories involve this type of conflict, where in the end the main character has to make a choice between love or career; moving to another town or staying; going back to school or staying in her job. In all cases, neither decision leads to dire consequences, but the choice still may be difficult to make if the character desires both equally.

For example, in the film *When Harry Met Sally*, Harry falls in love with Sally, but he is torn between commitment and freedom. While neither choice is inherently bad, they both present problems and conflicts.

DOUBLE-AVOIDANT CONFLICTS are more painful because the character has to choose between two negative goals. In Anna Quindlen's *Black and Blue*, the wife must choose between staying with her husband and getting physically abused, or leaving him and going underground with her son. If she leaves she'll be giving up her family, friends, job, and identity, and making her son leave his father. If she stays, she's afraid her husband will abuse her and eventually kill her. Both conflicts have painful consequences.

APPROACH-AVOIDANT CONFLICTS are decisions that involve choosing what you believe to be a pleasurable goal but which later leads to suffering and painful consequences. For example, a character who can't cope with her anxiety might choose to drink too much to calm her nerves. In the long run, this choice creates more pain for her and she could become an alcoholic. If your character suffers from anxiety and chooses not to turn to alcohol, that is another choice.

These types of conflicts usually involve individuals suffering from addictions. In Rebecca Wells's *Divine Secrets of the Ya-Ya-Sisterhood*, Sidda Walker's mother, Vivi Walker, drinks too much, and does and says outlandish things, especially to her daughter. Vivi uses alcohol to avoid facing her own reality and for immediate gratification.

In all stories, characters must make choices and decisions. The majority of their frustrations lead to conflict resolution by the end of the story. The characters deal with their frustration by taking direct or indirect actions involving fight or flight. These can be as innocuous as the silent treatment or as dangerous as killing another person.

DEFENSE MECHANISMS

Defense mechanisms are a person's unconscious attempts to protect himself against threats to the integrity of the ego, and to relieve tension and anxiety resulting from unresolved frustrations and conflicts. Deeply rooted frustrations and conflicts that can't be resolved lead to the development of defense mechanisms. Sigmund Freud considered defense mechanisms to be a set of psychological devices by which the ego distorts the perception of reality to protect the individual, thus allowing the person to achieve a sort of mental and emotional balance.

It has been formulated that people with high self-esteem can accept and adjust to frustration and stress better than individuals with lower self-esteem, who are easily threatened and need to protect their self-image by developing defense mechanisms. The following are some common defense mechanism:

1. **COMPENSATION:** You strive for perfectionism by overcompensating for weaknesses—real or imagined. For example, a child gets all *A*s in school or excels at sports, because she doesn't feel good about herself.

2. **CONVERSION:** You have an overwhelming sense of fear that manifests itself as a physical or mental disability. For example, GIs in war can suddenly become blind or crippled because they couldn't save a buddy or hid in fear during a battle.

3. **DENIAL:** You don't deal with frustration directly, but focus instead with other less painful issues. For example, a man in a dire financial situation may gamble on a football game instead of making a late house payment.

4. **IDENTIFICATION:** You lose a sense of self and begin to identify with those in control or power. For example, victims of kidnappings can begin to identify with their kidnappers so much so that they don't even try to escape.

5. **PROJECTION:** You protect yourself by seeing bad traits in another person who reminds you of these same undesirable traits in yourself. Projection involves not liking things about another person that you don't like in yourself but refuse to accept.

6. **REPRESSION:** You exclude from consciousness or memory an event that is too painful to deal with. Individuals repress desires, impulses, and feelings that are psychologically disturbing or arousing. However, such events or desires may continue to exist in the unconscious. For example, a priest who has sexual desires may be subconsciously motivated to preach about the dangers of sin and immorality.

7. **SUPPRESSION:** Unlike repression, suppression is when you consciously engage to control unacceptable feelings and impulses. For example, if you feel attracted to a stranger, you suppress the feelings rather than act upon them.

8. **UNDOING:** When you feel guilty about something you've done, you try to make up for it through gifts or acts of kindness. In

Divine Secrets of the Ya-Ya Sisterhood, both the mother and daughter erupt angrily and then call or send presents to make up. When Vivi is a young mother and feels guilty, she tries to undo her outbursts by being especially nice to Sidda.

9. **SUBLIMATION:** This is when you channel unacceptable feelings into other strong socially acceptable activities such as volunteering in a hospital or donating money to the homeless.

10. **OBSESSIVE-COMPULSIVE BEHAVIORS:** You escape frustrations through outside distractions and develop coping mechanisms through repetitive behaviors, such as constantly washing your hands, cleaning the house, or checking the electrical sockets again and again. A good example of a character with obsessive-compulsive behavior is the character played by Jack Nicholson in the film *As Good As It Gets.* Most of his behavior is so compulsive that he is unable to get along with anyone. He locks and relocks his front door, avoids stepping on sidewalk cracks, and follows specific rituals when he enters his home or eats out at restaurants.

11. **RATIONALIZATION:** You make excuses for other people or yourself. The rationalizer substitutes perfectly normal reasons for behavior because the real reasons are unacceptable to her conscious self. For example, a woman who stays married to a man who beats her might rationalize that her children need a father, when in fact the real reason is she's afraid that she can't make it on her own.

12. **ADDICTIONS:** You engage in behaviors that are compulsive, including addictions to drugs, alcohol, food, sex, gambling, or any behavior that reduces anxiety or frustration on a temporary basis and eventually stops working. These addictions lead to self-destruction. The solution to the original frustration and conflict eventually becomes a new problem.

Since all stories consist of characters in conflict, it's important for you to refer to these different types of defense mechanisms developed to protect one against conflict. When you create realistic characters, give them different defense mechanisms. For example, you could have a character who's in denial about her child's drinking. Or perhaps your character sublimates his sexual feelings for his teacher by getting on the honor roll.

PROTECTION FROM CONFLICT

You might have heard the saying, "Believe nothing of what you hear and half of what you see." That saying is applicable for your characters in that there's more to them than meets the eye. You and your characters are hiding secrets behind the myriad masks you wear. The masks are another form of self-protection against getting hurt and being too vulnerable. Just as you can't judge a book by its cover, you can't judge a person by the way she acts or looks.

In the ancient Greek dramas, actors wore masks to portray the different roles in a play. They literally rendered the facades of their characters through these masks. All of us wear masks in our own lives. We wear different masks for different people, situations, and relationships. Very few people get to know who we really are because we have many levels to our personalities and can decide in advance how we want to portray ourselves in certain situations.

All of your characters also wear protective masks. Throughout the course of the story, characters take off their masks when faced with different types of conflict.

Unfortunately most of us can't reach our powerful emotions because we wear our protective masks most of the time. Our masks keep us alienated from our inner selves and from developing intimacy with others. Only in rare moments are we able to connect on a deep emotional level to another person. If we're lucky, we have a handful of family and close friends who get glimpses of our true selves. In fiction, connections happen between a parent and child, or between lovers.

We learn how to put on our masks by the time we're young children, when our parents scold us for being honest. Can you remember an incident when your parents yelled at you for expressing your true feelings or opinions about someone or something?

After enough scolding, you learned to hide your true feelings behind a mask. After doing this for too long, your true self became completely hidden.

We've been mocked by our peers, reprimanded by the church, and disciplined by our parents, teachers, and relatives. Along the way, we have learned to put on our protective mask and not be who we really are. Even though we're spontaneous and free when we're very young, we eventually learn to hide our true self.

If you don't learn how to hide your feelings behind your mask, others may view you as strange or weird, and you won't be socially accepted. So you also wear your mask as a means of self-protection, which helps you from being too vulnerable or from getting hurt.

The problem is that many people also cut off their emotions and become detached from their feelings. They don't know who they are on the inside and are only able to identify with their masks.

What matters in your stories is who your characters are without the outer masks they wear. Are you able to answer the question, "Who am I?" beneath your own masks? Are you aware of the real you without a mask? How many masks do you wear? If you can't answer truthfully, then how can you unmask your fictional characters? You need to work on yourself first and become aware of all the masks you wear in your own life before you're able to take off your characters' masks.

To be a deeper writer, you must learn to separate yourself from the many masks you wear in life, work, and family. For now, you're going to remove your mask and write from the person you were meant to be. This is a very powerful way to write. It also helps you get beneath your persona or mask, and, in turn, get beneath your characters' masks to the real people inside.

F. Scott Fitzgerald's *The Great Gatsby* is filled with characters pretending to be people they aren't. When one character, Daisy Buchanan, is involved in a hit-and-run and kills a woman, Jay Gatsby, the man who loves her, takes the blame. In the end, the narrator Nick Carraway learns that even the wealthy Gatsby isn't the man he claimed to be—he actually made his money illegally. Like everyone else in the novel,

Gatsby was striving to be someone he could never become by facing the world from behind a mask.

CONFLICTS OR CHOICES

To be alive is to know conflict. Life is filled with conflicts as minor as which outfit to wear on a blind date or which entree to order in a restaurant. Such examples are usually considered to be choices rather than conflicts. In fiction, the characters' choices or decisions create the story, just as the choices you have made are responsible for the way your life is now. However, unlike the above examples, most choices aren't that easy.

We base our choices on past experiences, values, perceptions, attitudes, beliefs, and awareness. Many more unconscious aspects influence our choices. In fiction you need to build characters who make choices based on their backstory, inner motivation, and psychology so that their behavior is believable.

A Character's Persona: A Case Study of When Choice Becomes Conflict

Let's suppose that you're writing a story about relationships, and you create a single woman in her early twenties who's a stockbroker. She's dynamic and gorgeous, and she knows how to charm men. She has no trouble attracting men, but she has no luck in maintaining long-term relationships with any of them. None of her past relationships have worked out, and unfortunately her lovers are the ones who dump her.

Why does this happen to such a beautiful woman? Why can't she sustain a relationship? Why do the men in her life leave her? What is it about her that drives them away? What's wrong with her? It certainly isn't that she's not beautiful or physically desirable to men. She certainly has the opportunity to meet men through her job. So what is the problem?

Let's suppose a new man comes into her life at work who is interested in dating her. She is attracted to him, but she's also conflicted when he asks her for a date. She's scared to get romantically involved again. She's been burned one too many times. In this situation, your character isn't just going to make an easy choice on whether or not to accept a date with this man. She's coming to this relationship with a past. She's been hurt by men, and she's been cheated on by them. Each man she has dated ended the relationship while she still loved him.

Of course, she doesn't look at herself as the problem. She doesn't become introspective to see if there is anything she's doing to drive her lovers away. She just feels hurt and a lack of trust when they break up with her.

In this situation, do you think the character will make clear-cut choices about starting a relationship? Her choices will be based on her past affairs, her fearful attitude toward men, her negative emotions about trusting any man, and the fact that she never experienced a loving relationship that ended in marriage.

Her choices are now colored by her unsuccessful experiences that created the inner conflicts. Her conflicting emotions confuse her. She is torn between her need for love and attention from the opposite sex and her fear of getting hurt. Her desire for love motivates her to finally go on a date, and in spite of her fears, she is immediately smitten with the young man.

Now the character has to deal with her inner fears because she is once again vulnerable to a man. She still wears her smiling, confident persona, but inside she's worried about betrayal, pain, and fear. Her anxiety overwhelms her.

After only a few dates, she starts to act very needy. Instead of being the confident, beautiful woman he was initially attracted to, she now acts insecure and jealous. She starts asking him when she's going to see him again, when he's going to call, and what he did when he wasn't with her. Before long her confident persona has disappeared because her feelings of insecurity and mistrust have become stronger than her facade.

She becomes more frustrated. On the one hand, she desperately wants love, and yet she's waiting to be hurt and disappointed again. She begins to imagine the worse-case scenario—that her lover will lose interest and drop her. And that is exactly what happens—not because he was bad or untrustworthy, but because she has driven him away with her unpredictable behavior, her suspicious nature, and her neediness.

After he drops her, she becomes even more needy and insecure, and her lack of self-esteem continues on a downward spiral until she is thoroughly bitter and cynical about men. What originally attracted men to her now scares them away. She'll never have a decent relationship until she deals with her real self—her inner fears and anxieties.

If you were writing her story, you'd probably want her to realize that she is more than her looks and start to believe in herself by the end. But this emotional transformation would have to happen throughout the story. You would have to show her in situations that gradually make her emotionally stronger so that in the end her change and growth would be believable.

Characters are complex, just like you. They can experience extreme mood swings, from depression to happiness, from sorrow to joy, from love to hate. Your characters can be cautious, mistrusting, vulnerable, frightened, and adept at putting on a false front—smiling even though they're feeling fury, looking nonplussed when they're feeling emotional inside, acting sincere when they're lying.

RACHEL BALLON is a licensed psychotherapist who specializes in the personal and professional issues of writers, including overcoming rejection and procrastination while increasing confidence and creativity. The *L.A. Times* referred to her as "Doc Hollywood" for her work with struggling writers. Ballon is also a script consultant and the author of *Breathing Life into Your Characters: How to Give Your Characters Emotional & Psychological Depth* (Writer's Digest Books, 2003).

PART VIII

MOTIVATIONS & RELATIONSHIPS

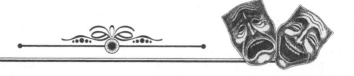

CHAPTER 28

MOTIVATION AND REALISM

BY CHERYL ST. JOHN

Nothing happens in a vacuum. People can't react without stimuli. Every action has a motivation—or it should.

You lean down and scratch your ankle. Why? It itched.

You go to the bank to make a payment. Why? You bought a car.

Your best friend bursts into tears. Why? Her boyfriend dumped her.

You gained five pounds. Um … Snickers bars.

You ate too many Snickers. Why? Stress eating over the rash of burglaries on the news.

You buy additional locks and install them. Why? You can't afford another five pounds.

A man jumps every time a loud noise startles him. Why? Post-traumatic stress disorder.

A woman wants six children and a big house. Why? She grew up in an orphanage. Of course that's not the only reason a woman would want six children. She may have been raised in a big family and wants to continue as her parents and grandparents did. She could have watched too many misleading episodes of *The Brady Bunch*. Everything depends on her personality—and her motivation, backstory, and prime motivating factor.

A prime motivating factor or prime motivation is an event or a series of past happenings that shape a character's personality. In *Jaws* we saw the incident that shaped Quint's personality. Leonard Hofstadter on *The Big Bang Theory* is another character that comes to mind. When his mother is introduced on the show, she is almost a female replica of Sheldon, with a complete lack of social conventions, strict adherence to details, and an obsessive need for order, routine, and punctuality. Leonard admits to his neighbor Penny that as a child he built a hugging machine because he lacked love and affection. These over-the-top traits are fodder for comedy, but it's easy to understand how Leonard's character developed.

Some people whose parents are alcoholics adapt a similar lifestyle, and for them drinking is "normal." Others go to extremes to keep alcohol from their home. A woman who grows up in poverty may vow never to raise a child in that environment. She might refuse to have children until she's wealthy, or she may indulge them too much. Another woman might unconsciously hold back emotionally and financially from her child so he'll grow up as tough and capable as she did.

The really exciting part about creating characters is that you can manipulate their lives in order to tell the story you want to tell. That means you manipulate their histories to shape them into the people you want them to be so they react the way you need them to react. It's your job to make their behavior and reactions believable.

CREATE CHARACTERS WITH BUILT-IN CONFLICT

Build in conflict as you personify your story people, and give them diversity. Use their pasts, their needs, and their fears as fodder for conflict. Use their strengths and their weaknesses *against* them. Their backstories, combined with characterization, will be motivation for everything they do. It will shape their goals and define the way they react to situations.

Weak, superficial motivations lead to weak, superficial conflict, which results in weak, superficial characters. Creating characters with embedded conflict from the planning stage will make your story strong and will ensure that you have enough conflict to carry the length of the book. Conflict that is superficial, external, or easily resolved will not sustain a plot. A cute premise makes for a great first meeting or introduction, but once that mistaken identity or initial problem is resolved, nothing is left to hold up the rest of the story.

I love to come up with an idea that seems impossible for the characters to overcome. If a situation looks impossible, it's a pretty good bet that the conflict will be strong. Occasionally I come up with something that looks so impossible that I have to put the idea on hold until I figure out a believable motivation and a resolution. A good example is my book about a large family who owns a brewery, *Her Colorado Man*.

My initial story idea involved a man arriving from a remote location and pretending to be my heroine's husband and the father of her child. I also wanted the man and the child to exchange letters before the man ever showed up. Why? Because that's the premise that stuck in my head and got me fired up. The problem was making the premise believable. I put this idea back on the shelf several times because I just couldn't bring it all together.

Obviously the heroine would know this guy wasn't her husband or the father of her child—unless, of course, she had amnesia, and I wasn't going there. So in plotting this story, I had to motivate both of the characters to make this premise believable. Eventually it came to me: I gave the heroine a son with a secret father and a grandfather who made up a husband in order to protect her and their family name. The heroine is content to live her life pretending there is a husband off in the Alaskan goldfields.

However, unbeknownst to her, the grandfather used the name and post office box of a real person. Wes Burrows gets caught in a bear trap while delivering mail in the Yukon and recuperates at the remote post office, where letters are piling up in his mailbox. An old man who used to read them and reply recently died. Because Wes was raised in an orphanage, the young boy's desire for a father strikes a chord in his heart, and he answers the letters. Eventually he gets on a steamer and heads for the States to meet this boy and to be a father to him.

You can see where this presents a big conflict for my heroine. Her family thinks Wes is really her husband, and now she has no choice but to let him into their family home—and pretend they're married. A lot of motivation planning went into making their actions believable to the reader. And this was definitely enough conflict to carry the length of the book. Marketing must have loved the premise because they sent out 750,000 sample packets of the first fifteen pages of this story in a reader mailing. I almost fell off my chair when I got that news. And reviewers specifically pointed out that they bought into the unlikely premise.

STICK TO YOUR GUNS

While writers must be open to change, suggestions, and new ideas, some factors should be considered sacred. I firmly believe this is critical to the plotting and brainstorming process. Before you ever brainstorm with another person or a critique group, lay down ground rules. Tell your partners that there are some elements from which you will not budge—those things that got you excited about the story. Keeping these elements sacred is imperative. You need that seed of excitement to grow throughout the book. You must have that excitement when you reach the middle and require motivation to move forward. Never compromise the initial spark of creative genius that fired your story into being. If a story simply won't come together for whatever reason, shelve it for a later date. I've done exactly that many times. Nothing is lost by waiting. Trust me—much is gained.

Because of the conflict in that plot idea, I was able to draw emotions from the characters. A story is feelings, and if you plan your story to engage your character's emotions, you will engage your readers. It's our job to help them identify, show them why they should care, and then force them to buckle their seat belts and hold on for the journey.

Conflict reveals your character's emotions, and it's emotion through which your reader identifies. If the conflict isn't emotional for the character, it won't be emotional for the reader. If you want the reader to care about these people—*and you do*—engage his feelings.

In my novel *Her Wyoming Man*, courtesan Gabriella is pretending to be Ella, a mail-order bride from a finishing school. Nathan Lantry, an attorney who aspires to be governor, marries her upon her arrival.

> "You, Ella Lantry, are one of the smartest people I've ever met. You never judge anyone by their appearance or on a first impression. You are appreciative of the smallest thing, down to the most

infinitesimal effort on another's part. You're quite curious. And you don't recognize your own value."

A niggle of panic rose up inside Ella at his intuitive assessment. She couldn't afford for him to look at her too intimately. She swallowed to keep fear from her voice. "Well-read on the subject of explorers and wines doesn't mean smart."

"I didn't say well educated, though you are. There's a difference. And I get the impression that you feel isolated, even here with our household or in a gathering."

She didn't care for his shrewd perceptions, but she understood that they made him a good leader. "I admire you," she admitted. "And everything about you. Your honesty and your ambition and even your idealism."

He raised his eyebrows. "Idealism?"

"Yes." And more than anything she wanted to be worthy of such an upright and principled man. He was as steady and unchanging as a rock in the middle of a raging river.

"No one has ever called me idealistic before."

"Perhaps I should stick to handsome."

He smiled, and this time it was a smile that crinkled his eyes and showed his teeth. He cupped her cheek and kissed her.

She liked everything about this man.

"This is new to me. Talking and enjoying each other, I mean. All along I was afraid to frighten you off. I didn't want to spoil what we had begun. Our marriage seemed so fragile."

It was more fragile than he imagined, but not for the reasons he thought. By taking this step and consummating their union, she hoped to strengthen their bond.

"Ella," he said, with an edge of seriousness that concerned her.

"You talk more than I might have anticipated," she said.

"I love you."

His words took her by surprise. *Love?* She blinked, hoping for comprehension. She threaded her hair back from her face without looking at him. "You didn't have to say that."

"No one ever has to say it. I told you because I felt it, and it was right to say so."

He loved her? Once she'd believed her mother had loved her, though, because the woman hadn't protected her from a life in the parlor house, she'd doubted her love, more now than even back then. After seeing children who were protected, she questioned what kind of love allowed a child to succumb to the fate Ella had. She'd seen the way Nathan safeguarded his children and planned for their futures. Her mother had never cared for her the same way. Of course the love he declared had nothing to do with parents and children. It was love between a man and a woman. No one had ever said those words to her before, and she didn't know how to receive them or to react.

He sat. "You don't have to say it," he told her. "I'm not expecting anything from you."

She recognized the pain in his voice, though. He wanted her to say it. "It's just ..." she began and groped for words to explain. "I'm not sure I believe in that kind of love."

He was silent for a few minutes. The clock on the bureau ticked.

"You don't have to say it," he assured her. "But just so you know ... I will make you believe."

Ella has never experienced a relationship other than one of servitude. Having been a prisoner her whole life, she has never enjoyed the most simple pleasures of everyday existence. Everything about her new life and the man who married her is unique and surprising. She can't reveal the shameful secrets of her past or she will lose this precious and tenuous new beginning. In this scene the reader sees Ella's well-protected vulnerability and recognizes that even though she wishes she could be honest with this man, her situation makes the truth impossible. The reader is experiencing this foreign concept of love along with her.

SIMPLE AND COMPLEX CONFLICTS

A simple conflict can be every bit as powerful as a complicated one; how the characters react and resolve it makes all the difference. A simple conflict relies more on internal conflict and characterization, while a complex conflict relies more on external conflict or plot.

The situation must be so important to the characters that it's intolerable unless they do something. You may have heard several of these terms, which basically cover the same thing:

- Motivation
- Backstory
- Prime motivating factor
- Prime motivating incident

This is the first sentence of the powerful prologue in Barbara Dawson Smith's *Fire on the Wind*: "Tonight his mother would finally love him." Seven-year-old Damien Coleridge garners all his courage to approach the mother who calls him a demon and a devil. He has spent hours on her Christmas gift—a picture he drew with scarred hands, which are a constant reminder of the fire two years previous that made his brother an invalid. His mother blames Damien for the harm to her favorite son.

While she's entertaining guests, Damien approaches his mother and accidentally breaks a vase, for which she verbally abuses him. He gives her the drawing. His mother takes him into another room where she tells him he's a devil who deserves to burn in the flames of hell. She rues the day he was born and wishes he had died. She throws his gift into the fire. That prime motivating incident drives Damien to spend his entire life living up to his mother's distorted opinion of him. He sees himself as totally unlovable. Her disgust and withheld love affects his every relationship from that moment forward. By knowing his vulnerability, the reader cringes when Damien faces rejection. Damien's internal conflict begins as a simple one and grows more complex as the plot develops over the years.

Your character's motivating factors don't have to be negative. He could be a person who can step in a steaming pile of doo-doo and come up smelling like freshly baked bread. You'd match this character with a jinx or an unlucky person. Or say your character had the perfect home life, with all the love and devotion a child could want. He believes in love and family, so you would pair him with a cynic and watch the fur fly.

When readers know about the experiences your characters have had, it makes the characters' goals and reactions motivated and believable.

Conflict must be personalized to the character. If you don't know your story people and how to motivate them, you won't have a strong conflict. A vague or general motivating force produces a vague and general plot. Being specific will increase the emotional intensity of your story.

DEVELOPING BACKSTORY

Everything that happened before the story starts is your character's backstory. Not all of it is interesting. Only a fraction of it needs to be revealed to the reader, and only the significant details are important to the plot.

When developing backstory, you will need to think about the prime motivating factors or the incidents that shaped your character. These are the memories you create for your story person and the basis for who they are now.

- **A BELIEF SYSTEM:** These are the precepts by which a person lives and may consist of faith, opinions on politics, philosophies, convictions, worldview, and ideals.
- **VALUES:** What is important to this person? Wisdom, skill, simplicity, reputation, order, independence, honor, freedom, discipline? Does your character look for the same values in others as in herself? By whose standards does she measure right and wrong?
- **FAMILY AND FRIENDS:** Family has fueled a good many plots and a lot of dysfunction, but family can also be held as a shining standard. Develop the history that results in the character you want.
- **FEARS AND PHOBIAS:** Some people are driven to succeed by fear, while others are crippled. What does your character avoid? What does she need to feel safe? Important? Loved?

Creating Characters

- **PRIME MOTIVATING INCIDENT:** This is the factor that kicks the character into action in scene one.

In *One for the Money* by Janet Evanovich, Stephanie Plum loses her job as a lingerie salesperson at Macy's in Trenton and has her car repossessed. She needs a job. Her mother mentions her cousin Vinnie has a filing position in his bail-bond business, but instead of taking the job, Stephanie blackmails Vinnie into giving her a job going after people who've jumped bail. If she can get Joe Morelli to turn himself in, she could get $50,000. Stephanie and Joe have a history (backstory). When she was sixteen, she had sex with him in the bakery where she worked and he never called her. She later ran him over and broke his leg in three places, but she claims it was an accident. The conflict is built in and the story is set is motion.

It is imperative to keep your character's history in mind as you unfold the story. However, beginning writers often lay out all of their backstory right off the bat to make sure the reader gets it. Big mistake. This is known as an info dump. The reader doesn't care yet, so he's not invested for the time it takes to get through the backstory.

Remember to spoon-feed your readers the backstory: At first, simply *hint* at the inciting incident. A little later, taunt the reader with just enough to tantalize. Make him *want* to know, and then—when he *cares*, when he's wondering—let him have it with both barrels.

....

CHERYL ST. JOHN is the author of more than fifty novels, in both contemporary and historical genres. In describing her stories of second chances and redemption, readers and reviewers use words and phrases like "emotional punch, core values, endearing characters, and on my keeper shelf." Visit her at cherylstjohn.net.

CHAPTER 29

SHOWING CHANGE IN YOUR CHARACTERS

BY NANCY KRESS

In addition to having multiple emotions at a given time, some of your characters may alter during the course of your story. Other characters may not change significantly in personality or outlook, but their motivation may nonetheless change as the story progresses from situation to situation. Both changers and stayers can have progressive motivations.

Confused? Don't be; it's really not hard. Characters come in four types:

- Characters who never change, neither in personality nor motivation. They are what they are, and they want what they want.
- Characters whose basic personality remains the same; they don't grow or change during the story. But what they want changes as the story progresses ("progressive motivation").
- Characters who change throughout the story, although their motivation does not.
- Characters who change throughout the story *and* their motivation progresses.

Because character and plot are intertwined, we'll refer to these four as "character/plot patterns."

THE POPEYE PERSONALITY: "I YAM WHAT I YAM"

Sometimes a character will have a single overriding motivation for the entire length of a story or novel, plus a strong personality that does not

alter much. James Bond is a good example. He's a stayer who starts out resourceful, suave, unflappable, and smart. At the end of each of Ian Fleming's novels, Bond is still resourceful, suave, unflappable, and smart.

Nor does his motivation alter. At the start of the book he receives a mission, and his goal is to pursue this mission until it's over, at which point the book ends. There may be interim temporary goals (not getting eaten by alligators, protecting the girl), but they are all part of the single overriding motivation.

It isn't only adventure fiction to which this applies. In John Steinbeck's classic *Of Mice and Men*, both protagonists, George and Lennie, retain the same motivation throughout. They want to earn enough money to buy a small farm of their own. Their personalities, too, remain the same: George is the planner and caretaker, dimwitted Lennie is the well-meaning bumbler who brings them both to tragedy.

If you are writing this type of book, your job is to present the character and the goal clearly and forcefully fairly early on. Then unfold your tale; we'll know who your man is and why he's doing what he's doing. This leaves us (and you the writer!) free to complicate other things, such as the plot, the conspiracies, or the hardware.

Please note, though, that an unfaltering character with an unfaltering goal can still feel more than one emotion *at a given moment*. James Bond might, for instance, feel attraction to one of the "Bond women" at the same time that he distrusts her (often with good cause). If your character feels two conflicting things toward another character, show this in the scene in which it happens. Then—and this is the important part—*return in the next scene to the main goal*.

Doing so tells us that the basic situation is unchanged. Although Bond, for instance, has just made love with a woman, she hasn't fundamentally changed him. He is not altered in either his personality or motivation as a result of her attractions.

PROGRESSIVE MOTIVATION: THE WORLD AS MOVING TARGET

Another type of story features a character who doesn't change in basic personality or beliefs, but what she wants changes as a result of story events.

These characters are often of two types: heroes or villains. The heroic ones are essentially admirable characters from the beginning of the story. They don't change because the author clearly doesn't feel they need to; they embody virtues he wishes to advocate. Two disparate examples are Charlotte Bronte's Jane Eyre (*Jane Eyre*) and Ayn Rand's Howard Roark (*The Fountainhead*).

Jane is spunky, plain, passionate, and moral, even as a child. She believes in the dignity of all individuals, including those at the bottom of the Victorian power structure. We see this early in the book when she stands up for herself, for school friend Helen Burns, or anyone being abused. At the end of the book, she's still doing it.

However, as Jane grows up, her immediate motivations change. At first, she merely wants to survive the brutalities of her terrible aunt and then of the boarding school that the aunt sends her to. Later she wants a new teaching position to broaden her horizons. Later still, she falls in love with her employer, Mr. Rochester, and wants him—until she learns the truth about him and wants to escape his home. Still more motivations follow.

Howard Roark, even more resolute and heroic than Jane Eyre, never really changes, either. He just rises, without flinching, above the failures and stupidities of the rest of the world. His initial motivation is to design buildings that suit him, with no outside influences dictating his designs; his next motivation is to blow up those buildings because the builders changed some of his architectural plans. Both actions proceed from an unchanged and unshakable conviction of his own superiority.

The point is that if your character is basically heroic, you may not want him to change. In that case, you construct the story this way:

- Your character is trying to live his life, but the outside world imposes an obstacle.
- The obstacle gives the character a motivation: fight it, flee it, change it, or adapt to it.
- That first motivation is met by a consequence, which in turn supplies another motivation (the consequence of Jane's seeking a new teaching post is meeting Mr. Rochester).
- That motivation encounters obstacles, etc.

You may recognize this patter; it's sometimes referred to as "the classic plot patter." (Actually, as we're discussing here, it's only one of four possible character/plot patterns.) Its success, as in the "Popeye" character pattern, depends on a strong, interesting character. Once you have that, you set up initial circumstances for her to cope with and then have her motivation change as consequences flow.

However, as with the first type of character, a basically unchanging personality may nonetheless experience changing or conflicting emotions at any given moment. When Jane Eyre's cousin, St. John Rivers, asks her to marry him in order to accompany him to India on his mission work, Jane has very mixed reactions:

> Of course (as St. John once said) I must seek another interest in life to replace the one lost: is not the occupation he now offers me truly the most glorious man can adopt or God assign? Is it not, by its noble cares and sublime results, the one best calculated to feel the void left by uptorn affections and demolished hopes? I believe I must say, Yes—and yet I shudder. Alas! If I join St. John, I abandon half myself.

During the rest of this scene, Jane will also feel awe, disdain, humility, dread, rebellion, scorn, and hurt. Mixed emotions indeed! But her basic personality and beliefs do not waiver: She is a person who wants more than a loveless marriage, even if that marriage is dedicated to God's work. Jane wants love.

At the other end of the heroism spectrum, some villains have unchanging personalities but changing motivations. They start out venial, greedy, evil, or destructive, and they end up the same way. This is true whether they win or lose. Along the way, however, their motivations often enlarge: They become greedier for greater things, destructive on a larger scale, or they want to succeed at different, grander schemes of evil. Or, as with heroes, their motivations may change as a result of story events.

Thus your villain may start out wanting to rob an armored car. He succeeds, but in the course of the robbery he kills a police officer. Now his goal is to elude capture. While pursuing him, your detective is forced to shoot the villain's nephew and protégé, who has drawn a gun on the cop. Now your villain has an additional motivation: revenge on the detective. The stakes have risen with each story event and its consequence.

CHANGERS WITH A SINGLE MOTIVATION: OREGON OR BUST

In many stories, a major character changes significantly. The character has a single motivation and may expand enormous effort to reach it, like those covered-wagon pioneers who risked everything to trek west. However, during the process of achieving (or not achieving) this overriding goal, the character's basic personality and/or beliefs alter. In fact, this alteration is often the point of the story.

For example, a young woman has as her motivation the desire to get out of prison. She forms this desire as soon as she is incarcerated, in the first chapter. The book ends when she gets out, for whatever reason: Her time has been served, she successfully escapes, or her lawyer wins the appeal. However, this character is a changer, which means that while her goal has stayed constant, her personality/belief structure has not.

For instance, as a result of her interactions with the other inmates, maybe she's changed from a superior, scornful snob to one who feels that she and the other women are basically the same. She's gone from scorn to empathy, from disdain to friendship. All the while that she's been working on getting out of prison, prison has also been working on her.

If you write this type of character, there are a few critical points to remember:

- Her character change must come about in response to story events. Create events that could logically lead the character to change in the ways you want. "Devise incidents," W. Somerset Maugham said when asked to divulge the secret of writing. This is what he meant: You must think up those plot events that will affect your characters enough for them to react with genuine change.

Creating Characters

- Your character must have emotional responses to these events.
- The character change, too, must be dramatized. We can't simply be told, "Abby now sympathized with her cell mate." We must see Abby's change of heart through things she does that she didn't do before, such as giving and accepting help from this once-despised cell mate. This is called *validation*, and it is essential for all changing characters.
- You must include a final validation at the end of the story so we know that your character's change is not temporary, but permanent. Usually this ending validation is on a larger scale than what has gone before. For instance, instead of just helping her cell mates with daily frustrations, your protagonist, now out of jail herself, does everything she can to improve the situations of those still inside.

Readers find this kind of story intrinsically satisfying. The single motivation throughout gives the book unity and comprehensibility, and the changing character satisfies the need for fiction to make a comment on life. In the case of the prison story, that comment is positive: People can grow nicer.

You might, however, also use the same character/plot pattern to make a negative observation about the world. In that case, the character with a single goal would, in the course of failing to achieve it, change from naïve innocence to "sadder but wiser." For example, this is the structure of Edith Wharton's *The House of Mirth*. Protagonist Lily Bart sustains the same motivation throughout the book: to marry for money. She does not succeed. Only at the end, both of the novel and of her life, do events force her to change, and then she realizes that she might have had a better life if she'd paid less attention to luxury and more to love. By then, however, it's too late.

The single-motivation, changing character also works in stories in which the character succeeds in getting what he wants but is disappointed in his success. These are the "be careful what you wish for" stories. The change in the character can be one of two types. In one, he realizes that he's paid too high a price for success, at which point he may or may not change his life. Or, he never realizes this (or at least never admits it), but he changes to grow regretful or bitter as a result of getting what he thought he wanted.

CHANGERS WITH PROGRESSIVE MOTIVATIONS: WHO AM I AND WHAT DO I WANT NOW?

This is the most complex fictional pattern. A character's goals change throughout the story, and so does her personality/belief system. This is confusing for the character. Your goal is to keep it from confusing the reader.

Consider, for instance, Ensign Willie Keith from Herman Wouk's Pulitzer Prize–winning novel of World War II, *The Caine Mutiny*. Willie undergoes a lot of personal change during the war. He also changes motivation often. In sequence:

- Willie wants to avoid being drafted, so he joins the Navy.
- Willie wants to avoid difficult duty, so he tries to avoid dangerous ships like minesweepers.
- Willie wants to transfer off the minesweeper *Caine*.
- Willie wants to survive the *Caine*'s tyrannical, irrational Captain Queeg.
- Willie wants to get rid of Queeg and joins a mutiny.
- Willie wants to avoid court-martial and dishonorable discharge.
- Willie wants, finally, to become a good naval officer and defend his country as well as he can.

From these changing motivations, you can also see Willie Keith's internal changes. He moves from being self-centered, looking for the easy way out, to an assumption of duty and, even more important, to feeling that duty is worthwhile.

If you have a character with both progressive motivation and internal changes, congratulations. You've got a strong character to carry an ambitious book. To keep all these changes from seeming arbitrary, however, it's important to follow all the guidelines set out above for single-motivation changers. Your character's changes must be dramatized, come about as a result of dramatized events, be accompanied by plausibly rendered emotions, and be validated by subsequent actions on his part.

PORTRAYING MOTIVATIONS

We've talked a great deal about dramatizing emotion. Now let's turn to dramatizing its source, motivation.

For characters with a single story-long goal and for characters with different consecutive goals, it is *your* job as writer to make sure we always know what those characters' goals *are*. There are several ways to do this:

- The character can think about her goal, as Jane Eyre does:

  I had no communication or letter with the outer world: school-rules, school-duties, school-habits and notions, and voices, and phrases, and faces, and costumes, and preferences, and antipathies; such was what I knew of existence. And now I felt that it was not enough: I tired of the routine of eight years in one afternoon. I desired liberty.

- The character can have his goal dictated to him by others: "Detective, you're assigned to the Riesling murder case."
- The character can talk about her goal with others, as Lennie and George do in *Of Mice and Men*:

  "I forget some a' the things. Tell about how it's gonna be."
  "Someday we're gonna get the jack together and we're gonna have a little house and a cow and some pigs and—"
  "An live off the fatta the lan'," Lennie shouted.

- Others can talk about the character's goals so we readers can "overhear" them. This works well for characters who are neither introspective nor talkative: "Jack is trying so hard to get his brother's approval, and Cal just ignores him."
- The character can demonstrate his motivation through two or, preferably, three attempts to accomplish something, such as getting Cal's attention. More than one attempt is necessary to estab-

lish that this is not just a habit, politeness, or rules but instead something the character really wants.

There are no hard-and-fast rules about which of these techniques works best for any particular plot. Try one in your story and, if it seems insufficient to illuminate motivation, add another.

THE KEY TO JUGGLING MOTIVATION AND CHARACTER CHANGE

All of this can, I know, sound overwhelming. Dramatizing motivation, dramatizing emotion, dramatizing change, creating sharp concrete details that characterize—and doing it all simultaneously—can seem too much to juggle (not to mention also "becoming the reader" to see how it all looks to someone else). But there is a way to keep control of your material. It is, in fact, the key to keeping control of many other elements of fiction as well, such as plot and emotional arc.

The key is this: *Write in scenes.*

You don't have to think about the whole book at once, the entire emotional arc, or the progressive motivations of six different characters. All you have to do right now is write this *one* scene. And the way you do that well is by knowing, before you write, exactly what the scene is supposed to accomplish.

Let us assume that you're writing a novel about a lady who left six million dollars to a veterinary hospital. You sit down at your keyboard to write the scene in which the woman's son finds a copy of her will in her desk (the original is with her lawyer). The son reads the will. Before you plunge into the action, take a moment to think about what you want this scene to *do*. If you're a list-making person, write it down. Purposes of this scene could include:

- conveying to the reader the contents of the will (the bequest to the veterinary hospital)
- characterizing the son as greedy, selfish, and furious
- giving the son motivation: he wants to prove that his mother was legally incompetent so he can break the will

Now you know what you need the scene to do. Ask yourself: How can I dramatize these things, not just talk about them? What can this guy do to *show* the reader what's going on inside him?

Ideas start to occur to you. Jot them down:

- He tears the room apart in his eagerness to find the will.
- He finds it and reads it. (Reproduce document in story text.)
- He kicks the cat, throws a chair, and curses.
- He makes himself calm down—takes a walk, has a drink or a cigarette—while contemplating a way to break the will. He decides on incompetence and realizes this is stronger if he sets the legalities in motion before anyone knows he's seen the will.
- He carefully replaces the will and puts the room back together.
- He calls the lawyer to ask "if Mama left a will" and to express concern to her about "the neighbor's reports" of his mother's failing mind.

Now you're ready to write this scene. Just *this* scene, in which you concentrate fully on specific, meaningful actions that will advance the plot, characterize the son, and set the stage for scenes to come.

As you write, ideas might come to you that differ from the ones on your list. If they're better, use them. The list is a guide, not a straightjacket. As a guide, it will keep you focused on motivation, emotion, character, and plot.

Our hypothetical scene involved only one person (plus a phone call). Most scenes, however, feature two or more people—and that means many more ways to develop character.

NANCY KRESS is the author of thirty-three books, including twenty-six novels, four collections of short stories, and three books on writing. Her work has won five Nebulas, two Hugos, a Sturgeon, and the John W. Campbell Memorial Award. Her most recent works are *After the Fall, Before the Fall, During the Fall* (Tachyon, 2012), a novel of apocalypse, and *Yesterday's Kin* (Tachyon, 2014), about genetic inheritance. In addition to writing, Kress often teaches at various venues around the country and abroad; in 2008, she was the Picador visiting lecturer at the University of Leipzig.

CHAPTER 30

ROMANTIC RELATIONSHIPS

BY VICTORIA LYNN SCHMIDT

Why are romantic relationships important?

If you want to build a story that will touch readers on a personal yet universal level, you need to add the element of love. Everyone longs for love on some level, and the best films and novels deal with the subject in one way or another.

All great books, movies, and entertainment have some sort of romantic theme running through them. Sometimes it is unrequited love. Sometimes it is passionate yet tragic love. Love is universal. It is something everyone desires, regardless of what they may say.

Keep in mind that many writers know how to write about the longing for love or unrequited love—great literature is filled with it—but the task of writing characters who have found love is much more difficult.

- How do they express their love?
- Who falls in love first?
- How will their relationship affect the rest of the story?
- Does the heroine's love for another effect or change her?
- Will they be together in the end?

As an author, you have several decisions to make up front regarding sex and love in your story. You may decide they have no place whatsoever in your story and that is fine, not every story has to have them. But writing about love and sex is still a skill every writer needs to learn. They are basic human functions, and love is a desire all your readers deal with in their daily lives.

Even action films include love in the subtext. Perhaps your hero is in love with a woman who has died. Such a situation adds a lot to his backstory—think of the *Lethal Weapon* movies.

After all, how many Heroes on the Masculine journey get the girl in the end? Many!

For all you skeptics out there, take a look at the following two love letters written by Napoleon and King Henry, and you will see that even a great solider, leader, or king can fall in love and reveal something of his character at the same time…

NAPOLEON BONAPARTE TO THE EMPRESS JOSEPHINE (FEBRUARY 1796):

"My waking thoughts are all of you. Your portrait and the remembrance of last night's delirium have robbed my sense of repose. Sweet and Incomparable Josephine, what an extraordinary influence you have over my heart.

Are you vexed? Do I see you sad? Are you ill at ease? My soul is broken with grief and there is no rest for your lover…

But is there more for me' when, delivering ourselves up to the deep feelings which master me, I breathe out upon your lips, upon your heart, a flame which burns me up? Ah! it was this past night I realized that your portrait was not you.

You start at noon. I shall see you in three hours. Meanwhile, mio dolce amour, accept a thousand kisses, but give me none, for they fire my blood."

KING HENRY VIII TO LADY ANNE BOLEYN:

"…No more to you at this present, mine own darling, for lack of time.

But I would that you were in my arms, or I in yours for I think it long since I kissed you.

Written after the killing of a heart, at eleven of the clock; purposing with God's grace, tomorrow, mighty timely, to kill another, by the hand which, I trust, shortly shall be yours. HENRY R."

ROMANTIC TENSION

Why are romantic interactions important? Because love is universal.

Romance novels make up the largest market in the industry for a reason! Most of the highest paid authors are romance novelists. In fact millions of women devour romance novels in an effort to experience the love and romance they can't find in their everyday relationships. Truth is we all are interested in love, which is why even manly action films have a love interest in them as a rule. There are very few films made without some sort of love interest.

Now that we've discussed the interactions between the sexes, I'd like to mention the three types of intimate scenes that exist. They are called Anticipation, Submission, and Empowerment.

ANTICIPATION occurs when the lovers want to be together but can't, so they anticipate being with each other. Usually there's an obstacle keeping them apart, and this obstacle creates anticipation in the reader as well. "When will they get to be together?"

For these characters, a job or other main focus will keep the attention on things other than on the relationship, thus causing problems for the couple. This "distraction" may also keep the pair apart much of the time. In such situations, great longing can set in, as well as deep fantasizing.

SUBMISSION means one person loves the other so much she or he would do anything to see that love returned. They will submit to almost any demand or requirement. Examples include the mistress who waits for years for her lover to leave his wife and the hero who has to prove himself to win over the heroine. The question is, "Will he find his love returned?"

EMPOWERMENT occurs when gender positions become reversed. In many cases, this means the woman gains a powerful position. She calls the shots, not because her male counterpart is submissive, but because she is willing to walk away from him if she has to. In most situations men have more power over circumstances than women do. It's not unusual for a man to leave a woman so that he can do his job—just watch a typical western—but it is unusual for a woman to walk away for the same

Creating Characters

reason. The question becomes, "Will she leave him?" On the flip side, the man can also decide to walk away from a woman when he finds his own empowerment. A good example is the dentist character in *The Hangover*.

These characters can be very independent. They know how to build an identity of their own. They can separate from their lover and still be secure with themselves.

You will use this information later when you start plotting your character's romantic story arc or subplot. For now I want you to write a love letter between your two main characters. You may be pleasantly surprised at what you discover about your character's psyche and past history as you do this exercise.

WRITING ABOUT LOVE

Love is a hard subject for most people to handle. It brings up our insecurities, makes us feel vulnerable, and subjects us to the possibility of deep pain.

Action Story Writers

Some of you may be writing action stories and are wondering why you need to read this part of the book. Love makes the world go round. How many heroes get the girl in the end? Many! Sometimes their motivation is to get the girl, or at least to impress her. He doesn't go after the girl merely for sex and often finds meaningless sexual relationships along his journey.

In these more manly stories, the romantic plot may take a backseat to the main storyline, but the stages listed in the following pages show up in the story on some level, even if it only takes place on one page in your script or novel.

Romance Writers

Some of you may be writing romance novels and wondering how the masculine and feminine journeys fit with the romantic journeys. Well, if you want to write a great romance, you should start with a traditional journey model as the plan for your main plot and use the romantic journeys as a plan for the subplot. This doesn't mean the romance will take a backseat to the main story. Romances are supposed to be about romance after all.

The main story becomes the spine on which the relationship is developed. Remember, the traditional journeys are very suitable to character-driven stories where the hero will face many obstacles to her goal and have to face hardships. The elements of the romantic journeys become the hardships. You can create an adventure plot and weave the romantic subplot into it.

Think of it this way: Most of Barbara Cartland's romance novels (which have collectively sold over a billion copies) are similar to the Cinderella romance model—the pretty, quiet, innocent girl meets the handsome, powerful, older man, who is usually a cynic. He falls in love with her and molds her into a beautiful princess, teaching her the art of love by the end of the story.

At the same time, though, most of Cartland's novels take place in exotic places and feature heroes who explore exotic lands, intent on saving the world. She purposely 'added a touch of James Bond' as she put it, to all her stories.

WHO SAID ROMANCE HAS TO BE BORING?

By analyzing the top three fairy tales—*Cinderella, Beauty and the Beast,* and *Sleeping Beauty*—you will see firsthand how to plot the romantic journey or subtext of your story. Fairy tales are universal. These stories are found in different variations across many cultures.

Very often in real life, love and power are intertwined. When you love someone, you are left vulnerable to the object of your desire. Likewise, when someone else loves you, you are placed in the more powerful position.

In the three fairy tales that follow, you will find three variations of how love and power manifest themselves in relationships. The suggested theme are not meant to be the rule, they are simply the themes that fit most easily into each romantic subplot. Mixing themes a bit may make it more interesting.

Creating Characters

Cinderella

In the *Cinderella* romantic journey, the heroine falls in love with the hero first and she is left at his mercy. Her actions are centered around him and whether or not he will save her. Very often these stories focus on the hero and how he's feeling. Hamlet and Ophelia come to mind.

Romantic Themes:

- **RAGS TO RICHES:** Getting your due against all obstacles. To go from a place of lack and dissatisfaction to a place of abundance and happiness. She's earned it.
- **ROMANTIC RESCUE:** Saving your partner from self-destruction, or needing to be saved or nursed back to health yourself. Love is lifesaving and life changing on a physical, emotional, mental, or spiritual level.

Beauty and the Beast

In the *Beauty and the Beast* romantic journey, the hero falls in love with the heroine first and is left at her mercy. The story often focuses on how the heroine is feeling. The hero is usually an extremely powerful man in every area of his life except where the heroine is concerned. Very often his whole life depends on her decision to love him back and save him from his meek existence. *The Phantom of the Opera* comes to mind.

Romantic Themes:

- **INDEPENDENCE:** Desire for someone different than the people you have previously dated, or desire for someone completely different from you. Wanting a life change and needing someone who is where you may want to go.
- **LOVE VS. HONOR:** What you want to do versus what you should do. Considering others' needs and your duty to your family. There is a major obstacle in your relationship and you have to learn to value your own needs. This fits well with paranormal stories as the hero is usually otherworldly and 'normal' people and family members may not accept him.

Sleeping Beauty

In the *Sleeping Beauty* romantic subplot, both the heroine and hero fall in love at the same time, a situation that puts them on equal footing. They save each other through their mutual love. *Romeo and Juliet* comes to mind.

Romantic Themes:

- **LOVE CONQUERS ALL:** You need someone to help you gain the courage to face yourself and your inner demons so you can heal. (Example: The hero has a drug addiction.) There's a tug between desire for the love of your life and a fear of commitment. Other things try to take precedence over the relationship.
- **SECOND CHANCES:** You try to recapture lost love and want to go back to a specific time in your life when things were better. This new person is a chance to recapture what you are missing in your life.

VARIATIONS ON A THEME

Of course variations on a theme always exist. The following outlines of the above fairy tales are not hard and fast rules, just interesting guidelines that can help inspire you. They can be used as a sort of road map as you plot your story.

Cinderella: The Hero Holds the Power

Unlike the two story models that follow this one, *Cinderella* gives full power to the hero as he rescues the heroine and changes her life.

- The Prince is going to throw a ball; it's time for him to find a wife.
- Cinderella is in a bad state of affairs. Her parents have died and she has no one to look after her except her nasty stepmother.
- Everyone but Cinderella is going to the ball. She has nothing to wear.
- A fairy helps her go to the ball, allowing Cinderella's outer beauty as well as inner beauty to shine forth.

- She goes to the ball and meets the Prince but has to leave at midnight or her whole world will fall apart. The Prince falls in love with her the moment he sees her.
- The Prince decides that Cinderella is the one for him and he stops at nothing to find her.
- The Prince finally finds her, proposes marriage, and changes her life. He will care for her now. He has saved her from her mean stepmother and sisters. He will teach her what a real family is all about.

Cinderella is an innocent heroine who has all the qualities the hero thought he'd never find in one woman. She is set apart from all the other women in the land. She is a special girl who needs to be schooled in the art of love, and the hero is the only man who is up to the job.

She goes out and meets the hero but doesn't expect much to happen. She runs away from him, and he enjoys the chase, determined to have her whether she wants him or not. She is often much younger than her pursuer and more inexperienced. She grows and blossoms because of his influence and help. He saves her. Often these stories are written from the hero's perspective.

This story focuses on the hero falling in love with the heroine, since she's in love with him from the start.

Beauty and the Beast: The Heroine Holds the Power

In *Beauty and the Beast*, the heroine saves the hero.

- Beauty asks her father for a rose when he goes out of town.
- Her father gets stuck in a storm and finds shelter in a strange castle.
- When he leaves, he picks a rose and the Beast comes out to yell at him and demands his life in payment.
- The Beast agrees to take Beauty as payment instead.
- Beauty agrees to live with the Beast to save her father.
- Beauty and the Beast become friends, but Beauty can't agree to marry him.

- Beast allows Beauty to go home to visit her sick father if she agrees to return in seven days.
- She forgets to return and the Beast gets sick without her. Beauty rushes back to his side to pronounce her love for him.
- The Beast is saved by her love and turned into a handsome prince.

The focus on this story is on the heroine and how she feels. She has to fall in love with the hero of her own free will. He cannot force himself upon her. He doesn't live in the normal world and can't make any claims upon her. Society's rules do not apply to him.

The Beast demands her in payment regardless of how she looks or who she is, sight unseen. He is not looking for the best woman in all the land but any woman who can truly love him for who he is.

Power, tension, and violence set the tone in this Gothic-style story. The Beast is like a child and Beauty holds the power to save him. She is the light to his darkness. She changes his life for the better in the end, and he feels unworthy of her.

This story focuses on the heroine falling in love with the hero, since he is already in love with her from the start.

Sleeping Beauty: Both the Hero and Heroine Hold the Power

Of the three stories outlined here, *Sleeping Beauty* walks the middle road, where the hero and heroine are true equals sharing in the same type of fate before they meet each other.

- Sleeping Beauty is the victim of a curse.
- No one can help her but the good fairy who changes the wicked spell of death put upon her. Beauty sleeps instead of dies and all the royal servants are put to sleep with her.
- The Prince, wandering the lands in search of something he can't name or find, happens upon her castle and enters.
- He finds her sleeping and falls in love with her. His whole world changes as he realizes this feeling of true love is what he was seeking all along.

- He kisses her and she awakens. She had been dreaming of him and waiting for him for centuries and is so happy he is here. They get married.

Both the hero and heroine are in dire straights. They are both 'asleep' before their chance meeting, lost in waiting and longing for something more. The Prince did not know what ailed him until he laid eyes upon her and felt love course through his heart.

They fall in love at the same time, and they both grow from the union. They are very much alike and on equal footing. Very often these stories use plot to keep the couple separated and battling obstacles.

This story focuses on the couple being able to stay together, since they fall in love with each other right away.

....

VICTORIA LYNN SCHMIDT (www.VictoriaLynnSchmidt.com) is the author of *Story Structure Architect* (Writer's Digest Books, 2005), *45 Master Characters* (Writer's Digest Books, 2007) and *Book in a Month* (Writer's Digest Books, 2008). She graduated from the film program at UCLA, and she holds a master's degree in writing from Loyola Marymount University and a doctorate in psychology.

PART IX

CHARACTER

ARCS

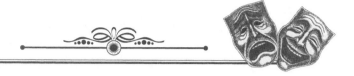

CHAPTER 31

CREATING A CHARACTER ARC

BY JOSEPH BATES

There are two types of motivation and conflict: internal and external. External motivation is the character's stated goal, what it is he or she hopes to accomplish by the end of the story, and external conflicts are those events and circumstances that (sometimes literally) stand in the character's way. Both of these are aspects of plot and are easy-to-spot, necessary components of story. Internal motivation and conflict can be a little more difficult to see, as these are often more subtle. Internal motivation is what the character wants on a personal level, what matters to him or her—which the external motivation and conflict help reveal more clearly. Internal conflict consists of what doubts or fears stand in the way … a realization of what's at stake for the character. This all may sound a bit complex when stated this way, but when all of the components work together in a story, they become difficult to separate from each other precisely because they all become aspects of the same thing.

By the way, please don't let any of this talk about motivation and conflict, internal and external, make you think we need psychology degrees to write fiction; what we're really talking about here is a character arc. In its simplest terms, this is about supplying a character with specific wants or goals and then putting obstacles in his or her way. And the degree to which the character is successful, or not, in achieving the goal tells us something about the character as a person and, ideally, tells us something about ourselves as readers.

Let's simplify these ideas even more by showing the basic form of a character arc—wants, what stands in the way, and resolution—and looking at a few examples everyone should be familiar with even if you haven't read the books.

THE WIZARD OF OZ

Character Arc: Dorothy Gale

WANT	WHAT STANDS IN THE WAY	RESOLUTION
External	**External**	**External**
To follow the Yellow Brick Road and find the Wizard of Oz, return home to Kansas.	The Wicked Witch, flying monkeys, a field of poppies, etc.	Finds Wizard, who can't help her. Learns from Glinda the Good Witch that she can return home by clicking her heels, could all along.
Internal (pre-twister)	**Internal (pre-twister)**	**Internal**
To find a place she feels at home and people she feels close to as a family. (Wants to be somewhere else "Over the Rainbow" and gets her wish.)	Dorothy is an orphan living with her aunt and uncle on their farm ... she's not sure if she fits in and is accepted.	Back in Kansas, realizes her aunt, uncle, and their farmhands are real family. Realizes this is where she belongs. Realizes she's been "home" all along. That both "home" and "family" mean the people you love and who love you back.

THE SILENCE OF THE LAMBS

Character Arc: Clarice Starling

WANT	WHAT STANDS IN THE WAY	RESOLUTION
External	**External**	**External**
To find and stop serial killer Buffalo Bill.	Bill's enigmatic clues and M.O.	Finds Buffalo Bill, has to face him alone, prevails.
To rescue Sen. Ruth Martin's daughter before she's killed.	Racing against time. Lecter's mind-gaming "help."	Finds and saves Catherine Martin.
To convince Hannibal Lecter to reveal what he knows of Buffalo Bill and the investigation.		Lecter's "mentorship" helps Starling solve case ... strange, equal relationship develops.
Internal	**Internal**	**Internal**
To prove herself worthy of being a full FBI agent.	Her self-doubt and inexperience.	Prevails, granted agent status, proves herself.
To escape the poverty of her past and upbringing and make something of herself.	Being marginalized by the FBI and other law enforcement (especially for her gender and youth).	Granted agency. Becomes full person.
To save an innocent and stop the "horrible screaming of the lambs" from a traumatic childhood memory.	Lecter's mind games revealing her fears and doubts.	Puts her doubts and demons to rest. Until the sequel, anyway.

THE LORD OF THE RINGS (TRILOGY)

Character Arc: Frodo Baggins

WANT	WHAT STANDS IN THE WAY	RESOLUTION
External	**External**	**External**
To destroy the One Ring at Mount Doom.	Orcs. Ringwraiths. Giant spiders! Gollum. Etc.	Takes the Ring to Mount Doom and finally destroys it.
Internal	**Internal**	**Internal**
Not just to save the world, but to save his world, to preserve Hobbiton and the way of life he loves. His strength of character, which leads Gandalf to entrust the Ring to him.	Doubts about whether he, as a simple Hobbit, is up to the important task. The Ring's influencing Frodo's mind, tempting him, trying to manipulate him.	Faces severe temptation and prevails. Returns to innocence in a sense but is nevertheless wiser as a Ringbearer.

You'll notice that in all of these character arcs—which closely parallel the novels' plot arcs—we begin not with the external motivation but the internal: in Kansas with the lonely Dorothy, or at Langley with the student Clarice Starling trying to prove herself, or in the Shire with Frodo and the Hobbits, enjoying a way of life that's about to be put in peril. We begin with the internal motivation because it shows what's really at stake for the characters, which will be further revealed, and tested, by the external motivation and conflict when they appear.

....

JOSEPH BATES is the author of *The Nighttime Novelist* (Writer's Digest Books, 2010) and *Tomorrowland: Stories* (Curbside Splendor, 2013). His short fiction has appeared in such journals as *The Rumpus, New Ohio Review, Identity Theory, South Carolina Review,* and *InDigest Magazine.* Visit him online at www.josephbates.net.

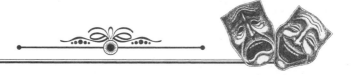

CHAPTER 32

THE ARC WITHIN PLOT

BY JAMES SCOTT BELL

What makes a plot truly memorable is not all of the action, but what the action *does to the character*. We respond to the character who *changes*, who endures the crucible of the story only to emerge a different person at the end. It may be a major difference, as with Ebenezer Scrooge in Charles Dickens's *A Christmas Carol*. Or it may be a subtle change, as when Scarlett O'Hara finally matures at the end of *Gone with the Wind* (just not soon enough to keep Rhett).

What deepens a plot is when characters grow. Events happen and should have impact on the characters. Are there novels where the characters don't change? Sure. But these are not usually classified as "enduring." In a detective series, for example, the main character may remain rather static, and the only change from book to book is the nature of the case.

Even in a series, however, subtle changes in the character over time can elevate the books from mere entertainments. Sue Grafton's Kinsey Millhone and Robert B. Parker's Spencer are examples.

So look to create character change in your novels in a way that deepens the plot and expresses a theme. For when a character learns something or suffers because he changes for the worse, it is an expression by the author about the larger canvas—not merely what happens in the novel, but what happens in life.

THE CHARACTER ARC

As opposed to the *plotline*, the character arc is a description of what happens to the inside of the character over the course of the story. He begins as one sort of person in the beginning; things happen to and around him, gradually moving him in an "arc" that ends when the story is over.

Your lead character should be a different person at the other end of the arc.

For example, in the film version of *The Wizard of Oz*, Dorothy begins as a dreamer, a farm girl with her head in the clouds. She dreams of finding a better life "over the rainbow."

At the end, she realizes "there's no place like home." We might describe this arc as going from *discontentment* to *contentment*, an arc of 180 degrees. Or from *dreamer* to *realist*.

However we put it, we are saying that Dorothy has grown because she has learned a life-changing lesson.

The character arc has a build to it. It must, or the change will not be convincing. A good character arc has:

- A beginning point, where we meet the character and get a sense of his interior layers (more on layers in a moment)
- A doorway through which the character must pass, almost always reluctantly
- Incidents that impact the layers
- A deepening disturbance
- A moment of change, sometimes via an "epiphany"
- An aftermath

Let's take a look at each step in more detail. We'll use the example of Ebenezer Scrooge in Dickens's *A Christmas Carol* as our prime example. This is the greatest character-change story ever written. It's a good model.

Beginning Point

When we first meet Ebenezer Scrooge, he is described as a "squeezing, wrenching, grasping, scraping, clutching, covetous old sinner!" Dickens goes on to provide a biting physical description of Scrooge, and then proceeds to *show* us what Scrooge is like. In one instance, some men have stopped by Scrooge's place of work to seek donations for the poor. Scrooge snaps:

> "Since you ask me what I wish, gentlemen, that is my answer. I don't make merry myself at Christmas and I can't afford to make idle people merry. I help to support the establishments, I have mentioned: they cost enough: and those who are badly off must go there."
>
> "Many can't go there; and many would rather die."
>
> "If they would rather die," said Scrooge, "they had better do it, and decrease the surplus population."

A bit later, Scrooge's clerk, Bob Cratchit, once more requests Christmas day off. It is, after all, only one day a year. As you know, however, Cratchit's simple request is denied, further illustrating the heartless nature of Scrooge.

The Layers

We all have a *core self*, which is the product of many things over the years; our emotional makeup, our upbringing, our traumas and experiences, and so on. Most of the time we're not really thinking about who we are. Yet the core is there.

And we will do what we can to protect this core because, by and large, people resist change. So we surround that core with layers that are in harmony with our essential self. Working from the core outward, these layers include: (1) beliefs; (2) values; (3) dominant attitudes; and (4) opinions.

If you think about it, these layers get "softer" as they move away from the core. Thus the outer layers are easiest to change. It is much easier to change your opinion, for example, than one of your deeply held beliefs.

But there is always a ripple effect when a layer experiences change. If you change an opinion, it will filter through to the other layers. Initially there may not be much effect. But change enough opinions, and you start to change attitudes, values, and even beliefs.

On the other hand, suddenly changing a core belief automatically affects the other layers because it's such a strong shift.

How might we describe Scrooge's core self at the start of *A Christmas Carol*? He is a miser and a misanthrope. He loves money and hates people.

His *beliefs* include the pointlessness of love and charity.

He *values* money over people.

His *attitude* is that profit is more important than good works.

In his *opinion*, Christmas is a humbug, clerks are always trying to take advantage, and so on.

To make Scrooge into a new person, these layers are going to have to be disturbed. How is that to happen?

Ghosts, of course.

Scrooge is to be visited by three ghosts. The first, the Ghost of Christmas Past, takes Scrooge to a familiar scene:

> "Good Heaven!" said Scrooge, clasping his hands together, as he looked about him. "I was bred in this place. I was a boy here!"
>
> The Spirit gazed upon him mildly. Its gentle touch, though it had been light and instantaneous, appeared still present to the old man's sense of feeling. He was conscious of a thousand odours floating in the air, each one connected with a thousand thoughts, and hopes, and joys, and cares long, long, forgotten.
>
> "Your lip is trembling," said the Ghost. "And what is that upon your cheek?"
>
> Scrooge muttered, with an unusual catching in his voice, that it was a pimple; and begged the Ghost to lead him where he would.

Scrooge is crying! This hard-bitten man who seems so intractable has, at a scene from his boyhood, connected with long-forgotten emotions. They affect him. He attempts to divert the ghost's attention. It is the first, small indication that somewhere inside Scrooge's cold, uncaring body is a warm person who may reemerge.

The ghost takes Scrooge to see the shop where he was a young apprentice, Old Fezziwig's. Scrooge remembers how generous Fezziwig was to his employees, how he brought joy into their lives. This brings

Scrooge to another moment of reflection on his own relationship with his employee, Cratchit. The moment results in a softening toward Bob Cratchit, whom we met earlier in the story when Scrooge barked at him. Some of the outer layer of Scrooge has been affected.

And the plot advances.

Impacting Incidents

The Ghost of Christmas Present takes Scrooge for a look at the Cratchit family. What Scrooge witnesses there is the joy of Christmas as shared by a poor family, including Tiny Tim:

> "God bless us every one!" said Tiny Tim, the last of all.
>
> He sat very close to his father's side upon his little stool. Bob held his withered little hand in his, as if he loved the child, and wished to keep him by his side, and dreaded that he might be taken from him.
>
> "Spirit," said Scrooge, with an interest he had never felt before, "tell me if Tiny Tim will live."
>
> "I see a vacant seat," replied the Ghost, "in the poor chimney-corner, and a crutch without an owner, carefully preserved. If these shadows remain unaltered by the Future, the child will die."
>
> "No, no," said Scrooge. "Oh, no, kind Spirit! say he will be spared."

We are starting to get into deeper levels with Scrooge here. There is an interest "he had never felt before." The shadows are doing their work.

Before the Ghost of Christmas Present leaves, Scrooge sees one more image that sears into him—under the Spirit's robe are two young children tainted by poverty and want:

> "Have they no refuge or resource?" cried Scrooge.
>
> "Are there no prisons?" said the Spirit, turning on him for the last time with his own words. "Are there no workhouses?"
>
> The bell struck twelve.

Notice how Scrooge's own words (the references to prisons and workhouses), planted early in the story, now come back to haunt him.

This is a powerful technique for character change. If you can repeat a motif, or have the character somehow come face-to-face with his "earlier self," the reader will see the pressure to change powerfully conveyed.

It is best to underplay such moments. In Dickens's time a bit more on-the-nose writing was acceptable. Don't overdo it, or you may lapse into melodrama.

Deepening Disturbances

We are fast coming to the point where Scrooge will try to become a new man. The ultimate disturbance is when the Ghost of Christmas Yet to Come shows the dismal aftermath of a despised man's death.

And then Scrooge is shown the Cratchit family again, where he learns that Tiny Tim is dead.

The Ghost next takes Scrooge to a graveyard and points to a headstone. With this shock to his system, Scrooge finally snaps:

> "Spirit!" he cried, tight clutching at its robe, "hear me! I am not the man I was. I will not be the man I must have been but for this intercourse. Why show me this, if I am past all hope?"
>
> For the first time the hand appeared to shake.
>
> "Good Spirit," he pursued, as down upon the ground he fell before it: "Your nature intercedes for me, and pities me. Assure me that I yet may change these shadows you have shown me, by an altered life!"
>
> The kind hand trembled.
>
> "I will honour Christmas in my heart, and try to keep it all the year. I will live in the Past, the Present, and the Future. The Spirits of all Three shall strive within me. I will not shut out the lessons that they teach. Oh, tell me I may sponge away the writing on this stone!"
>
> In his agony, he caught the spectral hand. It sought to free itself, but he was strong in his entreaty, and detained it. The Spirit, stronger yet, repulsed him.
>
> Holding up his hands in a last prayer to have his fate reversed, he saw an alteration in the Phantom's hood and dress. It shrunk, collapsed, and dwindled down into a bedpost.

Aftermath

Scrooge has declared that he is a changed man. But that is not enough. We must see some action that demonstrates the change, shows that it has truly taken effect.

First, we see a Scrooge we haven't encountered before, bounding out of bed and rejoicing in his own happiness. Then he goes to the window and stops a boy running by. He engages the lad to buy a prize turkey:

> "I'll send it to Bob Cratchit's!" whispered Scrooge, rubbing his hands, and splitting with a laugh. "He shan't know who sends it. It's twice the size of Tiny Tim."

There is an action. Now we know Scrooge is different. We've been shown. The showing continues when he finds the two men whom he rebuffed who had solicited a donation from him the day before and makes it up to them. Scrooge then dines with his nephew, and the next day raises Bob Cratchit's salary and asks to assist him with his family.

So, when we get to the final words of the great Dickens classic, we believe them:

> Scrooge was better than his word. He did it all, and infinitely more; and to Tiny Tim, who did not die, he was a second father. He became as good a friend, as good a master, and as good a man, as the good old city knew, or any other good old city, town, or borough, in the good old world. ... [A]nd it was always said of him, that he knew how to keep Christmas well, if any man alive possessed the knowledge. May that be truly said of us, and all of us! And so, as Tiny Tim observed, God Bless Us, Every One!

The Epiphany

Since *A Christmas Carol* is a character-change story, the beats are clearly designed for that purpose. In many novels, the character arc may be quieter and shown in a subtler fashion.

That's fine. You can still use the steps above. But be ready to work hardest on that *moment of change*, which we might call the *epiphany*—that realization that comes to us and shifts our way of viewing the world.

What we want to avoid with such moments is melodrama—the overplaying of the emotion involved. Epiphanies and realizations are often best when underplayed.

In fact, it is quite possible not to play it at all! Yes, the moment of change can be *implied* by what happens *after it*. In other words, the proof of the change (what author Nancy Kress calls "verification" in her book *Dynamic Characters*) can follow pressure. That is one way to avoid being "on the nose" with the change.

In my novel *Deadlock*, a Supreme Court Justice, Millie Hollander, is an atheist. But pressure has been applied in a big way. So much so that something major happens on her plane trip back to Washington D.C. Let's take a look:

> The plane rose into fog, a gray netherworld. Millie took a deep breath, looked out the window, feeling as uncertain as the outside.
>
> In so many ways this day should have been a relief. Her body was good again. She'd spent precious hours with her mother, connecting with her in a way that she'd never dreamed was possible. And she was going back to Washington to assume the job of a lifetime—Chief Justice.
>
> So why the disquiet?
>
> She put on the earphones the flight attendant had passed out earlier, clicked the dial until she got classical music. And what music. They were right in the middle of Beethoven's Symphony No. 9 "The Ode to Joy." The beauty of Beethoven.
>
> Beauty.
>
> She put her head back, just letting the music wash over her. And then she looked outside again. Bright sunlight hit as the ascending plane topped the fog. Suddenly, there was clear sky, the bluest of blue, and soft clouds seen from above, like an angel's playing field.
>
> The music swelled.
>
> Inside her something opened up. There was a flooding in, an expansion, as if she were a sail filling with wind. And it terrified her.

She put her hands on the earphones, pressing them in, making the music even louder to her ears, as if she could crowd out
all thought, all sensation.

But she could not. For one, brief moment—but a moment of
almost unendurable intensity—she felt like a door was opening,
and thought she might go crazy.

That's where the scene ends. The book then cuts forward in time, and
we see the results of this moment. Instead of spelling out the change
when it happened, the writer leaves room for suspense, and only later
pays off the scene.

A CHARACTER'S CHANGING BELIEFS

Another way a character can change is by learning a lesson that will change
the way he looks at life. At the end of Harper Lee's *To Kill a Mockingbird*,
Scout, the narrator, realizes what her father Atticus has been trying to
teach her. Most people are decent "when you finally see them."

Consider your character's primary beliefs. Can you design incidents
that will teach the character a new "life lesson"?

Character-Arc Table

A simple way to map character change is to create a table that covers the
main beats of your story. This will enable you to describe the character's
inner life at each juncture.

Let's say your novel is going to emphasize four major incidents in
the life of a criminal—the crime, time in jail, a trial and sentence, and
an aftermath in prison. Create a table with four columns.

Begin with the first column, "the crime." Describe in a few words
who your character is on the inside. Next, go to the last column, "prison." Describe how you want your character to be at the end. What will
be his life lesson? How will he have changed?

Now you can fill in the other columns to show a progression toward that final point. Come up with adequate pressure in these places
to justify the outcome.

The character-arc table will give you ideas for scenes that illustrate what's happening inside the character, which in turn will help you deepen your story.

THE CRIME	JAIL	TRIAL AND SENTENCE	PRISON
Without pity, cynical	Mistreated here, but helped by another con	Has to face the victims of his crime	Compassion and empathy are what is needed in the world
	Changes his opinion of other prisoners	Witness testimony shows him how he's wasted his life so far	Proved by how he treats a prison guard
		His inner layers are affected	

A strong character arc will enhance any plot. It is well worth your time to create memorable changes that flow naturally from the story. It is not always easy, but your readers will thank you for the effort.

....

JAMES SCOTT BELL is a best-selling and award-winning suspense writer. He has authored four WD Books: *Plot & Structure* (2004), *The Art of War for Writers* (2009), *Conflict & Suspense* (2012), and *Revision & Self-Editing for Publication* (2012).

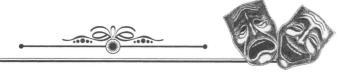

CHAPTER 33

THE KNOT

BY JEFF GERKE

Your main character needs a problem.

Maybe it's adultery, like Mistress Prynne from *The Scarlet Letter*. Maybe it's unresolved anger. Maybe it's selfishness (this is a favorite in Disney movies of late, as in *Frozen* and *Brave*). Maybe it's a classic tragic flaw like hubris or narcissism or ambition or unwise trusting. Maybe it's a more "modern" sin like drug addiction or pornography or child predation. Perhaps it could be something mundane like discontentment or jealousy or a weakness for chocolate.

It's okay if you haven't thought of one yet. The problem you choose for your character is something anyone could have, so it is important first to establish who this person is, independent of what may afflict her as the story begins. When you have the character's personality firmly set in your mind, it's time to add a problem.

TYING THE KNOT

I refer to your character's problem as his knot. If you've worked with ropes much, especially in a nautical setting, you know they have to run smoothly through eyelets and pulleys and across capstans. A knot in the wrong rope at the wrong place can result in irritation, delay, or even disaster.

So it is with your character. There he is, going along fine, minding his business, when something causes a knot to form in the rope of his life. Maybe he sees it and begins working on untying it. Maybe he sees it and doesn't work on it. Maybe he doesn't see it at all and the problems it's causing are happening in his blind spot.

Whether he knows about it or is working to correct it or not, the knot is messing up his life.

In Mark Spragg's novel *An Unfinished Life*, protagonist Einar is living a solitary life on a ranch. His unresolved grief over the death of his beloved son—and the fuming anger at his daughter-in-law, who was driving the car at the time of the accident—has left him poisoned, bitter, and stunted. Einar doesn't know it. He can't see it. He's stuck in the delicious sadness, if he thinks about it at all. It isn't until he meets a granddaughter he never knew he had that his uneasy truce with life is broken. Old wounds are opened and he is forced to face his crippling anger.

In my novel *Operation: Firebrand*, my protagonist is a Navy SEAL who is involved in a mission that goes wrong. Because of a hesitation during the mission, his best friend is grievously wounded. The story proper begins with him consumed with guilt. He quits the Navy and takes the kind of low-life jobs he feels he deserves. What he's really looking for is a way to kill himself, to end the self-recriminations once and for all. When he is recruited for a new team and a new mission, he believes he's found a way to commit suicide by enemy fire. But he encounters something unexpected that offers him a reason to hope, to live again … if he will take it.

What knot could you give your character? With the clear sense of who she is as a person (and you might read over your notes to make sure you have that firmly in mind), you can begin thinking about what problem you might want to give her.

HOW TO FIND YOUR KNOT

It's time to have some fun with your character. It's time to put on your Hawaiian shirt and a silly hat and get a little crazy.

When it comes to picking a problem for your hero, the sky's the limit. It's really up to you. Be wacky. Brainstorm. Don't shoot down any idea; just toss 'em all out there.

Do you want her to be afraid of commitment? Addicted to gambling? An out-of-control spender? Go for it. Do you want him to beat his wife? Do you want him to cheat on his taxes? Do you want him to be obsessed with a movie star? Do it.

Here's one guideline: *Go deep.* Play junior psychologist. Maybe you think it would be fun to have a main character who is scared to go outside. Alex Rover is a character you can appreciate—she's a novelist in Wendy Orr's *Nim's Island.* Alex writes about an Indiana Jones–style adventure hero, but she herself is scared of the mailman, spiders, disease, and just about everything else.

Cool. Good idea. But here's the go-deep question: Why? Why is she scared to go outside? It's not enough to show a symptom like that. You need to know what has caused it.

If you think you'd like to give your character a fixation with ducks, that's okay, but it's not a knot. That's a quirk. You could dig a little deeper and decide that he's obsessed with ducks because his dad was a duck hunter and his one great memory of his dad is a duck-hunting trip. But now his dad has abandoned the family, and the character thinks that if he collects the right duck-hunting gear, his dad will come back.

Now we're getting into knot territory. He's feeling sad and angry and adrift and thinking his father left because he wasn't a good enough boy. Aha! When you feel yourself treading into that Freudian, tell-me-about-your-mother land, you know you're getting close to a knot.

Most important: You need to find something that can carry a full novel. If your character's knot is that his shirt is untucked and everyone's laughing at him, the solution to which is simply to tuck in his shirt, that's not going to propel a whole story.

That doesn't mean it has to be something earth-shattering, though. The knot doesn't have to be that your hero has a fear of saving the earth but the earth needs saving and somehow he must overcome his fear or the earth is doomed. The fate of the universe doesn't have to hang in the balance. Your knot just has to be significant to the character.

Note that the knot doesn't have to be a fear, though I seem to keep going back to fears because they make for good knots. Other great—and deep-enough—knots are extreme hurt, a lack of forgiveness of someone else, or a lack of forgiveness of self (which we call *guilt*). It can be a deep wound, as when a parent has lost a child to death or abduction. It could be unresolved anguish or a horrible secret. It could be a heavy sense of regret over having done something unwise. It could be awful shame over something done or suffered.

The beauty of it is that it's wide open. So long as it's deep and large enough, it can be anything you wish. Want to explore loyalty between siblings? Give your character the knot of feeling that she's never been loved by her family. Want to investigate the nature of courage—or what it will take to turn a coward into a hero? Then make your character a quailing heart (just be sure you know *why* she prefers flight over fight).

If you're a plot-first novelist you may be feeling pretty good right now. Finally, your comfort zone! If you're a character-first novelist, you might be equally as comfortable because you love thinking about what makes people tick, or change.

If you're feeling a little nervous now, go back to your party hat and crazy shirt: Relax and have fun with it. Dream. Is there a theme you've always wanted to explore? Consider your own life: Is there a loss or fear you'd like to finally grapple with, or an ideal or extreme you'd like to imagine? How about a time when you've failed someone or someone has failed you—want to explore what that must've been like for the other person? Here's your chance to write the ultimate book—the story that finally gives you freedom to tell the tale of your heart.

SAMPLE KNOTS

Here are some knots drawn from an array of novels, movies, and real-life experiences:

- The belief that life has dealt him an unfair hand
- A fear of being alone (caused by abandonment as a child)
- A willingness to break any rule to achieve the ultimate approval of her mother
- An overpowering desire to exact revenge
- A fear of commitment (caused by parents' divorce)

Creating Characters

- A hoarding of clothes and food (caused by living through the Great Depression)
- An unwillingness to let a child have fun (because she lost another child through indulgence)
- A willingness to endure continued abuse (because his parents were abusive and that's the only way he understands love)
- A loner mentality (caused by being hurt by someone she relied upon)
- A belief that he is worthless and a resulting self-sabotage to make his reality line up with his belief

Get the idea? You want to wound your character in some way or give her a tragic flaw or "besetting sin" that causes her life to be less than it should be.

It might even help to think of it in medical terms. The patient has a tumor. She doesn't know it yet—or maybe she does but doesn't want to deal with it—but it's killing her all the same. You, as her surgeon, want to get it out quick, but she keeps missing her appointments with you. You can see how it's hurting her and how it will hurt her if left untreated.

What kind of wringer do you want to put your poor character through? What kind of tumor do you want to give him?

CONSIDER THE ALTERNATIVE

As you're thinking about the particular kind of misery you're going to sic on your main character, also be thinking about what Door No. 2 should look like.

Let's say you're thinking you'd like to make your protagonist scared to be around children because when she was young she dropped her baby brother and he's been a vegetable ever since. She is beset with guilt, though she goes to see him every weekend. She won't hold anyone's baby, ever. But the guilt has exceeded normal bounds. She intentionally has deprived herself of any good thing in her life. She didn't go to veterinary school, as she'd always dreamed, because that would've meant moving away from her brother. She hasn't dated, much less married, because she feels she doesn't deserve such joys in her life if her brother will never get to have them.

The Knot

Pretty interesting character, actually. You can just see her wearing ratty clothes and frumpy hair, and maybe she's even intentionally unhygenic so as to dissuade any would-be suitors. It's definitely a knot that is big enough to propel an entire novel.

Now it's time to imagine what the alternative could be. If you are Fate in this story and you're not going to let her remain in her miserable stew, what are you going to try to get her to change into? What is the happy other possibility you'd like her to see and possibly seize?

Maybe you'd like to see her forgive herself and finally give herself permission to have a life. That's a radically different existence than what she's currently embracing. It would take a lot of convincing for her to let go of the self-loathing she has such a death grip on. But it would make for an interesting novel! Already you can begin thinking of ways you might bring that optimistic possibility into her life. That's what you're looking for.

In *An Unfinished Life*, Einar begrudgingly allows his daughter-in-law and granddaughter into his world. The more they hang around, the more he glimpses what it would feel like to love again, to care again, to invest again in a young person's life. The crypt of his soul is pierced by a shaft of light, and for a moment it feels good. For a moment he is almost tempted to let go of all this cancerous anger and become the kind of man he was before he lost his son.

As you're looking for a good alternative to your hero's problem, *make sure it's the opposite of her knot*. It's great that you present a happy option of your hero getting promoted to organizer of the homecoming parade, but if that promotion isn't the antithesis of her knot, it will have no impact. It would work great if she sees herself as a nobody who is capable of nothing good. But if her knot is that she feels abandoned, the parade job won't be therapeutic to her in any way. It will just feel like more work.

So, what will it be for your main character? Given the following knot, what would be the most attractive substitute outcome? If he's addicted to online role-playing games (and you'd of course want to delve into the *why* behind his addiction), what would be the best alternative in his eyes? Maybe it's the ability to go through a day free of the tyranny of those games; the ability to make his own choices and spend his days—and his money—as he pleases.

GETTING THERE

Getting to that happy destination will not be easy. One doesn't lightly walk away from addictions or negative strongholds. Your character has become comfortable in her dysfunction. Forget your crowbar—it will take something akin to a nuclear blast to get her to leave it.

Ah, fiction. It's good to be a god.

Find a great knot for your main character. Then find an equally powerful promised land to offer in exchange. The bulk of his inner journey—and of your book itself—is going to be the interplay (more like battle) between these two options—all leading up to that breathless moment when he decides once and for all which door he's going to step through.

....

JEFF GERKE is the author of three books from Writer's Digest: *Plot Versus Character* (2010), *The First 50 Pages* (2011), and *Write Your Novel in a Month* (2013). He is the founder of Marcher Lord Press, the premier publisher of Christian speculative fiction. He currently freelances for clients: editing, creating book cover designs, and typesetting (at www.jeffgerke.com). He lives in Colorado Springs with his wife and three children.

CHAPTER 34

THE MOMENT OF TRUTH

BY JEFF GERKE

> The light sprang up again, and there on the brink of the chasm,
> at the very Crack of Doom, stood Frodo, black against the glare,
> tense, erect, but still as if he had been turned to stone.
>
> "Master!" cried Sam.
>
> Then Frodo stirred and spoke with a clear voice, indeed with
> a voice clearer and more powerful than Sam had ever heard him
> use, and it rose above the throb and turmoil of Mount Doom,
> ringing in the roof and walls.
>
> "I have come," he said. "But I do not choose now to do what
> I came to do. I will not do this deed. The Ring is mine!" And
> suddenly, as he set it on his finger, he vanished from Sam's sight.
>
> —J.R.R. Tolkien, The Lord of the Rings

This is the climactic moment. Frodo and Sam have traveled together for
endless miles and endured tragedy and peril to get them to this place,
the inside of a volcano, the only place where the treacherous Ring of
Power may be destroyed. Frodo need only drop it into the lava below
and the deed will be done and all free peoples saved.

Tolkien has done a marvelous job of bringing the main character's
inner journey to its pinnacle at the same moment that the external story
is at its apex, thus doubling the tension. The fate of the world literally
hangs on what one character *decides* to do.

And that, dear writer friend, is what you need to do with your novel.

WE'RE AT THE END ALREADY?

Don't worry if you haven't yet written the end of your book. By considering the point you are trying to reach, you can then work backwards to figure out the steps you need to take to get there.

The power of your story will be the strength of this central dyad, the moment of truth. In a way, your entire story is just a vehicle to transport the reader to the moment of truth. The Lord of the Rings was about many things, but the crucial bit, the part when moons and stars paused in their orbits (literally speaking), was the passage quoted above: Frodo's moment of truth. In a broad sense, everything else in the entire epic was simply setup for that moment.

In the previous chapter you picked your main character's knot, the "sin" that the story god has decided to purge her of. All the events of the story are the tools Fate is using to cause her to get to the moment of truth. Figuring out where your hero's character arc is headed will enable us to find the whole structure of the story.

You don't have to decide now which path the character is going to take at the moment of truth, by the way. For now, it's all about getting her there.

WHAT IS THE MOMENT OF TRUTH?

Simply put, the moment of truth is when your character makes her decision.

She's been going down Path A for a long time. She would still be happily (or miserably) going down that path if the events of the story hadn't come along. Now there's that pesky Path B to consider. "Man, it looks pretty good. It would sure solve a lot of problems if I went that way. It comes at a price, though. Am I willing to pay? Ooh, I hate decisions."

Throughout the course of the story she's been making minor choices, little moments of truth. For months, Frodo has been dealing with the temptation to use or even keep the ring for himself. Each time, he avoids the temptation. And even when he doesn't, he regrets it and recommits to his original purpose to destroy it. Those have been play-off games leading to the Super Bowl, so to speak. Each has been important, and if he had chosen poorly before, he wouldn't have gotten to the big game, but in the end it's all been lead-up to the main event.

So it will be with your character. Because you know the old way, the way of the knot, and the new way that leads to the promised land, you will be able to bring both into play in escalating intensity as the story goes along. Both sides will have their say. Reps from both companies will have their turn to tout their wares. Evangelists from both sides will get their turn in the pulpit. And like an undecided shopper at a middle-eastern bazaar, called this way and that by earnest criers, your hero will be tempted.

At each juncture, your main character learns more and more what is at stake. He begins to glimpse just how poisonous his current way is—and just how wonderful the other way might be, if it truly is as advertised. He comes to understand both the promise and the price of the two ways. He comes, in other words, to truly understand his choice.

It is that moment—when his last reason for staying the same has been knocked away and he must choose once and for all—that you are heading toward. It's the reason you are writing your novel.

That is your book's moment of truth.

Your hero is standing at the crossroads. No, let's make it more picturesque. Your hero is balancing on the end of a girder one hundred stories above the pavement. She can't go backward because ... because an alien creature is coming toward her down the girder. If she stays as she is, cold and alone and clinging to balance, the creature will consume her—or worse. But that *is* one of her options. Her other option is to try to leap to a rooftop across and below. If she takes a running start, she can probably make it. Firefighters have set up a fall pad for her and are standing by to administer first aid.

Whatever she's going to do or not do, it has to be now.

This is the moment of truth.

FAMOUS MOMENTS

We've already looked at the moment of truth from The Lord of the Rings. Let's see some others to help illustrate what I'm talking about.

- Romeo's moment comes when he's in the tomb beside his (supposedly) dead Juliet. Now that he believes he's in the world without her, what will he do?
- Darth Vader's moment of truth comes in *Return of the Jedi* when the Emperor is killing Luke Skywalker: Will the evil Emperor win his ultimate allegiance or will Vader betray his dark master to save his son?
- Elizabeth's moment of truth in *Pride and Prejudice* comes when she realizes Mr. Darcy, whom she has snubbed, has actually saved her family from great shame. Suddenly he's not what she thought he was, and he's asking her to marry him—what is she going to do?
- In *Pirates of the Caribbean: Dead Man's Chest*, Captain Jack Sparrow is in a rowboat paddling away to safety, leaving his crew and friends to die. He puts his oars down, turns back to look, and … has his moment of truth.
- In *Of Mice and Men* George's moment comes when he's alone with Lennie after Lennie has killed Curley's wife. If George—who has a gun—lets Lennie go, the lynch mob will get him. Yet he knows Lennie can't be allowed to be free anymore. What will he do?
- Captain Ahab's moment of truth comes when Starbuck tells him that the chase for Moby Dick is blasphemous and people are dying. Will Ahab see reason or pursue the whale to the doom of himself and his entire crew?

Do you see how the author brings the main character to the brink? The hero fully understands what will probably happen if he goes through Door #1 and what will probably happen if he goes through Door #2. The choices are clearly laid out before him. He understands the risk and consequences. Then he chooses, and the impact of the choice plays out from there.

That is the moment of truth.

THE CONTENDERS

If your hero's knot is a bitterness that has left her sad and lonely, perhaps the alternative you pick for her is to release her anger, forgive the person who wronged her, and rejoin the human race. So if you locked those two options in a room together and let them fight it out, what would happen?

Maybe at first the pleasant alternative just looks like foolishness to her. Maybe you personify it by having a special needs child move in next door. The child is always happy despite his many handicaps. *Silly, stupid child*, she thinks. But of course you have the child insinuate his way into her life. Subtly at first, and then with more vigor, she tries to get him to face his impediments and get angry about it. But his positive outlook proves indefatigable. She smiles at him in spite of herself. She begins to appreciate his visits, to hear in her head his outlook on things.

Finally you bring the journey to a crossroads. The woman is faced with a major decision. For the first time in a long time she can imagine herself making a positive choice. It would mean giving up her hatred. It would mean taking a chance to trust someone else and possibly be hurt. But it would get her something she longs for, perhaps a reconnection with the boy, since he has now stopped coming over.

And so she has a choice to make: Stay with the old way (and enjoy its safety but endure its continued toxins) or go with the new way (and risk failure or ridicule but have a chance at joy).

Okay, that's a hypothetical example. Let's look at The Lord of the Rings. The story gives several characters their moments of truth, all regarding the One Ring. It's almost a study in the variety of reactions to the ring, a litmus test for character quality. Gandalf has his chance at the ring, as do Farimir, Borimir, Aragorn, Sam, Gollum, Bilbo, Galadriel, Saruman, and more.

But the main one is Frodo. He carries it for the bulk of the trilogy. His knot is to use the power of the ring to serve his own interests. The cost of doing that would be the destruction of all he holds dear—even as he seeks to save it—and the loss of his own soul to the corrupting power of the ring. He knows this, but still the siren song is appealing.

The alternative, the "right thing" to do, is to deny himself the temptation of the ring and instead bring about its destruction.

It's a great conflict woven into the fabric of the story. You can see that at every step he is torn in opposing directions. To have the means of your salvation as near as your hand and yet refuse to use it, even when in danger or when friends are in danger, to serve a larger but more distant good ... hoo boy. Not sure I could be as strong as our surprising little hobbit.

During the story, the two desires vie for Frodo's loyalty. The Black Riders are sending out psychic signals, urging the Ringbearer to put it on and use its power—because by doing so he reveals his location to them. The ring itself longs to be found and taken back to its evil master. Situations come in which it is almost impossible *not* to use the ring's invisibility to escape danger. And yet on the other side are Gandalf and Aragorn and Galadriel and others urging him to never use it, for the safety of his own soul (not to mention everyone else's life). It is a powerful internal conflict and it propels both Frodo's inner journey and the reader all the way through the story.

The goal of the novelist is to bring these two choices, these two options, together in an ultimate moment of choosing for the main character. We've seen how Tolkien did it. There stands Frodo at the edge of the Cracks of Doom, having surmounted incredible obstacles to arrive here at the place of the ring's potential destruction, facing the final choice at last. Compounding the tension is that his friends are at that very moment fighting for their lives on a battlefield not far away, a battle whose outcome rests on what he does with the ring inside Mount Doom.

In *Star Wars* (Episode IV), you could build a case that Luke Skywalker's knot is a faith in technology and what man and science can do. His happy alternative is to put his faith in the Force, a more spiritual solution, which—if true—supersedes the abilities both man and science can bring to bear. Luke experiences his moment of truth as he's speeding through the trench on the surface of the Death Star, with bad guys all around him and good guys dropping like flies, with the good guys' secret base almost within range of the Death Star's weapons.

He turns on his targeting computer, which denotes his reliance on technology. The goal is to shoot an energy weapon (a proton torpedo) into a very small portal at the end of this trench. Everyone else in his position would try to use the targeting computer to guide the missile into the hole. That's the way he's leaning, too. Except that he's been getting a taste of the power of the Force throughout the film. This spiritual thing that promises to be better even than technology. Plus he has the voice of his mentor in his head telling him to trust the Force.

With the fate of the free galaxy in the balance, Luke has a choice to make. It's his moment of truth.

PICKING THE MOMENT OF TRUTH FOR YOUR CHARACTER

To find the moment of truth for your main character, bring to mind your hero's knot. You've got her "problem" already figured out. You've also chosen the alternative, the sunny land of promise she could get to if she lets go of the old way and embraces the new way. With this dialectic in hand, you're ready to figure out your hero's moment of truth.

Here are some things to keep in mind as you craft this all-important moment:

- **MAKE IT FIT:** It (almost) goes without saying that the moment of truth has to be the collision of the two contenders in the hero's life. You've got the old way and the new way. In your character's moment of truth, she decides between those two options.
- **MAKE SURE BOTH OPTIONS ARE COMPELLING:** Your hero is stuck in the old way, which is hurting him on some level, and yet it gives him something he values. The new way has to be at least as attractive to him as the old way, even if he doesn't see the attraction at first. It must give him everything the old way is not giving him, and it must solve problems for him—but not without cost.
- **INCLUDE THE COST OF PURCHASE:** The moment of truth is not complete unless the hero understands not only what he stands to gain by choosing one option over the other, but also what he stands to lose. If he lets go of his self-loathing to embrace a posi-

tive view about himself, it will be a betrayal of his father, who always said he was worthless. If she lets go of her fear and moves on with her life, it will mean risking failure again.

- **PROVIDE SMALLER MOMENTS OF TRUTH ALONG THE WAY:** Keep in mind that you will need to think of ways for these two opposing options to skirmish before the decisive battle. Just as Frodo was tempted to use the ring at multiple junctures in the story (and in some of these, he chose *wrong*) and as Luke saw the promise of the Force over the limits of technology, your character will need to make minor yes/no choices between these two options before the big moment of truth.

Now it's time to choose the moment of truth for your book. Fill in these blanks for your main character:

- My main character's knot is _____
  _____.
- This handicaps him in this way: _____
  _____.
- My main character has chosen or allowed this state of affairs because it gives her this benefit: _____
  _____.
- The happy alternative (the "new way") I'm going to set before my main character is: _____
  _____.
- It's a perfect foil or counterbalance to the old way because ____
  _____.
- The new way will provide these benefits to my main character: __
  _____.
- But my main character will not initially consider this new way to be a real option for him because _____
  _____.
- After a while, though, my main character begins to see that she would probably enjoy the following benefits if she went with the new way: _____
  _____

- The cost of going this new way will also become clear to my main character over time. He will come to see that if he does this, she will have to _____.

It's a price she is not entirely sure she is willing to pay.

PULLING IT ALL TOGETHER

With all these ingredients bubbling in the stew, you're ready to add the final element.

The question is, why now? Why does your character have to make this choice right now? In our steel girder example, there was an alien monster barreling down on our hero, so she had to make a choice in a hurry. What will it be in your character's life that is forcing her to choose without further delay? It's up to you to force this choice. It's what everything has been pointing to from page 1.

I'm not saying you have to know your plot as of yet. You may not have a clue whether your book is going to be more like *Jaws* or *Gone with the Wind*. That's fine. What we're looking for is the corner you're going to back your hero into—metaphorically speaking—that forces her to choose now.

You'll find your "why now?" component in the nature of the two contenders themselves. If the knot is an overdependence on technology and the alternative is a reliance on something spiritual, your moment of truth will have to be something that forces the character to choose between those two options. Sounds obvious, I know, but it's important to say it clearly. And your "why now?" will be some factor that puts a time limit on the decision.

If the knot is a bitterness that has left the hero isolated and lonely, and the alternative is letting go of the anger to forgive and embrace what's left of his family (*An Unfinished Life*), the moment of truth will be something that makes him jump off the fence one way or another. Maybe the granddaughter is going to leave if he doesn't reach out to her. The moment of truth becomes what he's going to decide to do—hold on to the old way and be miserable or let go of his delicious anger to embrace the new way—and the "why now?" element is what's forcing him to finally take action without further delay. Act now or forever regret it.

Often the moment of truth will come when the hero's last resistance has been knocked away. He's hit rock bottom and he realizes the depravity of his old way. It has finally cost him too much. His eyes have been opened at last, and now he's able to make a sober choice.

As we've seen, characters don't change until it hurts too much to stay the same. A woman may not be willing to leave her family homestead, despite the rising floodwaters. But when the water comes in and her infant daughter is almost swept away, suddenly Granny's old quilts don't seem so important.

So bring on the pain. Be willing to throw lightning bolts at your character, zapping away his arguments, until he can finally compare both options and evaluate them as equals, as real, valid choices for him.

What will be your main character's moment of truth? You can always adjust it later, but what are you thinking right now?

To quote Master Yoda, "Upon this, all depends."

....

JEFF GERKE is the author of three books from Writer's Digest: *Plot Versus Character* (2010), *The First 50 Pages* (2011), and *Write Your Novel in a Month* (2013). He is the founder of Marcher Lord Press, the premier publisher of Christian speculative fiction. He currently freelances for clients: editing, creating book cover designs, and typesetting (at www.jeffgerke.com). He lives in Colorado Springs with his wife and three children.

CHAPTER 35

REVISING FOR STRONG CHARACTER

BY JACK SMITH

Even if the impetus for your story is an idea and not a character, the characters you create must be more than mere pawns to carry out this idea. Fiction isn't a treatise on idea or perceived truth. It's an experience that your reader must be able to enjoy imaginatively, by entering the lives of very real characters. Your fiction can certainly be rich with ideas, but *characters* attract most readers to fiction—strong characters. By "strong," I don't mean heroes or heroines. I mean characters that are richly developed—complex characters.

In this chapter we will look closely at key revision issues for characterization with an emphasis on main characters, but with some attention to secondary characters as well.

RETHINKING CHARACTERIZATION

Your main character must be a strong character—one who captures the reader's attention. Strong characters are complex; they exhibit range as well as depth. And because of this range and *depth*, we find them compelling. They are also called "round" characters. Like human beings, round characters are multifaceted: in their overall makeup, their motivations, and their actions. They are believable to readers because they possess the fullness of life and all of its wellsprings and depths. But how do you achieve such characterization? The following section of the book addresses the techniques you need for solid character revision. Beginning with roundness...

The Round Character
Creating a Fully Human Character

A character's overall makeup includes physical appearance, personality, attributes, habits, quirks, mannerisms, speech intonation, and typical behaviors. A character without any of the above is merely a series of actions and a disembodied voice with nothing distinctive about it— hardly a character at all.

But even a draft without a shred of characterization could be substantially improved by adding details to help the reader visualize this character: his or her physical appearance, maybe a few gestures, or a distinctive tone of voice. How much more is needed? You must add whatever it takes to make this character a living, breathing human, so alive to the reader that she could step right out of the pages of the story or novel.

Consider this character description by a first-person narrator from Saul Bellow's short story "Zetland: By a Character Witness":

> Max Zetland himself had a white face, white-jowled, a sarcastic bear, but acceptably pleasant, entering the merchandising palace on Wabash Avenue, neat in his office, smart on the telephone, fluent except for a slight Russian difficulty with initial aitches, releasing a mellow grumble when he spoke, his mind factual, tabular, prices and contracts memorized. He held in the smoke of his cigarettes as he stood by his desk. The smoke drifted narrowly from his nose. With a lowered face, he looked about.

This descriptive passage certainly covers a broad range: physical appearance, personality, behavior, and ability. And in this range, we discover a human being, not a stock character. On the heels of this general portrait, the character's distinctive personality is revealed in his smoking of the cigarette and his final gesture.

Or consider how human—and comic—Vladimir Nabokov makes Professor Timofey Pnin:

> Ideally bald, sun-tanned, and clean-shaven, he began rather impressively with that great brown dome of his, tortoise-shell glasses (masking an infantile absence of eyebrows), apish upper lip, thick neck, and strong-man torso in a tightish tweed coat, but ended, somewhat disappointingly, in a pair of spindly legs (now flannelled and crossed) and frail-looking, almost feminine feet.

These portraits make these characters very real, and what is immediately apparent is how detailed they are. This is a matter of style. For now, suffice it to say that not all writers depict their characters—whether protagonists or secondary characters—with such profuse detail. Some are much more sparing in their use of such direct methods as description and exposition. They select representative details and rely more on the dramatic method of scene.

A good example of the dramatic method is Cormac McCarthy's postapocalyptic *The Road*. McCarthy provides no concrete description of his protagonist. His protagonist's personal attributes—his bravery and commitment in the face of terrible odds—come through not by authorial commentary but by action and speech only. Note the minimalistic style in this short excerpt:

> This was not a safe place. They could be seen from the road now it was day. The boy turned in the blankets. Then he opened his eyes. Hi, Papa, he said.
> > I'm right here.
> > I know.

More is suggested than stated. But clearly we feel the father's protective role in assuring his son he's right there.

So, as you revise, consider these two methods of characterization:

- **OPTION 1: THE DIRECT METHOD:** You ratchet up description and exposition to capture your protagonist's appearance and distinctive qualities or attributes. Two things to consider: 1) If your point of view is third person, be as careful as you can not to *intrude* as author—keeping the reader as much as possible inside your character. 2) Be sure that your character's actions match up with, and don't seem at odds with, any descriptive passages about this character—or any expository passages covering character attributes.

- **OPTION 2: THE INDIRECT OR DRAMATIC METHOD:** You rely almost exclusively on scene; readers depend on the details of action and speech to visualize your protagonist. Expository passages do not directly mention key character attributes; instead, you impart them via character thought.

You may decide to combine parts of each method. Describe your character physically but do not explicitly name personal attributes. Or don't describe your character physically but do explicitly name personal attributes. It's best to try these things out, and then decide.

Now that we've looked at two useful methods of characterization, let's look for specific ways to make your character fully human. As you revise, give your character:

- More than one primary goal, behavior, or attitude
- Several interests—practical, romantic, intellectual, etc.
- Some inner conflicts—about goals, about self, about others
- A personal quirk, odd gesture, or noteworthy habit
- Distinctive speech patterns or qualities

In other words, individualize your character—but don't overdo it. The character must be multidimensional but not global in dimensions. If you pile on too many inner conflicts, the story will lose focus. If your character possesses too many distinctive traits or quirks, he may seem over the top. If this is what you intend—if you're writing farce or satire, for instance—that's a different matter. But generally speaking, more is not necessarily better. Develop range and depth, but be selective.

Look for contradictions that can be explained at one level. For instance, John Harvey Kellogg of T.C. Boyle's *The Road to Wellville* reads as a truly complex human: He has an altruistic vision for his flock at the Battle Creek Sanitarium, yet many of his methods, shortsighted and extreme, contradict his impulses for good. Kellogg's grandiose dream of health at his turn-of-the-century clinic accounts for his contradictory nature. Boyle, in spite of his savage satirical thrusts, has created a fully believable, convincing human being.

Believable Motivations

As you revise for character motivation, keep in mind three things, each of which has to do with predictability. Strong characters with range and depth are not predictable—at least not generally.

First, characters, like real people, are not governed by the laws of logic. Boyle's Kellogg is an instructive example. We feel in the presence of a true-to-life character when the character's motivations are complex and even contradictory—but nonetheless believable because they are contradictory. Humans, after all, have contradictory impulses. We have two sides: the emotional and the rational. We are driven by both egoistic and altruistic concerns. Conflicts between these needs are inevitable. When you revise, make sure that you look for the possibility of contradictory motives in your character—contradictions that can be explained or understood in some way.

Second, some readers might not believe your character would do what she, in fact, does. Make sure to build the context fully enough so your reader will believe that this character would do *this thing* at *this particular time*, even if it goes against conventional wisdom. Who can say what a character might actually do, given the right motivations or the right circumstances?

Third, like real people, characters might not be clear themselves as to why they do certain things. As complex human beings, we often try to figure out our own motives. If we analyze our past actions, they might make some sense; yet, we can't fully account for why we did what we did. Were our motives mixed? In human motivations, there are always gray areas—areas not defined by reason or logic—and that's what makes round characters more interesting than flat, predictable ones.

Having ended on the above note, I don't mean to suggest that it's all up for grabs as to what a character will or will not do. Several factors and influences help to explain character motivation, however ambiguous such motivation might at times be. Think about each of the following as you revise:

- **CHARACTER'S PERSONALITY AND TEMPERAMENT:** Depending on the conflict (for example, speaking in public), an introvert may react one way, an extrovert another. We can't be sure, of course. People surprise us, and characters should surprise us, too. But personality is certainly a contributing factor in character motivation. So is temperament. A person who is easily riled may react differently than a person who is slow to anger. A person who is easily frustrated may react differently than one who takes things in stride. Can you connect your character's motivations to his personality or temperament in some way?

- **ANTAGONISTS:** Antagonists of every stamp—personal, societal, natural—are an important factor in character motivation. Is your character affected enough by this antagonist to react in the way you have shown? Do the antagonist's beliefs or actions affect your character in convincing ways?

  This raises, at least in part, the question of character make-up. Different people react differently to different events. Some people are vulnerable to certain statements made by particular antagonists. Others would not be. As readers we should see connections between a character's basic makeup and her reaction to an antagonist. A complex character may or may not react in predictable ways toward antagonists. Whatever the outcome, we should see a deeply human engagement between opposing parties, and the protagonist's personality, attitudes, and personal attributes should be evident in some way—if not crystal clear.

- **CHARACTER'S PAST:** A character's past can affect how she acts in the present and can help clarify certain choices. But be careful not to oversimplify cause-effect relations. Did this past event really cause your character to do what she did? Cause and effect is, of course, a complicated matter, and it's easy to make hasty conclusions. But if you've made this past event, as well as your character's psychological reactions, compelling enough, the reader may suspend disbelief. Look for opportunities to link backstory, if you provide it, to character motivation in a believable, convincing way.

- **CHARACTER'S ACTIONS THEMSELVES:** It may seem paradoxical to say that actions can both reflect character (motivations) and affect or *develop* character. But actions have effects, not only on others but also on the person who performs these actions. Ask virtue theorists. Once one acts, one's character may change in some way. Minor crimes, if they are committed often enough, can change a person. More serious crimes can certainly affect one's thinking about oneself, others, and the world as a whole. If one commits murder, isn't it credible to say that this person may never be quite the same person again? In a complex character, we see how actions aren't simply rooted in given motivations—they're more complex than that. Characters given to edgy behaviors have a way of spiraling out of control as one action leads, almost lockstep, to the next.

As you revise for character motivation, make convincing ties between your characters—their complex makeup, what influences them, affects them, and so on—and their resulting behaviors and actions. But *convincing* doesn't mean utterly logical—so allow for surprises. Don't nail everything down like the answer to a math problem; leaving your reader with some questions is a good thing to do.

Speech That's Real

To make your characters real, you must make your dialogue convincing. Perhaps your character is complex and real in all the ways we've discussed so far. But if he speaks in calculated phrases, he won't seem human or real.

How do you revise your dialogue so that it creates strong characters? Consider the following:

- **MAKE SURE YOUR DIALOGUE DOESN'T SOUND LIKE A PRE-PARED SPEECH:** Unless your character speaks this way—perhaps to comic effect—the character will be very flat. How does "real" speech sound? Dialogue is artifice, as all art is, and yet it must have interesting speech rhythms that hook us and make us feel like we're in the presence of a real human being.

- **BE CAREFUL WITH DIALECT:** If you try to capture an accent, whether it's regional or ethnic, you will probably need to do some fieldwork. Otherwise you risk the character coming off as both unbelievable and hackneyed. A true-to-life character imparts a distinct air of reality. Well-researched and accurate dialects, accents, and colloquialisms will help achieve this realism.
- **MAKE SURE YOUR DIALOGUE ISN'T CANNED:** If the dialogue seems typical of what everyone says all the time about this subject or conflict, your character won't seem very unique—or complex.
- **REVEAL CHARACTER ATTITUDES:** Look for ways to let dialogue illuminate character traits and motivations. And think about this as well: Sometimes what is not said is more revealing than what is said.

Dynamic Versus Static

A round character is one who changes, while a flat character isn't likely to change—this may mean a change in behavior or a change in vision, or both. Oftentimes the change a new way of seeing things. Sometimes it's almost imperceptible, and yet we know this character will never be quite the same.

What's the point of a story in which the character doesn't change? If the character is a certain way at the beginning and at the end is exactly the same way, what has really happened? Is the reader expected to come to a new realization, as in *Billy Budd*? Let's consider this novella more fully. Billy Budd doesn't change at all, unless one argues that Billy's act of striking Claggart reflects change. But striking Claggart was not intentional; it was more visceral, like a leg kicking out after the knee has been struck. Billy Budd remains purely good, a sacrificial lamb; Claggart is the snake in the Garden. Both Billy and Claggart are one-dimensional characters. This fiction is much more allegorical than realistic.

In contrast, consider Charlotte Perkins Gilman's "The Yellow Wallpaper," where the protagonist does change. She descends increasingly into madness due to the oppressive regimen her husband inflicts upon her in response to a diagnosis of so-called hysteria. He encloses her in the house, discourages any mental effort, and casts her into utter dependency and isolation. Thus the seeds of her madness are planted and ripen in the story. She changes, bit by bit, before our eyes. The story is the impact this regimen has on her sanity.

In another oft-anthologized short story, Kate Chopin's "The Story of an Hour," the protagonist gains new vision, new insight. At first, she grieves when she learns of her husband's death, but then she realizes, upon further reflection, that she is in fact now free. But when her husband appears, quite alive and well, she drops dead. Is it because of her heart condition or because she cannot tolerate living with her husband now that she has entertained the idea of being liberated from him? Surely, the latter. Chopin makes both sudden realizations—that she is free, and that she's not after all—quite compelling.

It isn't necessary for characters to change significantly. If they change too much, the reader will wonder how it happened. Even in dire circumstances, people may learn something new about themselves and others, but it's unlikely that their entire outlook on the world or personality will change. It's not easy to gain a completely new vision overnight or to change old habits. Ask yourself, is your reader likely to buy that your protagonist suddenly becomes an absolutely new somebody in the course of ten to twenty pages, perhaps spanning a few weeks or even a year? You must make the transformation convincing and real. As extreme as it might seem, we accept the transformation of Gilman's protagonist because of her intolerable situation and because Gilman meticulously dramatizes the woman's descent, by degrees, into madness. We accept Chopin's protagonist's sudden realization—symbolized by her sudden death—because the marriage had little substance to begin with. When characters are granted new insight, this realization must be earned. Also, the realization can't be over some utterly trivial event. The stakes must be high enough that the reader cares.

Here's a revision checklist to consider for the dynamic character. Look for the seeds of this change in:

- Your character's overall makeup
- Your character's past, if relevant

- Other characters, including antagonists
- Major incidents and how they have affected your character in terms of emotions, behavior, and so forth

As you head into revision, allow me to harp on it again: Don't attempt to work out character change with mathematical certainty. That your character would come to this new insight, whatever it is, should be believable. But if it's a little vague or obscure, that air of mystery will be interesting to your reader and probably more satisfying than a totally obvious ending—or worse yet, a tidy explanation.

THE COMPELLING CHARACTER

A round/dynamic character grabs our attention and holds onto it. We care about this character's actions. If we don't entirely sympathize, we at least empathize. We find the character engaging—compelling.

If the character is sympathetic, then this is a real plus, but be careful. Is this sympathy based on sloppy sentimentality? Stories about teenagers dying in car wrecks or children dying of cancer, though tragic and horrible in real life, tend to be thin in fiction because they quickly turn sappy. They involve *bathos* instead of *pathos*. With the former, the desired emotional response is not genuinely earned, while in the latter, it is because of the intellectual component within the story.

The central event in Tim Johnston's title story in his Katherine Anne Porter Prize-winning collection, *Irish Girl*, is a car accident and the death of a teenage boy. Johnston deals with the tragic aftermath, but the story takes on more than this. Johnston's focus is on the parochial and confining nature of a Midwestern town from which teenagers try to escape. The story moves beyond the predictable sad tale of teenage death to address this larger cultural issue. The narrator, the younger brother of the dead boy, thinks back to an occasion when his cool older brother was speaking of his girlfriend, the eponymous Irish Girl. Captured in his brother's eyes the narrator saw "...the blue light, the wild secret rush when William said the words 'Irish girl.'"

This passage, taken in context, gives the story an emotional and intellectual dimension beyond the tragic accident itself. It's about youthful spontaneity versus adult restraint: wayward youth's need to break free from the constraints of dull conformity to parental rules and societal conventions. This is something we can think about intellectually. It transforms the story beyond the simple bromide that it's so sad when young people die so needlessly—which is indisputably true, but it's a truth that depends on an emotional appeal only. Johnston makes his characters sympathetic and compelling, but he doesn't do so by manipulating us emotionally.

Putting aside the question of bathos, let's consider the larger question: What is it about your character that will make your reader sympathetic? We may or may not sympathize with Henry Fleming in *The Red Badge of Courage* when he enlists to go off to fight in the Civil War; he wants to earn honor, and he is quite naïve in terms of what he's about to undergo. But if we don't sympathize with his reasons for joining up, we probably do sympathize with his profound psychological distress in confronting grisly war death. And if we don't sympathize with his running off, we can at least empathize with his choice and find something compellingly human in his need to do so, and in his need to rationalize doing so.

It's when readers can neither sympathize nor empathize that characters need real attention. If readers can find no human qualities within your characters with which they can relate, you must find ways to impart these qualities. This takes us back to the question of a complex character—a complex character will certainly be empathetic, if not sympathetic.

Yet, what about those characters who commit despicable acts? What about murderers? What about Raskolnikov, the protagonist of Dostoyevsky's *Crime and Punishment*? Raskolnikov is certainly a character with depth, and we might be able to empathize with his troubled soul, if not sympathize with his actions. We don't have to approve of what he does, yet on one level, what he does, though monstrous, can be understood in human terms. It's undoubtedly the author's deep psychological study of his crime and punishment that keeps us interested. The treatment is dramatically intense and realized fully in human terms;

we want to discover more and more about this character because we find him compelling.

Largely, then, roundness, sufficiency of motivation, and adequate dramatic treatment produce compelling characters. Be attentive to the following in your creation of a compelling character:

- **MAKE SURE YOUR MAIN CHARACTER IS COMPLEX.** Very likely if your character is complex, he will be empathetic; if not sympathetic, he will at least be interesting.
- **CHOOSE PATHOS** over bathos.
- **KNOW THIS:** Even if the ideas in your story or novel are compelling, if the character is a turnoff, the reader will likely put your work down.

SECONDARY CHARACTERS

Thus far, I have discussed only main characters, or protagonists. Main characters must be developed with range and depth, but secondary characters are a different matter. Secondary characters that are developed too much overshadow main characters. The possibility of doing so is always a risk. Sometimes we might feel that our secondary characters are actually more interesting than our protagonists. And that's fine, as long as the main character engages the reader and is quite compelling. The opposite—when the protagonist is not engaging or compelling—is certainly a problem.

The same fictional techniques apply to creating secondary characters as to main characters, except secondary characters are far less complex. But you certainly do not want one-dimensional secondary characters unless they play really minor roles—or perhaps serve some comic role. Give them a few dimensions. Those with a somewhat important part in the plot deserve some range and depth—as much as they need to fulfill their respective roles in the story. The greater the role, the more sides of that character need to be seen. But add just enough to support their secondary part in the story.

AUTOBIOGRAPHICAL FICTION

Many writers draw largely from their own experiences, and some draw almost exclusively from personal experience. They may find support in the old catchphrase, "Write what you know." This is fine as long as you keep your fictional character separate from you, the author. You are not this character. Even if you *are* alike in some or even many respects, this character is not you. You must realize that this character is a fictional creation. If you don't, you will tend to confuse fiction with fact. This will lead to more than one of the following bad results:

- **YOU WILL ROB YOUR CHARACTER OF ITS VITALITY:** You will try to make your character fit you, the author—your traits, your attitudes, your mannerisms—but your character needs a life of her own. She may be a bit like you, but make sure you give her plenty of room to grow—to be unlike you.
- **YOU WILL ROB THE STORY OF ITS IMAGINATIVE POWER:** Your character wants to go in a certain direction, and you hold him back. Your character must have his own energy and be empowered by your imagination—not by "true" life events or the way things "actually" happened.
- **YOU WILL LIMIT YOUR SETTING:** If you stick to the facts too much, you will avoid taking certain, perhaps important, risks; for example, setting your story in a city if you're from a small town, or a small town if you're from a city. Setting your story away from your own origins or present location might free up your imagination more. If you feel you've limited yourself in this regard, it may be good to rethink or change the setting, though it may take some research and a field trip or two. It's possible to energize your story by simply changing settings, unless you find they are too integral to your present storyline to change without great disruption. Even so, you should feel free to change details about the setting you've chosen. What's "true" about the setting is what's true for the characters, not you as author.

JACK SMITH is the author of the award-winning novel *Hog to Hog* (Texas Review Press, 2008), *ICON* (Serving House Books, 2014), as well as numerous short stories and reviews. He is a frequent contributor to Writer's Digest's Writer's Market series and is the co-editor of *The Green Hills Literary Lantern*.

PERMISSIONS

"25 Things You Should Know About Character." Excerpted from *The Kick-Ass Writer* © 2013 by Chuck Wendig, with permission from the author.

"Amp Up Your Antagontists" © 2013 by Laura DiSilverio. Originally appeared in *Writer's Digest*, July/August 2013. Used with permission of the author.

"The Arc Within Plot." Excerpted from *Write Great Fiction: Plot & Structure* © 2004 by James Scott Bell, with permission from Writer's Digest Books.

"Character Concepting." Excerpted from *The Nighttime Novelist* © 2010 by Joseph Bates, with permission from Writer's Digest Books.

"The Character Hierarchy." Excerpted from *Elements of Fiction Writing: Characters & Viewpoint* © 1988 by Orson Scott Card, with permission from Writer's Digest Books.

"Character Objective and Conflict." Excerpted from *Writing Irresistible Kidlit* © 2012 by Mary Kole, with permission from Writer's Digest Books.

"A Character's Emotional Thread." Excerpted from *Make A Scene* © 2007 by Jordan E. Rosenfeld, with permission from Writer's Digest Books.

"Choose a Name Wisely" © 2003 by Nancy Kress. Originally appeared in *Writer's Digest*, November 2003. Used with permission of the author.

"Coping with Conflict." Excerpted from *Breathing Life Into Your Characters* © 2009 by Rachel Ballon, with permission from the author.

"Crafting Effective Supporting Characters." Excerpted from *Writing and Selling Your Mystery Novel* © 2005 by Hallie Ephron, with permission from Writer's Digest Books.

"Creating an Anti-Hero." Excerpted from *Bullies, Bastards & Bitches* © 2008 by Jessica Page Morrell, with permission from the author.

"Creating a Character Arc." Excerpted from *The Nighttime Novelist* © 2010 by Joseph Bates, with permission from Writer's Digest Books.

INDEX

WRITER'S DIGEST

Is Your Manuscript Ready?

Trust 2nd Draft Critique Service to prepare your writing to catch the eye of agents and editors. You can expect:

- Expert evaluation from a hand-selected, professional critiquer
- Know-how on reaching your target audience
- Red flags for consistency, mechanics, and grammar
- Tips on revising your work to increase your odds of publication

Visit **WritersDigestShop.com/2nd-draft** for more information.

CREATE STORIES THAT CAPTIVATE YOUR AUDIENCE
Crafting Novels & Short Stories

FROM THE EDITORS OF WRITER'S DIGEST

Learn how to keep your plot moving, create a rich setting and backstory, master the art of dialogue, revise like a professional editor, and more with *Crafting Novels & Short Stories*. Whether you are developing an epic trilogy or putting the finishing touches on a piece of flash fiction, this book will provide strategies and advice from leading experts to help you master the art of storytelling.

Available from **WritersDigestShop.com** and your favorite book retailers.

To get started join our mailing list: **WritersDigest.com/enews**

FOLLOW US ON:

 Find more great tips, networking and advice by following **@writersdigest**

 And become a fan of our Facebook page: **facebook.com/writersdigest**